Feminist Amnesia

Is academic feminism intellectually sound? *Fem* [...]
contemporary feminist thought, like much cont[...]
is muddled. Jean Curthoys argues that the cont[...]
presenting radical credentials and pursuing the conservative and insti-
tutionalised life of today's academia have produced a particular sort of intellectual distortion, and one reminiscent of 'Lysenkoism' in the former
Soviet Union.

Jean Curthoys makes an analogy between the increasingly popular notion
of 'patriarchal' versus 'feminist' thought and the idea of 'bourgeois' versus
'proletarian' science which came to prominence during the course of 'the
Lysenko Affair'. Both are cases of ideas found in political movements apparently opposed to obvious injustices and thereby able to evoke widespread
support; in both movements the original aims have been corrupted by
opportunities for gaining power, and both movements give rise to the contradiction of having to espouse radical ideas whilst enmeshing themselves in
positions of authority.

Moreover, some intellectual confusion has stemmed from the repression of
the early thinking of the Women's Liberation movement. Curthoys argues
that the radical implications of these ideas had to be avoided by an essentially
power-seeking movement. None the less, they still inform dominant trends in
feminist theory because they provide the moral appeal necessary for its wide
support. *Feminist Amnesia* brings these forgotten ideas to light again.

Feminist Amnesia will provoke intense debate amongst all those interested
and involved in feminism, gender studies and philosophy.

Jean Curthoys was a pioneering member of the Women's Liberation movement. She was one of two teachers of the first course in feminist theory at
Sydney University in 1973. This course is notorious in the history of universities for having been instituted only after one of the biggest strikes ever
of staff and students. After the resulting split in the Philosophy department,
she lectured in the 'radical' department of General Philosophy for some
years. Her increasing opposition to 'radical' academia culminated in her
transfer to the 'conservative' department of Traditional and Modern
Philosophy, where she continues to lecture now.

Feminist Amnesia

The wake of women's liberation

Jean Curthoys

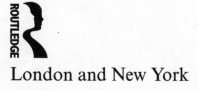

London and New York

First published 1997
by Routledge
11 New Fetter Lane, London EC4P 4EE
29 West 35th Street, New York, NY 10001

Typeset in Times by
RefineCatch Limited, Bungay, Suffolk

Printed and bound in Great Britain by
TJ Press (Padstow) Ltd, Padstow, Cornwall

British Library Cataloguing in Publication Data
A catalogue record for this book is available from the British Library

Library of Congress Cataloging in Publication Data
Curthoys, Jean
　Feminist amnesia / Jean Curthoys.
　　p.　　cm.
　Includes bibliographical references and index.
　1. Feminist theory.　2. Political correctness.　I. Title.
HQ1190.C875　1997　　　　96–20529
305.42—dc20　　　　　　　CIP

ISBN 0–415–14806–5 (hbk)
ISBN 0–415–14807–3 (pbk)

Contents

I stood on a hill and I saw the Old approaching, but it came as the New.

It hobbled up on new crutches which no one had ever seen before and stank new smells of decay which no one had ever smelt before.

The stone that rolled past was the newest invention and the screams of the gorillas drumming on their chests set up to be the newest musical composition.

Everywhere you could see the graves standing empty as the New advanced on the capital.

Round about stood such as inspired by terror, shouting: Here comes the New, be new like us!

And those who heard, heard nothing but their shouts, but those who saw, saw such as were not shouting.

(Bertolt Brecht, 'Parade of the Old New')

Preface

It is unfortunate that I did not come across Russell Jacoby's *The Last Intellectuals* (Jacoby 1987) until after I had completed the manuscript for this book. For when I did read it, I realised that Jacoby had posed the question (although he put it more generally) to which, in effect, the argument inside is an answer. The question is this: why has the generation of student radicals of the 1960s and 1970s failed to produce any genuine intellectuals? I think it was an achievement of Jacoby's just to have articulated this question. It brings into focus one of those features of a situation which, once seen, appear to be so obvious that it is difficult to believe they were ever missed – the kind of feature which is immediately explanatory at the same time as it calls out, itself, for explanation.

Jacoby tackles this question differently than I do and so a comparison of our respective approaches will help to situate what I have done here. First, we have some things in common. We are both rather more interested in the 'why' than the 'that' of the intellectual degeneration of university faculties of the Humanities over recent decades and we are both also specifically concerned about the substantial contribution made to this by the 'radicals'. Moreover, for both of us, the reason for the latter focus is a commitment, although I suspect of different kinds, to broadly left wing opposition and an enormous disappointment, in this respect also, with the gap between the promise and the actual achievements of what is our own generation. While we both concede the truth of conservative criticisms of contemporary academic 'political correctness', neither of us would regard the intellectual and political failure of the present radical intelligentsia as an argument for conservatism. Rather, I think we would both see this failure as pointing to the fact that there is an indissoluble connection between a disciplined and authentic life of the mind (at whatever educational level) and the realisation of egalitarian and libertarian social values. It is the angles from which Jacoby and I argue for this connection which are different.

Jacoby tackles his question sociologically, producing an analysis of intellectual mediocrity very much in the vein of Max Weber's. The key to the unexpected conformism and lack-lustre intellectual performance of the ex-student radicals, he suggests, is to be found in the fact that so many of them found employment in universities at a time when, associated with their rapid expansion, the process of bureaucratisation was being intensified. This in turn, he shows, is partly due to the fact that the economic and social conditions which had hitherto supported 'independent intellectuals' (intellectuals who, being economically independent of an institution, can function as independent thinkers) had disappeared. This thesis (although Jacoby does not present it this way) instantiates two of Weber's more general claims – first that the bureaucratic life, with its promise of security, its orientation around established and regular procedures and its well laid out career paths promotes the development of a conformist and rule-bound personality and second, that the bureaucratisation of universities in particular results in pervasive intellectual mediocrity, encouraging as it does the attitude of living 'off' rather than living 'for' science. The point, made differently by Jacoby and Weber, is that genuine inquiry cannot be bureaucratically managed or squeezed into a steady promotion path since, necessarily, it is performed for its own sake, in its own time, and not primarily for external rewards.

My argument is not sociological, for it is concerned with the character of the present intellectual mediocrity. It developed out of a curiosity about the kind of thinking which, as a university teacher, I saw all around me and which seemed to more than accidentally involve conceptual muddles and basic ignorance. I was deeply puzzled about how my peers could think that way, how they could present such thinking as profound, innovatory and involving great learning and about how such thinking could have appeal for keen, intelligent and apparently genuinely 'socially concerned' young students. My approach, then, is more philosophical than anything else because it is concerned with the internal workings of the mode of reasoning itself.

Nevertheless, different in kind as they are, Jacoby's analysis and mine extend each other. Because I treat the problem internally, reconstructing the conceptual moves involved in prevailing patterns of thinking, I inevitably end up highlighting quite different factors from Jacoby. What he is content to describe in general terms as mediocrity I see more as systematic intellectual confusion. This specific quality of thinking is, perhaps, not so accessible to a predominantly sociological approach. However, in pursuing the question why those who see themselves as intellectuals have what seems to be an actual interest in confused reasoning, I was lead to identify as crucial an ambivalent attitude to status and power. So Jacoby's account, which reveals how and why this generation of intellectuals became more interested in acquiring status than opposing it and why so many of them now fill professorships and other important senior academic positions, provides sociological background for my argument.

On the other hand, my own focus on the way this group reconciles, 'in the head', its attachment to its radical past with its present managerial reality, highlights the significance of a socio-historical factor which is not particularly emphasised by Jacoby. For if it is the conflict between a radical self-identification and a conformist life which is behind the fact that conceptual

slides and equivocations are intrinsic properties of its theoretical productions, then it follows that the key to this generation is its radical past. Not
only did this past constitute the credentials which first gained it access to
university appointments as university administrators tried to contain the student rebellions of the late 1960s but also, and naturally enough, its self-image
was fashioned in those days when it stormed various kinds of barricades.
Many who did not actually storm any barricades, being perhaps a few years
too young, nevertheless adopted the radical identification made so attractive
by those who did. We have here, then, a more distinctive phenomenon than
the straightforward institutionalisation of intellectuals which Jacoby discusses. We are now seeing, especially in universities, the culmination of the
career of a distinct socio-historical group, one which emerged with an intense
youthful idealism and which, finding no obvious avenue to pursue its very
moral and very radical aspirations, succumbed in rather indecent haste to the
more immediately viable pursuit of a career. I suspect that there is a specific
sociology to be undertaken of radicals who become elites and yet need to
maintain that they are still radicals.

In any case, behind the intellectual failure of this generation I find a political and moral failure whereas Jacoby finds a changed economic and social
environment. The two analyses are complementary. It is the changed social
conditions which have produced the political failure – although this judgement itself underlines just how little, despite what it thinks of itself, this
generation has managed to shape its environment and how much it has
responded blindly to it.

What, then, of feminism? The development described above has received
its clearest manifestation in the fortunes of feminism of the second wave.
Very much the creature of the radical 1960s and 1970s, this emerged in the
form of 'Women's Liberation', a popular, though socially powerless, moral
and political movement. However, in the 1990s second wave feminism constitutes one of the most powerful networks operating in social institutions. And
the women's studies movement, which reaches hundreds of thousands of
tertiary students, is one of the strongest parts of this network. My explanation of the general character of the intellectual products of this women's
studies movement is, along the lines described above, in terms of the
unrecognised betrayal of earlier principles. However, as my title suggests, my
discussion is directly only about contemporary feminist thought, not about
contemporary radical thought. I am introducing it as an instance of a more
general analysis, that is, as a contribution to Jacoby's question of the failure
of a whole generational grouping, because most of the argument can be
readily extended.

But there is a substantial point in this. Such a presentation assumes the
rejection of a prevailing (academic) feminist view that there is something
special and unique about the emergence of recent feminist thought, something which would make it qualitatively different from other recent theory.
The reason given for this view is that 'truly' feminist thought is different in

kind from 'male' thought. The idea is that 'sexual difference' extends so far that it affects the way in which we think, where this means not just a predisposition to be interested in certain kinds of issues and/or to search out certain kinds of connections, but the way in which we properly think about these things. It is the idea that 'knowledges are sexualised', where this means that the very way in which we decide what is true and false is a function of 'sexual difference'. I devote some space to criticising this view.

Nevertheless, I *have* made feminism my focus, so I must find something special about it. In fact, there are two things. The first is that academic feminism, despite being pedagogically the most influential strand of recent radical thought, has been the least subject to the sort of criticism which the very fact of its political success makes necessary. Let me be clear what I mean. In recent years, there has been a small growth industry of more competent feminist minded academic women criticising various aspects of the less intellectually sound academic feminism. This is to be welcomed. But the assumption perpetuated is that the theory criticised is a worthy object of the activity, that it has a legitimate place both in universities and in the wider world of intellectual debate. It is as though specific theses or arguments of, say, creationism were to be refuted without showing the pseudo intellectual nature of the whole project. Respectability is implicitly conferred on theories which deserve rather to be exposed as failing to constitute serious intellectual contributions (which does not mean that a necessary aspect of any such exposé is not the specific criticisms of specific theses).

At the same time, in that small but growing body of literature which does express concern about the authenticity of much of what presents itself as our intellectual life, there is some reluctance to expose the feminist instances of what is revealed to be widespread substandard reasoning (Callinicos 1989, Ellis 1989, Windshuttle 1994 and, too, Jacoby 1987 – an exception is Gross and Levitt 1994). It is not too difficult to guess at the reasons for this reluctance. The significant exception to what I have just said, Christina Hoff Sommers' impeccably researched and very witty *Who Stole Feminism?* (1994) – a book which completely demolished the alleged statistical basis of many of the common assertions of feminist academics – was so hostilely received that it is clear that, at the very least, this kind of criticism is a high risk activity.

I take it on because of the second way in which 'second wave' feminism is very special. The specialness concerns what I claim is both its original and continuing basis, that from which the corrupted form emerged and that from which corrupt and non-corrupt forms alike still draw much of their strength. This, I argue in Part I, is a traditional but little understood morality which was brought vividly to life by Women's Liberation and which is now largely forgotten. It is this moral understanding which supports taking certain risks against the status quo. So it is what I gained from the earlier women's movement which now seems to require that I take a stand against its subsequent corruption. I suspect the same is true of Helen Garner's writing of *The First Stone* (1995) where she questions the revenge seeking, victim mentality of some current forms of feminism. But since I work in a university the corruption which immediately confronts me is more specific. It is that which manifests in the undermining, rather than what should be the strengthening, of the critical abilities and independence of mind of students of philosophy, which is my discipline.

It happens that the forgotten morality of Women's Liberation – or rather the fact of its distortion – throws some light on this situation. So in this case, acting on this morality provides me with an opportunity also to present it, to recover it from the mountains of feminist literature beneath which it has been hidden. I am pleased to be able to do so because I think it was a moral understanding which was precious in a way which was not fully understood at the time of Women's Liberation even by those of us who gained so much from it.

I want to be clear, however, that I am not suggesting an immediate way forward for the present women's movement in any of this. The morality itself is enduring, but the specifically feminist way into it discovered by Women's Liberation would, I think, constitute the basis of a movement only in the specific social circumstances of the late 1960s and early 1970s. In any case, the future direction of feminism is a question for another generation than mine.

As for acknowledgements, in an activity one regards as risk taking, one does not expect or want others to pay the cost of risks taken by oneself. There are those who deserve my thanks for support, encouragement and ideas whom I shall not mention here. Those I can mention are the following. Because no personal connection is implied, I can thank Rick Benitez for his inspiring lectures on Plato which introduced me to a Socrates I had not known but who is deeply relevant to my own thinking. Because he has already paid the price for his defence of philosophy, I can thank Ted Sadler also for insights into the relevance of Greek Philosophy to my argument. I should mention that it was Lloyd Reinhardt who made me (and many others) aware of the virtues of Simone Weil. (And it was the people of the Charleston Inn in Charleston, Angus, Scotland who showed me, while I was writing the book, that Weil's aspirations for humanity are not purely utopian.) I am very grateful to my two anonymous readers at Routledge, both of whom displayed an intellectual generosity which is now quite rare and of which I was badly in need. I appreciate the assistance of both Veronica Leahy and Anthea Bankoff with the printing and layout of various stages of the manuscript at a time when they were under pressure of too many tasks. My thanks, also, to my parents, Barbara and Geoff Curthoys, for encouragement and for hunting out their old copy of the full 1948 Lysenko report which prompted much of my thinking. Adrian Driscoll, Emma Davis and Sarah Hall from Routledge, and Jacqueline Dias, who copy edited this book, have been pleasant, co-operative and efficient – it has been a pleasure to work with them.

My major intellectual and personal debt is to my husband, Alan Olding. Much of the argument, particularly in Part II, was worked out in discussion with him and although I have tried to be meticulous in my referencing, there are still likely to be some points I incorrectly present as my own. My debt to Alan extends well beyond the fact that he listened to me as I tried to work out the argument and that he put me on to books and references of which otherwise I should have remained ignorant. There is a depressed mentality one can get into when one is working in the area of contemporary radical thought, in which it seems that the one acceptable way of entering the discussion is by endless descriptions of the ideas of others, only after which it may be permissible to make some sketchy suggestions of one's own. Alan is one of those academics who actually thinks – it is beside the immediate point that he is extraordinarily good at this – and through him I relearned what academia had stifled in me, that one can just straightforwardly put one's mind to a problem and try to work it out, that one can use the insights of others to this end without becoming stuck in them (as those which really are insights were intended to be used) and that there is more to thinking than being apparently knowledgeable about intellectual trends. I owe him the liberation of my mind.

Acknowledgements

I am grateful to the authors and/or their publishers for permission to quote from the following:

John Anderson (1962) *Studies in Empirical Philosophy*, Sydney: Angus and Robertson.

Bertold Brecht (1976) 'Parade of the Old New' in *Poems 1913–1956*, Part Three (1938–1956) (eds John Willett and Ralph Manheim), Eyre Methuen (permission received from Reed Books, London).

Lorraine Code (1991) *What Can She Know? Feminist Theory and the Construction of Knowledge*, Ithaca: Cornell University Press.

Ros Diprose 'A "genethics" that makes sense' in R. Diprose and R. Ferrell (eds) (1991) *Cartographies: Poststructuralism and the Mapping of Bodies and Spaces*, Sydney: Allen and Unwin.

T.S. Eliot 'Little Gidding' (1959) *Four Quartets*, London: Faber and Faber (permission for USA rights received from Harcourt and Brace, New York).

Shulamith Firestone (1979) *The Dialectic of Sex*, London: The Women's Press (permission received from Laurence Pollinger Ltd, London).

E.A. Grosz 'Philosophy' in Sneja Gunew (ed.) (1990) *Feminist Knowledge: Critique and Construct*, London: Routledge.

E.A. Grosz and Marie de Lepervanche 'Feminism and Science' in Barbara Caine, E.A. Grosz and Marie de Lepervanche (eds) (1988) *Crossing Boundaries*, Sydney: Allen and Unwin.

Julia Kristeva (1986) (ed. Toril Moi) *The Kristeva Reader*, Oxford: Blackwells.

Primo Levi (1986) 'Story of a Coin', *Moments of Reprieve*, London: Michael Joseph Books.

Alan Morton (1951) *Soviet Genetics*, London: Lawrence and Wishart.

Terry Threadgold 'Introduction' to Terry Threadgold and Anne Cranny-Francis (eds) (1990) *Feminine/Masculine and Representation*, Sydney: Allen and Unwin.

Introduction

The losing of wisdom

The most dreadful condemnation stray feminists have to fear here is dismissal with the last dinosaurs of the late sixties.

(Meaghan Morris)

Gentlemen of Athens, I got this name through nothing but a kind of wisdom. What kind? The kind which is perhaps peculiarly human, for it may be that I am really wise in that. And perhaps the men I just mentioned now are wise with a wisdom greater than human – either that or I cannot say what.

(Plato)

In the late 1960s and early 1970s the Women's Liberation movement took over from the Black Power movement and adapted to its own needs a set of ideas about the psychological dynamics of oppression which, for want of a better name, I shall call 'liberation theory'. Liberation theory was less concerned with the virtues of oppressed groups than were the subsequent radical theories which soon displaced it. Its focus was on the deforming effects of oppression, the most central of which were identified as the psychological dependence of oppressed people and their intense mutual antagonism, the characteristic 'division of the oppressed'. This emphasis was partly due to the fact that the theory understood itself as a 'critical theory' where the point of explanation is more to change the world than to interpret (or to represent) it.[1] For the aim of liberation theory was to demonstrate the possibility of a psychological transformation, namely the transformation of the distortions due to oppression into the virtues of personal autonomy and loyalty to one's fellow oppressed.

Liberation theory fused psychology with politics in so far as the conditions of the desired transformation were understood to be intimately bound up with the workings of power. Here, too, its stance was in sharp contrast with that of the theories which replaced it.[2] The effects of oppression, it was maintained, could not be eliminated from the psyche by way of the oppressed seeking power, although this was understood to be a likely, if not necessary, transient development. Ultimately a stand would have to be taken against power. Liberation theory, then, was based on the anticipation of human relationships without power, in the specific sense in which it understood power and which I shall shortly define.

Critical theories of this general psychological/political kind have since become an industry and it might seem as though what is now distinctive about this liberation theory, as I call it, is only its naïve 1960s flavour, consisting in the use of concepts like 'oppression' and its utopianly optimistic stance. Certainly, as the later theories go, liberation theory is comparatively unsophisticated, at least with respect to its content. If, however, we look more closely at the kind of theory it is, we find that there is something very strange about it and it is this strangeness which I would show is worthy of further consideration. It is a function of the distinctive features of the theory – of its straightforwardly oppositional stance and of its conception of psychological development – but it consists in the fact that these are developed within very peculiar epistemological assumptions. They are peculiar because the more we reflect on them, the more we come across deep and unlikely affinities with the philosophy of Socrates,[3] a philosophy which is itself regarded as very strange.[4]

Liberation theory, like critical theory more generally, is a theory very much of the modern world, based on largely modern assumptions about human beings, while the philosophy of Socrates is usually thought to operate on distinctly premodern assumptions, appropriate to social life in ancient Greece. Furthermore, liberation theory at least looks like a political theory – in any case it was the theory of various political movements whereas the Socratic way of life is classically posited as an alternative to the political life.[5] Nevertheless, it will emerge that liberation theory could be legitimately proposed as an answer to Socrates' version of the question: what is virtue? By this I mean that it is an answer essentially within the terms of reference of the famous Socratic paradoxes and one which could, indeed, be seen as containing a solution to them. If the philosophy of Socrates is strange, then even more strange must be such a spontaneous and unwitting emergence of a potential answer to its fundamental question, expressed in the radical language of recent liberation movements.

Central to the Socratic paradoxes is the intriguing identification of knowledge with virtue and vice with ignorance.[6] We could well redescribe this in terms of the identification of virtue with wisdom, in order to emphasise the distance between the kind of knowledge which would have to be at issue in order to make such an identification and what we presently take to be knowledge. For any knowledge which counts as virtue must 'run deep'. Far more than mere intellectual assent, it must be so deeply inscribed in us that it cannot fail to manifest in right action – it must be a knowledge of the emotions and of the desires as well as of the mind. 'Wisdom' is a notion which has long fallen into disuse and which could appropriately be used to refer to such knowledge. The point would then be that the strangeness of liberation theory consists in that it not only gives some sense to this ancient concept of wisdom but that it also counts as such.

But it is not only its Socratic resonances which make liberation theory a radically different kind of theory from other theories, perhaps with superficial similarities, which we meet with more commonly. It also has equally unintended and deep resonances with Christian morality – or at least with some interpretations of it. Its central moral notion of 'solidarity' could be readily represented as an account of the Christian concept of 'love' and the theory as a whole could be seen as an elaboration from a 1960s political perspective of an essentially Christian account of spiritual transformation – although one without any notion of a transcendent God.[7] That is, it retells with a bit of a modern twist and certainly more than the traditional amount of social theoretical explanation what is at bottom an extremely old story. It is a story, though, which for the most part those involved are unaware of having told. I shall show that liberation theory, more or less despite itself, contains a broadly Christian answer to the ancient Socratic question but that this answer is given in the language and concepts of a revolution of oppressed groups.[8]

Liberation theory does not only recapitulate central themes from these two ancient philosophies – it also reproduces something of their fate. An aspect of both the Socratic and the Christian world views is that they contain an account of the nature of the forces which would destroy them and the sort of moral life which they advocate – the philosophic life in the one case and the Christian life in the other. (For when interpreted, the stories of the deaths of Socrates and of Christ provide just such accounts.) The genuine Socratic and/or Christian ways of life are, then, on their own respective self-understandings, such as to be continually driven underground by the sorts of forces whose more dramatic manifestations were in the execution of their two famous martyrs but whose less dramatic manifestations would be in more everyday modes of repression – such as simply discrediting what is experienced as threatening. A striking fact about liberation theory's own history is just how quickly and thoroughly its widespread popularity was undermined. Despite the intense impact that this theory – or the more general kind of understanding contained in it – had on a whole generation of feminists, radical blacks and radical gays, it was displaced after a very few years by a range of theories, many of the 'postmodern' kind, most of which proclaimed their own superior radicalism and almost none of which had any direct moral content. I shall argue that this overly quick disappearance is intrinsically connected with the status of the theory as 'wisdom' and that it is in the pattern, therefore, of the repression of 'real' Christianity and of Socratic philosophy. More generally, how liberation theory disappeared, what was lost and the effects of this loss are the subject of this book.

THE REPRESSION OF LIBERATION THEORY

The extent (and limitations) of these strange and deep associations of liberation theory will be developed in Part I. Let me leave them, then, for the

moment – except for the passing reference – in order to formulate my question more precisely and in more contemporary terms. I began with the claim
that liberation theory came to Women's Liberation via Black Liberation in
the 1960s. I would go further than that and claim that it also contained ideas
which were, among others, formative of Women's Liberation. There was,
of course, at that time an abundance of theories, ideas and explanations of
male dominance, many of them enthusiastically excessive, but it was the
understanding in liberation theory which gave the movement much of its
tremendous energy. For it was this understanding which was implicit, if not
explicit, in the activity of 'consciousness raising' which was itself formative
of the early movement. Although Women's Liberation was itself short-lived,
it initiated the still flourishing 'second wave' of feminism and so indirectly
liberationist ideas could be said to have provided a significant part of the
conceptual basis for the emergence of contemporary feminism itself.[9] This
fact has left its strong marks on contemporary feminism. But not in any
straightforward way.

It is the way in which liberation theory ceased to be 'the' understanding of
Women's Liberation which suggests that there may have been more at stake in
this than either the poverty of the ideas themselves or a simple change in
theoretical fashion. What is unusual – or at least distinctive – about this is
that any accurate awareness of the true character of these ideas also virtually
disappeared.[10] This is not due to a lack of discussion about this period of
feminist history. On the contrary, a disproportionate amount of feminist
theoretical writings contain a reference to what are taken to be the ideas of
this early movement, a reference which is almost always made in order to
draw the contrast with the purportedly more sophisticated and appropriate
ideas we have now developed. But these references are nearly always either
inadequate or inaccurate.

When feminist theorists look back on this early period they almost always
focus either on what was the (real) presence of what is described as 'grand'
theory (one which purports to identify fundamental social causes), missing
the existence of the more significant 'liberation theory' which was not of this
kind, or alternatively and far more commonly, they recount (for the most part
in good faith) what is in fact an invented history.[11] The almost universal
description of this period is under the heading of the 'feminism of equality'
or of 'the feminism of sameness', a kind of feminism which I shall show in
Part I simply did not exist in anything like the way in which it is claimed. The
false description having been given, however, the argument very often proceeds, now relying on the assurance of the superiority of the later 'feminism
of difference'. In short, to adapt what has become one of the most popular
concepts of recent feminism, the ideas of this period appear to function as a
kind of theoretical 'Other'. They are the object of a set of projections, falsely
attributed, the purpose of which is to reveal the superiority of another set of
ideas.

It is this 'Otherness' which suggests that what is at issue may not be a straightforward forgetting of ideas which are, after all, now a quarter of a century old. This suggestion is reinforced when we realise that what we have is not only a forgotten history and a false history, but also, in some ways, an enforced false history. I mean by this that there is an effective prohibition in feminist intellectual circles of any positive identification with the early movement. Meaghan Morris, quoted above, expressed it clearly: no self-respecting feminist can afford to be associated with the politics or ideas of that time. To an extent this is due to an understandable distaste for some of the excessive and simplistic ideas proposed then, as well as for the authoritarian personal politics which quickly developed – although these features are hardly absent from later feminism – but the important point is the compulsory nature of the dissociation, for it is this which prevents any recognition of the more positive aspects of Women's Liberation. (It also prevents there being any real explanation of that movement, for if the thesis of a feminism of equality or sameness is true, then it remains mysterious how such basically orthodox ideas were able to provide the focus for the enormous enthusiasm and excitement which, it is generally accepted, were generated by Women's Liberation.) This suggests that the rewriting of early second wave history is not just a mistake but performs the function typical of such rewriting, that of diverting attention away from the real history.

(One of the specific arguments I shall develop in this connection will show that despite liberation theory being, in some ways, very much of the enlightenment mould in so far as it would advocate the 'big three' of enlightenment thinking (namely the interrelated goods of freedom, reason and autonomy), it nevertheless very clearly escapes what can be made of postmodern objections to this thinking. For this reason, an awareness of its very existence would reveal the 'universalisation' and 'essentialising' of this very common postmodern argument, that is it would reveal the way in which the features of some very specific ideas have been taken as characteristic, not only of the thinking of a whole historical period, but also as necessary for any theory seriously concerned with ideas of autonomy and freedom.)

We could see here the first of the parallels with the philosophy of Socrates – not in itself that remarkable but worth noting in view of the stronger affinities to come. It is clear from Socrates' account of the reasons for his own death as given in Plato's *Apology* that he understands the falsity of the accusations against him to be an essential part of his story. If, as he maintained, what he was really condemned for is the fact that he questioned people's false certainties, their convictions that they 'knew' and that they were, already, virtuous, then it follows that the only way such a threat could be met would involve misdescribing it. A correct recognition of what was troubling about Socrates would be as troubling as Socrates himself in so far as it would itself require acknowledgement of an uneasiness concerning one's knowledge and one's virtue. The specific reasons why liberation theory may have been threatening will be discussed briefly in a moment and in depth in Chapters 1 and 2. My immediate suggestion is only that there is an analogy between the two situations where it is in the nature of the case that a certain sort of understanding – 'wisdom', perhaps – will be met, not with rational debate, but by misrepresentation.

Reverting to a more contemporary formulation, I would maintain – and this is the major thesis of Part I – that liberation ideas have been repressed. By this I mean that they were abandoned, not because there was a conscious and reasoned move away from them, or because they became irrelevant, but rather because of factors in the situation which require that they not be articulated. If this part of feminist history has been repressed – and this would be consistent with its role as theoretical 'Other' – then the accepted history spelled out in terms of the feminism of 'sameness' would function somewhat in the manner of Freud's 'screen' memories. It would be a set of ideas which, in purporting to describe significant historical events, prevents their genuine memory from emerging. This is the point of my title, *Feminist Amnesia*, where 'amnesia' is used in the same sense as in Russell Jacoby's *Social Amnesia* (1977), meaning the systematic and necessary forgetting of socially threatening ideas. There is no suggestion that the process of rewriting the history of Women's Liberation has been conscious, in the way, say, that the continual and notorious rewriting of *The History of the CPSU* was deliberately undertaken. Rather I should think that it has been the unconscious result of certain political forces. These forces are in opposition to the original and far more valuable aims of second wave feminism.

THE DIFFICULTY OF BEING MORAL

The question now concerns the reasons for this feminist amnesia. What is it about liberation ideas which could be threatening? At issue here is not, as in Jacoby's *Social Amnesia* (1977), a controversial concept like that of the 'unconscious' which it is claimed radically psychologically unsettles us by challenging our everyday ideas about ourselves. Moreover, one of the characteristics of liberation theory is that it is simple and readily accessible and while it draws on several different philosophies it can be, and most often is, presented in ways which presuppose no more than an everyday level of theoretical sophistication. So the explanation for the repression of liberation ideas can have nothing to do with the intellectual or the psychological difficulty of the concepts involved, because these are uncomplicated. The problem, I suggest, is in terms of the moral difficulty they pose.

What liberation theory contains is an account of the psychological workings of power, where power is seen straightforwardly as the ability of one person or group to determine the behaviour of another person or group. (In what follows, then, 'power' does not refer to the resources available to someone in the sense of 'power to' but is used in the more common sense of control over people, that is, as 'power over'.) The account is of the destructive psychological effects of power but it is also about how it can be confronted and undermined. It clearly presupposes a principled opposition to power as such and not just to this or that kind of power, the power that men have, say, in relation to women. This opposition is the content of an ethical or moral strand in the theory which is fundamental to it. And it is this moral strand which I think could be taken as a rendering of the Christian ideal of opposition to the 'ways of man'. But however interpreted, the moral implications of liberation theory are very demanding and it is here that the difficulty arises.

Liberation theory identifies as the psychological key to power our very ordinary and very pervasive assumptions of human superiority and inferiority – the simple idea that some people are more 'important' than others. The implicit moral position, then, is that it is these assumptions which must be abandoned. Such a moral position may be simply stated, and Simone Weil amongst others has done so: 'respect is due to the human being as such and is not a matter of degree.' (Weil 1987: 15). But it is not so easy to live up to. Weil herself, intensely religious, believed that what was required was 'to experience non-being . . . the condition for passing over into truth . . . a death of the soul' (McLellan 1989: 284).[12] Liberation theory, more oriented to 'everyday life', puts it differently, insisting that the pressures to collude with those who are 'acceptable', having status and power, and to disassociate from or patronise the 'unacceptable' are extremely strong, more simply because the costs of not doing so are high, either psychologically, economically or politically. But on both accounts what is sought is something like T.S. Eliot's condition of 'complete simplicity' the cost of which is everything,[13] and both accounts understand that it might well cost everything in worldly terms to refuse this collusion which operates on a fundamental disparity in the evaluation of the worth of human beings. Not to flatter the powerful and to patronise the powerless is recognised as a dangerous activity. It must be counted, then, an achievement of Women's Liberation and the parallel liberation movements of the time to have made this ethic of the irreducible value of human beings come alive for large numbers of people for a brief while and to have done so, not by means of some extraordinary religious intensity, but by making it understood as a necessity of ordinary life. It is this ethic, I maintain, which remains the significant moral truth in feminism and its avoidance and repression is an essential aspect of the latter's intellectual and political corruption.

At this point, what I am claiming in general terms may appear to be just the obvious. There is a simple morality to the effect that there is something absolute about the value of human beings such that judgements of relative superiority or relative importance cannot be made. This morality is deeply embedded in Western culture, mainly in the form of the Christian idea that we are all 'equal before God' at the same time as it is completely at odds with the way we live, our societies being organised largely around status. Such a contradiction can be expected to generate all kinds of repression, equivocation and uneasiness and we know that it does. The moments, therefore, when significant numbers of people try genuinely to implement such a morality are extraordinary. Even in general terms, however, I think there is something new about my argument, which is that I want to take this contradiction seriously and explore its effects. We are so used to it that we forget about it and think that to do otherwise is simply to moralise. Its significance is disguised by its obviousness. But if we do take it seriously as a contradiction and follow through the twists and distortions by means of which we try to cope with it, we can disentangle many of the intellectual, moral and political confusions which surround us. What is new about my specific argument is its approach to this general problem by way of the history of recent feminism. I shall return to the argument.

THE IMPORTANCE OF APPEARING MORAL

We have established, then, that liberation theory contains a basic but demanding moral position. This may partly explain why it was abandoned but not why it has been repressed, why its very existence has been so effect-ively covered over. The reason for the repression, I shall show, is that despite – indeed because of – their lack of direct expression the essential ideas of liberation theory continue to provide contemporary feminism with its enor-mous moral appeal. For without this moral appeal it could not function so successfully. It is this moral appeal which inhibits criticism and which enables contemporary feminism to identify itself as the opponent of obvious injustices. It is its moral appeal which gives contemporary feminism the same sort of hold over our conscience that Stephen Spender identified as crucial to the success of Marxism in the 1930s.[14] The reason repression is necessary is because it is a quite different, indeed opposed, set of ideas which is drawing its credibility from the powerful force of the morality embedded in liberation theory. These ideas would be revealed as fraudulent if 'liberation' ideas were directly articulated. (The aim of Part II is to expose this fraudulence.)

These opposed ideas are ones, I shall argue, which sit quite comfortably with the aspiration for power and which can be readily made use of for such ends. But before we look at what, more specifically, they amount to and how they draw on the appeal of liberation theory, the question must be answered: why is this moral appeal necessary at all? The puzzle here is that there is nothing in principle which prevents a self-interested political movement declaring its self-interested character, since Western democracies are home to lobby groups of all kinds. It is not at all necessary to present a political case as a moral case as well. The situation of the power-oriented kind of feminism I am discussing is complicated for the following reason. The confusions and repressions developed because 'second wave' feminism (and this transform-ation probably occurs in almost all liberatory movements) made the switch from genuinely opposing power to seeking power for a highly specific group-ing, only in the course of it becoming clear that emerging from this very opposition were a growing number of opportunities for power.[15] For this reason it was unable to come clean even to itself about its newer aspirations, because the possibilities for attaining these were actually based in the unexpectedly widespread and growing positive response that the earlier, simpler moral position had elicited. This kind of power-seeking feminism necessarily, then, expresses two contradictory sets of aspirations. On the one hand, there is an expression of the desire for power – an aspiration which speaks mainly, I should think, to those who are actively engaged in the movement and benefit from it. On the other hand, there is a moral and principled (albeit repressed) opposition to power which conceals the self-interested character of much that occurs and which provides it with a much wider basis of support. The strength of contemporary feminism lies in the fact that many people have had an essentially decent response to what has become recognised as a clear injustice. This support is not intended to be for a few women 'making it' but is given on the basis of a morality which rejects arbitrary privilege. This is why so much current feminism, with no particular moral commitment at all, has been forced to capture the moral ground laid down so successfully by Women's Liberation and why, therefore, the ideas of the latter in a clear and direct form have been forced underground.

It is for this reason, also, that the historical dimension of my argument is necessary. From what has been said so far it may seem that the case could be put in purely structural terms. The structural argument is simply that some self-interested political movements operate by way of confusing their constituency with a tacit moral appeal. And what stronger moral basis could be sought in predominantly Christian cultures than one with strong Christian resonances? One should often expect to find, then, in such movements a covert appeal to these sorts of ideas. And it would not seem to matter much whether these were historically acquired or drawn upon from the culture at large. However, the opportunities for widespread support and therefore for power are usually learned about historically, by witnessing the actual influence of a movement which successfully presents a moral position. This is why many movements which do emerge as very genuine 'liberation' movements seem to transform so rapidly into vehicles for careerists. It is because of this same kind of development in the old communist movement that I have been able to find significant analogies between the kinds of intellectual moves made there and those made in contemporary feminism. It is also clear that this general analysis of power-seeking movements appealing to a moral opposition to power could be extended to explain aspects of the wider phenomenon of 'political correctness' although I shall not myself attempt this.

Anticipating my argument that liberation theory counts as a piece of Socratic wisdom, it is worth noting again the emerging parallels with the fate of Socrates and his thought. As I said above, according to Socrates himself the reason for his execution lay in the need of his accusers and judges to appear to be moral and in the fact that that appearance was challenged by Socrates' probings. I am suggesting here something similar but stronger about liberation theory – that the reason for its repression was the requirement that another theory not only appear to have moral credibility but appear to have precisely the moral power of liberation theory itself. And that appearance, clearly, could not be maintained if liberation theory itself were to be freely articulated. The general point is simply that a primary investment in the appearance of morality cannot co-exist with the genuinely moral, for the latter in one way or another threatens to expose the former for what it is.

MADNESS IN THE METHOD

Where, then, are those ideas to be found which avoid the moral implications of liberation theory at the same time as they draw upon its moral credibility? In fact, I believe this broad description would apply to a wide range of the more strident feminist responses which work on a sense of moral outrage but equivocate when it comes to questions of consistently applying the principles they advocate to groups other than the ones they choose. But I shall analyse in depth only one such set of ideas. This, however, is an extremely influential way of thinking, belonging to that kind of academic feminism which largely, although not exclusively, presents itself as postmodern or poststructuralist. It is a kind of thinking most clearly discernible in one of the common pre-occupations of contemporary feminist thought, the concern with what are variously called dichotomies, dualisms, or binary oppositions. It often associates itself, therefore, with the movement known as 'deconstruction', although I shall argue that it should be distinguished from the latter, which is found much less frequently than its derivative, on account of its greater degree of intellectual seriousness. For the thinking in question is characterised by systematic and pervasive confusions, logical slides and a mode of argument which I can best describe by borrowing the concept of 'surrational' theory from David Joravsky (1970: 213), who coined the term to describe the intellectual character of Lysenkoism (a subject to which I shall return). Finding it necessary to distinguish this mode of thought from a more blatant irrationalism, Joravsky defined 'surrationalism' as 'a show of rational discourse, camouflaging a basic refusal to meet the tests of genuine reason'. With this kind of academic feminism, too, the 'show' of genuine and profound intellectual endeavour is a crucial feature.

'Surrational' feminism cannot be simply identified, however, because it appears in a wide range of contexts and in different degrees. Some pieces of writing are almost completely dominated by it. Others are predominantly intellectually serious but will in passing fall into this mode. I shall reconstruct, with examples, the main kind of argumentation which constitutes this kind of feminist thinking in Part II.

My thesis in Part II and the central thesis in the book is that 'surrational' feminism manages to effectively poach moral credibility from the almost antithetical ideas of liberation theory and that the price of this is an actual interest in intellectual confusion. The reason for this is that it is also a mode of thinking which both expresses a desire for power and is primarily suited to exercising power and so the source of its moral appeal is directly at odds with its appropriate function. It is a mode of thinking, therefore, which is typically generated within the kind of political movement described above – erstwhile liberation movements which become career and opportunity vehicles but which are also constrained by the necessity to present themselves as being genuinely opposed to power. To a significant extent 'surrational' feminism can be understood as an attempt in theory to hold together two contradictory positions in a context where both positions seem to be necessary.

The confusions and illogicality, however, are not right on the surface, where they could be seen to be between a principled opposition to power on the one hand and a desire for it on the other. Rather they are generated by the (presumably unconscious) manoeuvres which prevent this basic contradiction from becoming obvious. What happens is that only one of the two positions (that which functions for power) is directly expressed while the other (liberation theory) is repressed. This implies that liberation theory is covertly expressed, that we have, it could be said, a 'return of the repressed'. This 'return' is particularly manifest in the contemporary 'surrational' treatment of dualisms or binary oppositions. A large part of my argument is directed to showing how a straightforward, coherent, and very revealing treatment of these oppositions in liberation theory is transformed into a highly abstract and incoherent approach by those who attempt to go beyond 'patriarchal binary logic'.

This covert expression of liberation ideas can be shown to amount to a projection of the political and moral conflicts with which it deals onto a different plane than that in which they really occur. The resulting picture, reminiscent of the official dialectical materialism of the old Communist world, is of political struggles taking place between metaphysical categories, or between different 'logics', or between signifiers, rather than between human beings who may use these categories, signifiers, or 'logics' in different situations.[16] The move allows for the simultaneous expression and avoidance of the difficult moral position. (In somewhat the same way some would understand psychotic thinking as a projection onto a different plane of a conflict which is too difficult to handle on the 'real life' plane where it occurs.[17] In psychosis, however, the characters are changed from maybe Mum or Dad or some other immediate acquaintance to Napoleon or Hitler, or even God. In the kind of thinking I am describing the shift is from the plane of human action to an abstract one, that of metaphysics, logic or language.) More generally, when a contradiction threatens to become apparent the strategy is to jump to a higher level of abstraction.

The first part of my argument is that much was lost with liberation theory. Here I emphasise its character as 'wisdom' in the Socratic sense. The second part of my argument concerns the way this loss was dealt with by way of a repression necessary to maintain contradictory political orientations. There is also a third part, necessary to complete the argument. It concerns the fact that if 'surrationalist' feminism draws its moral credibility from a repressed liberation theory, it draws its theoretical credibility from varieties of post-structuralist theory, mainly that commonly described as deconstruction. A discussion of the last and its different, although also distorted, relationship with the ideas of liberation theory becomes the content of Part III. I shall begin in Part I with a reconstruction of the ideas of liberation theory, stressing their moral content in order to show exactly what is being avoided, repressed and exploited in the later ideas.

Part I
Liberation theory

... respect is due to the human being as such and is not a matter of
degree ...

(Simone Weil)

1 The psychology of power

... we too are so dazzled by power and money as to forget our essential fragility, forget that all of us are in the ghetto, that the ghetto is fenced in, that beyond the fence stand the lords of death, and not far away the train is waiting.

(Primo Levi, 'Story of a Coin' in *Moments of Reprieve*)

Aspects of what I am calling liberation theory can be found in many and diverse contexts, from that of the Chinese People's Liberation Army of the 1940s to some forms of contemporary Western psychotherapy. The main route by which it became so influential in Women's Liberation would appear to be as follows. To begin with (remembering that Women's Liberation was born in the USA) the ideas were taken over from the Black Liberation movements.[1] But the emphasis on consciousness in black liberation movements was not itself entirely home-grown. In that rather strange solidarity that existed in the late 1960s between the armed struggles of national liberation movements based in the peasants of the 'Third World' and radical movements of predominantly European societies, it is clear that the original base of liberation ideas was, in fact, the former.[2] The major theorist was undoubtedly Frantz Fanon of the Algerian National Liberation Front (FLN) whose most influential work, *The Wretched of the Earth* (Fanon 1967b), was said by Eldridge Cleaver to be 'now known among the militants of the black liberation movement in America as "the Bible"' (Gendzier 1973: 28). The reason why such a striking difference in context did not affect the reception of Fanon's thought is partially explained by its content. There are two central ideas. The first, as Irene Gendzier describes it, was Fanon's assumption 'that the perfect coincidence of an internal struggle accompanied by a political fight would invariably lead to a total regeneration of the social order' (Gendzier 1973: 28). (It is worth noting that Fanon was a psychiatrist and that for him the conviction that political confrontation was necessary for psychological health was not an a priori ideological commitment but developed out of his attempts to treat Arab patients in Algeria before his own political ideas were formed (Gendzier 1973: Part Two).) So it was the insistence on the general necessity of internal, psychological change for effective political change and vice versa which was taken up by Black Liberation and later by Women's and Gay Liberation, becoming one of their defining character-istics.[3] The specific kind of political change sought, which of course was largely context dependent, did not affect this general proposition. The second idea, now unpopular because of the emphasis on 'difference', was that dom-ination by human beings of each other induced a common psychological dynamic of power. In so far as this was assumed and what was thought to be at issue was domination, there was no barrier to one movement taking over from another the general analysis of the psychology of power and adapting it as necessary. And in the late 1960s the awareness of the psychological, experiential aspects of power – the 'politics of experience' – was very much in the air.[4]

The other important theorist of liberation theory was (and still is) Paulo Freire, a Brazilian educator with a strong Christian identification and emphasis, whose work began and evolved amongst the peasants of Latin America although, as with Fanon, the main reception of his ideas has been in the West. It might be thought that these two sources of liberation theory, one the ideas of a Christian educator and the other of a militant of an armed liberation movement, are distinct. In fact, however, Freire was very influenced by Fanon,[5] and so it was for similar theoretical reasons that they shared a faith in the ability of peasants to achieve a revolutionary consciousness (for which Freire had the more moderate description of 'humanisation').[6] What Freire did, however, was to systematise the ideas found in Fanon's writings in an untidy form and to clearly distinguish the elements I am describing as liberation theory, the aspects concerning the transformation of conscious-ness, from the rest of the theory (Freire 1972). The latter purported to be an objective analysis in quasi-Marxist terms of the different political potential of the various social groupings in the nations undergoing decolonisation. Outside of the black movements where Fanon was read directly it was prob-ably mainly through Freire that liberation ideas became known. Or rather became known in the form of theory. For more important, although not to my immediate purpose here, was the fact that the general ideas were widely expressed in the very popular radical literature of the time. Their strongest perpetrators were in fact writers such as James Baldwin, Richard Wright, Eldridge Cleaver, Robin Morgan, Fay Weldon, Ti-Grace Atkinson, etc.

The reconstruction I am about to give of liberation theory is, with respect to its content, essentially an amalgam of the ideas of Freire and Fanon as formulated in the 1950s and 1960s. But the analysis of its epistemological status, of its humanist implications, and the implications concerning the 'logic' of binary oppositions are my own. Indeed the last is only appropriate because of the issues raised in the intervening period by the dominance of what is loosely described as postmodern theory. The general theory, when applied to male/female dynamics, constituted much of the theory of the con-sciousness raising groups which were so fundamental to Women's Liberation. It was also, therefore, the theory which informed many of the short experiential writings, on topics ranging over housework, aging, humour, beauty ideals, race relations, etc., which grew out of these groups and which were the main literary output of the movement. Nevertheless, the only well-known systematic theoretical articulation of these ideas from within Women's Liberation is to be found in Shulamith Firestone's *The Dialectic of Sex* (Firestone 1979) and there it is intertwined with a quite different kind of theory, a supposedly Marxist account of reproduction as the fundamental material basis of social life, the kind of theory which is now often rejected as 'grand theory'.[7] Unfortunately it is for the latter theory that the book has been remembered although it is on account of the former that it changed lives.

(Catharine Mackinnon's radical feminist analysis of male/female relations in terms of the patriarchal control of sexuality is presented by her as the theory which has emerged out of feminist consciousness raising. Her theory, also, is of the kind which would fall under the postmodern classification of 'grand theory' whereas liberation theory, as I shall show in a moment, is not. (To repeat, 'grand theory' is usually defined as that which searches for fundamental causes.) And although, unlike postmodernists, I can find no objection in principle to this kind of theory as such (although I am more than sceptical about Mackinnon's specific example of it), clearly Mackinnon and I are in conflict over just what ideas are centrally at issue in feminist consciousness raising. We are not, however, in conflict over the fact of its epistemological significance upon which Mackinnon also places much emphasis (Mackinnon 1991: 83–105). My disagreements with Mackinnon are, however, peripheral to my line of argument and so I shall confine them to a note.[8])

PRELIMINARIES

My reconstruction of liberation theory is in two parts. The first, the content of this chapter, explains how power relations are maintained and the second, the content of the following chapter, how they might be destroyed. Both parts are concerned with the mechanisms of power, specifically with its psychological mechanisms. The theory makes no attempt to explain the origins or the structural basis of power and it is for this reason that it cannot be considered as any kind of 'grand theory'. Rather it assumes the existence of power and restricts itself to examining how it operates. It is important to note these restricted aspirations of liberation theory so that it is not misinterpreted as offering a psychological explanation for the existence, rather than the mechanisms, of power.[9]

I have said that liberation theory is a comparatively unsophisticated theory. Those familiar with psychoanalytic discussion may recognise in it an extremely simple account of the same phenomenon which Freud deals with under the concept of femininity.[10] They will also recognise very general aspects of Luce Irigaray's attempt to reinterpret and denaturalise the classic Freudian account in a way that makes possible an optimism concerning the possibilities for psychological change, most importantly in our ability to relate to others on a basis other than that of our compulsive requirements for a certain kind of validation.[11] In no way do I propose this simple liberation account as an alternative to a more complex psychoanalytic approach, although I shall argue in Part III that it provides a broad framework or general orientation within which the psychoanalytic discussion could take place. It is in that context that I shall discuss the overlaps and differences with Irigaray's analysis as well as with those other psychoanalytic accounts popular with feminists. However, if I do expect that some may recognise in liberation theory elements of more recent psychoanalytic theories, I very much hope that no one sees here a theory which falls within the scope of current postmodern criticisms of the category of 'experience' (their quotation marks). It may well be, I think, that some vaguely recollected idea of the politics of experience is the intended object of these criticisms, but that they simply do not apply to liberation theory, one of the main theories referred to by this name, should be obvious from my reconstruction. I shall in any case make it obvious, although once more I shall do so in a note, for the criticism is widely off the mark and I do not want it to intrude on the development of my argument.[12]

It is in the following chapter that the Socratic character of the theory becomes apparent. The analysis of the destruction of the operations of power within the psyche is at the same time an analysis of the acquisition of a certain kind of understanding – an understanding which combines self-knowledge, knowledge of the workings of power and a strong ethical stance and which qualifies, therefore, as what I would describe as wisdom. The beginning of a Socratic understanding, though, can be discerned in the argument of the present chapter in so far as it reproduces the theme that respect for power and status is accompanied by ignorance.[13]

The broadly Christian morality, however, is evident throughout the whole argument. The key to liberation theory is a basic ethic according to which people should not judge each other as superior or inferior, as better or worse than each other – an ethic, it could be said, according to which we are all 'equal before God'. The first part of the theory could be understood as an analysis of what is involved in failing to adopt this moral position and the second part as an analysis of what is involved in trying to adopt it.

POWER MAINTAINED

We begin with an apparently simple and widely accepted thesis but one whose implications go much further than is usually thought. The claim is that the conviction (not necessarily conscious) of the relative superiority and inferiority of human beings is both the main psychological effect of power as well as, and more importantly, its main psychological mechanism. (This is excluding relations of coercion by pure force.) It is crucial here that the superiority/inferiority is attributed to the human being as such, so that what is at stake is one's relative worthwhileness or worthlessness as a person, as opposed to, say, a recognition that certain of one's specific abilities may be greater or lesser than someone else's or that aspects of one's behaviour are more or less worthy. For it is only here, in the relative evaluation of the person as such, that the existence of a moral 'category mistake' can be demonstrated, and in opposition to which Weil's thesis shall be maintained that 'respect is due to the human being as such and is not a matter of degree'. It should also be noted that the thesis is that it is the comparative evaluation of human beings as such which is the mechanism of power and so it follows that while this evaluation will very often latch onto cultural attitudes about sex, race and class it does not necessarily have to do so. In other words the claim is that what is essential is the evaluation of the powerful as 'better' than the powerless and that the further 'deductions' from this that men are 'better' than women, whites 'better' than blacks, etc. are secondary. Relations of power, therefore, can also hold outside of these secondary determinants and sometimes partly reversing their normal implications. All that is required is that both parties believe that one of them simply *is* 'better' than the other, that they are the more 'important' one. This point will become pivotal in the next chapter in my confrontation with postmodern notions of 'binary oppositions', where what will be at issue is precisely whether the more fundamental problem of power is this comparative evaluation of people which then latches onto various definitions and perceptions of their specific attributes or whether it is the character of the latter definitions themselves.

What, then, is the basis of the thesis which links comparative evaluation of human beings with power? Here the argument is very familiar and I will be brief. First, it is easy to grasp why living within relations of domination would be thought to produce experiences and ideas of personal superiority or inferiority. When one is systematically treated in a certain way the immediate, unreflective, assumption is that the reason for this lies in one's own nature. Since the important differences in treatment concern status it seems as though these differences in nature must be to do with our overall 'worthwhileness' and not our specific attributes. (Although the former can be thought to be based in the latter.) It is only a little more difficult to see why the experiences and ideas which arise in this way would then be thought to function as the central psychological mechanism of power. They do so by way of concealing the very existence of relations of power. The reason for differential (status) treatment of different people is assumed to lie in their different degrees of worthiness and so the relations of domination which are in fact responsible are rendered invisible. And, the argument goes, power works best when its character as power is obscured. (Or, as I said above, power is necessarily accompanied by ignorance.) So the first thesis of liberation theory is an empirical claim about the causes and the effects of failing to live up to the idea that we cannot measure the worth of human beings. We are some distance yet from having any moral argument for this position for all we know is that, metaphorically speaking, the 'ways of man' are the ways of power and these are not 'God's ways'. The question why we should choose one way rather than the other is yet to be addressed.

Liberation theory aspires to explain more than these elementary causes and effects. It aims also to reveal the inherently unstable dynamics of power. In doing this it begins to develop a case for opposing power. There is an argument that one of the two above ways, 'the ways of man', will not work. This would be the first part of the case for 'God's ways'. (If the argument were left there the implication would be that 'God's ways' are good because they work. But this pragmatism would scarcely count as 'wisdom'. The second part of the argument in the next chapter will show that this is not the case and that 'God's ways' work because they are good.)[14] The theory begins to develop the complexity necessary for this first part of the argument when the nature of the assumptions of superiority and inferiority is further explored and found to have the form of the now notorious 'binary opposition'. Since what is involved here is not at all part of the indiscriminate attack on binary oppositions which is now so popular, but rather the discussion of a very specific 'binary opposition' whose causal role depends on its specificities and since, furthermore, I want to argue that the former kind of indiscriminate attack is the result of an unrecognised abstraction and displacement of the latter specific analysis, I shall proceed carefully at this point.

We have seen that our everyday ideas of personal superiority and inferiority are applied to the person as such and not in the first instance to our specific pieces of behaviour or to our specific attributes. The subject, then, of comparative evaluation is our goodness or worthiness as a person or – and this formulation will soon take on significance – the degree of our 'humanness' itself. Now this comparative evaluation of persons takes the famous binary form when one, and necessarily only one, of the two people or groups at issue is itself taken as the standard of measurement of the 'fully' or 'properly' human (or as the standard of normality). Instead of there being an independent standard with respect to which both terms are evaluated, one of the terms becomes the standard of evaluation for both. What occurs then is that these attributions of higher and lower human status become logically dependent. The evaluations are mutually exclusive and therefore of the binary form, in the sense that if one party is seen to be fully human then the other one cannot be.[15] So long as there is a hidden assumption that one of the two terms will be the standard of evaluation then one party in the relationship can be seen as fully human only because the other is seen as lesser and vice versa. So the second thesis in my reconstruction of liberation theory is that this is precisely what does happen in situations of domination. The reasons why it does we shall explore in a moment, but for now there is more to say about the 'logic' of the assumptions.

What is at issue in situations of domination – and this part of the account is also standard in postmodern accounts – is that the operative assumption of relative superiority/inferiority is an aspect of the more complex assumption that there is one right, proper and normal way to be human and that this way is the way of the controlling or powerful group. De Beauvoir, for example, complained about the assumption that 'A man is in the right in being a man: it is a woman who is in the wrong' (de Beauvoir 1972: 15). If we continue with this example it can be seen that the two sexes are said to measure their human 'value' not independently but in relation to the other, in a way that is most damaging to women. The male sex is established as 'properly' human and therefore as the standard of what it is to be human, while the female sex is implicitly measured by this standard and is as a consequence found to be wanting. There is a destructive linking of the way the two sexes value themselves, such that a positive evaluation of one can only be attained by way of a negative evaluation of the other. The two are not, as the psychotherapists might say, psychologically separate. There is an exploitative exchange of experiences of self worth, the recognition of which is in fact central to the very notion of a politics of experience. So if, as we shall see, the 'deficient' person or group begins to lay claim to the status of the 'fully' human, then the other person or group feels that *their* status is immediately threatened. Given the assumption that there is only one way to be human, only one of the two parties can be in the 'up' position.

This can be put in a way that highlights the convergence on this point with the deconstructionist strand of postmodern thought (in both its 'surrational' and 'serious' varieties). If we look at the attitudes which people in relationships of power have to each other, we first identify the shared conviction that the person in the 'up' position is a better person than the one in the 'down' position. The two aspects of the judgement of relative merit, namely that the one person has so much 'worth' and the other a greater or lesser amount of 'worth', appear to be made independently of each other and so prior to their comparison. This is because an essential aspect of these sorts of notions of superiority/inferiority is that they are believed to be objectively based. We experience ourselves as having whatever degree of 'worth' which is tacitly conceived to be a real property. However, when it is recognised that a change in the alleged 'worth' of one person affects the alleged worth of the other in a see-saw situation we see that the two judgements cannot be objectively based and therefore independent in this way. If they were, then an improvement in the status of one would not affect the status of the other. Contrary to appearances the two evaluative judgements are in fact interdependent and this is because the standard of evaluation is not independent of the people in question but is identified with one of them, or rather with the attributes of one of them. The point is that comparative evaluation of persons appears not to take the binary form which in fact it does take.

The convergencies with deconstruction are these: first, it is agreed that we have a situation in which one of two parties is taken as the standard of what it is to be fully and properly human and the other, therefore, being different, has to be seen as deficient. There are only two possibilities and these are exhaustive and exclusive; either one is 'normal' or one is 'deficient'. Differences can only be seen as deficiencies. Second, it is agreed that the two evaluations so made have an appearance of independence which conceals a deeper dependence.

The non-convergencies with deconstruction are these: first, deconstruction regards this kind of comparative evaluation as arising from the humanist project itself. Humanism, it is maintained, must define what it is to be human and any such definition must take the above form. Humanism, in other words, necessarily posits its 'Others'. It is necessarily in the binary mode and this is because of the alleged domination of Western thought itself by such binary oppositions, dichotomies, or dualisms, as they are variously called. (More on this in Chapter 4.) Liberation theory by contrast, we shall see, understands this 'Otherness' as arising from the particular character of situations of power and more specifically from the form which the comparative evaluation of human beings must take in these situations. Second, the fact that we have two dependently defined terms which appear to be independent is taken by deconstruction to be an instance of the perfectly general character of the allegedly dominating dualisms. Liberation theory explains what is at issue as a very specific case of the form of a comparative evaluation, made in specific circumstances. So one approach focuses on a specific binary opposition and the other on the binary form itself, a fact which will become crucial later in the analysis of the procedures of some varieties of deconstruction as avoidance. These criticisms of deconstruction will be further developed throughout but for now I want to look at liberation theory's own very specific explanation for the 'binary form' of the way we evaluate each other, so making others into 'Others'.

Why, then, do people unconsciously measure their worth as the negation of someone else's? Why does my sense of my own goodness, importance, or 'humanness' depend on you being seen as bad, insignificant or as 'lesser' in some way? The puzzle is why we don't evaluate each other in the more straightforward, non-binary way where your worth is thought to depend on you and not on my worth. Now the striking feature of these binary evaluations is that they express relations of dependence in so far as two people making them will be tied together in respect of their sense of self worth by such an understanding. For if you are 'fully' human and I am 'lesser' then I will depend on you who have real worth so that some of it may rub off on me. (The details of this will be developed below.) And if you are 'lesser' and my sense of my own worth depends on this comparison then I am still dependent on you. Clearly, such conceptions will be generated by and will reproduce relations of dependence. So if the first thesis of liberation theory was that notions of the superiority/inferiority of human beings are mechanisms of most power relations, then the second thesis that these evaluations take the binary form is necessary to explain the dependent character of such relations. If the assumptions of relative merit did not take this form then relations of power would not bind its parties together in any stable way. If the standard of evaluation was independent then the essential judgement of relative superiority/inferiority would be too easily weakened or undermined. The evaluations are dependent because the relations in which they operate are ones of dependence. But more than that, this second thesis of liberation theory, unlike the general positing of binary oppositions we find by deconstructionists, will turn out to have powerful explanatory force. This is in relation to the way power psychologically deforms people, how these deformities maintain power, and also why they are inherently unstable. This explanation, however, works only in conjunction with another thesis of liberation theory concerning human needs.

The third thesis in this reconstruction of liberation theory is that human beings have a fundamental need to be recognised as human by other human beings. (By 'fundamental' here is meant that this need is to be counted as constitutive of what it is to be human. The full significance of this idea will not emerge until the next chapter where, broadly following MacIntyre (1985), this thesis will be shown to provide the beginnings of a theory of human nature able to provide objective grounds for the moral position: 'respect is due to the human being as such'.) The idea that human beings intrinsically require recognition from others can be found within developed philosophical positions such as those of Hegel, Sartre, and others who would develop a dialectic of 'self and other' in terms of a philosophy of consciousness. But it does not have to be. It can also be stated in the straightforward terms of Simone Weil who simply asserts that such a need is one of the 'needs of the soul' (Weil 1987). The idea is essential to liberation theory, the specific framework in which it might be formulated is not. (However, the distinctive epistemological basis upon which the claim is made is discussed in the next chapter, for it is of that self-referential kind which presupposes aspects of liberation theory itself.)

What does it amount to, then, this 'need of the soul' for recognition as human? It is distinctive about the liberation account – and this will enable it to avoid some of the difficulties usually involved in talking about 'human nature' – that no specific quality is posited in the definition of 'the human' other than the satisfaction of this need itself. Recognition as human does not by definition imply recognition of one's autonomy, or of one's rights, or of one's capacity for reason or whatever. It implies only a recognition that one is of the same species as others. There *is* here a claim concerning 'human nature' for it is asserted both that humans have this need and that it is constitutive of their 'humanness'. But it is a minimal claim. It amounts to the idea that we are 'species-beings' in something like the nineteenth century sense used by Feuerbach and the young Marx, meaning that we can only fulfil whatever specifically human potential we may individually have if we do so as members of the species. There are two aspects to the version of 'species-beings' implied in liberation theory: the claim that we can only act as specifically *human* beings if we are recognised as such by others of our species whom we similarly recognise and the claim that there is a need to be human. And while we shall see in the next chapter that there is further content to the notion of what it is to be human, this is argued to consist in the empirical consequences of seeking satisfaction of the fundamental need. But if liberation theory gives only a minimal definition to the content of the notion of 'the human' it does place restrictions on the manner in which this recognition as human can be given if it is to satisfy the need for recognition.

It is implied by the above account that the need for recognition as human is prior to any further identification of what it is to be human. It follows that the need is for recognition as something which is not dependent upon the possession of any other qualities. It is therefore a need for unconditional recognition as human which is recognition as unconditionally human. (If it seems strange to insist that the need for recognition as human is more fundamental than any other kind of aspiration to humanness such as autonomy, maybe, or the possession of rights or duties, remember that the theory appears to be unpacking what is assumed by Christian themes which place love at the centre of human life.)

Now the thesis is clearly a humanist one and humanism traditionally centres on the notion of equality. The claim concerning the need for unconditional regard could be cast in terms of the claim that what we need from each other is recognition as being equally human to others, but only if we are extremely careful about what is meant by equality. The equality of human beings cannot be understood here as the result of some kind of measurement of our respective worth, a measurement which finds us all equal, for such a measurement could only be made on the basis of some further quality which renders us all 'the same'. Recognition as unconditionally human or as equally human must then be understood as implying the absence of possibility of such measurements. The point is that the worth of human beings is considered to be absolute, unchangeable and not subject to comparison. It is 'not a matter of degree'. (This does not mean that human actions are not subject to evaluation and moral judgement or that different human dispositions may not be counted amongst the virtues, but only that that judgement in no way mediates the value of the person as such.) We have here a version of the humanist notion of equality which runs counter to the interpretation upon which much of the postmodern rejection of humanism is based.[16]

This thesis and its 'non-measurable' interpretation of the notion of equality suggests the possibility of a return to humanism which would escape many of the objections to it put by the advocates of 'difference'. Moreover, such a version of equality is in accord, though not identical, with those found in Locke and Marx, who are respectively *the* major figures in the founding of the liberal and socialist traditions. Locke clearly specifies that by 'equality' he means nothing like 'sameness' but only an absence of any qualities which would subordinate one person to the will of another.[17] Marx's criticism of liberalism was precisely that it could only achieve its ideals of equality in the form of 'sameness', that is, in a form which inserted everyone in the same way into the social/legal fabric regardless of individual differences.[18] In this sense both philosophers insisted that humans ought to be regarded as having an irreducible value which is not affected by differences and that neither in any way thought of equality as sameness or in terms of measurement but rather as the absence of these. Finally, that such a humanist tradition is not yet dead is suggested by the fact that these rival and incompatible accounts of the notion of equality are also central to Simone Weil's much more recent and increasingly influential attack on the central importance given to the notion of rights: 'The notion of rights is linked with the notion of sharing out, of exchange, of measured quantity' (quoted in McLellan 1989: 79). Weil's concern is that the emphasis on rights is an emphasis of one's welfare in relation to the next person and not with the good of the soul as such which is essentially non-comparative.

We have three theses, that power both engenders and requires comparative judgements of human worth, that these judgments take a binary form and that there is a basic human need for recognition as human. We can now move on to explain the psychologically deforming consequences of power and its inherent instability. These explanations are straightforward but they are also the ones which, in speaking directly to personal experience in the context of Women's Liberation, were powerfully effective in changing lives. The more theoretical point that I shall stress here is simply that these theses do have explanatory force. I stress this because it is in this way that liberation theory can be seen to contrast positively with the postmodern discussion in which the alleged pervasive presence of binary oppositions can neither be satisfactorily explained nor itself perform any explanatory role.

Let me briefly recapitulate the 'liberation' account of the much discussed 'dependency' of oppressed people. This dependency is something more than the mutual dependence of both parties on an oppressive context (as described in the second thesis, pp. 20–3) for it specifically characterises the psychology of the oppressed, whether this be women's 'clinging behaviour', the so-called 'dependency complex of colonised people', 'dependent personalities', or whatever. The dependency is in no way denied by liberation theory, which on the contrary identifies it as a major psychological problem, but what it does do is to reveal it as an intelligible response to oppression, one which anybody would have in these psychological circumstances and so one which, therefore, cannot stem from the specific psychology of women, or of peasants, or of the colonised.[19]

Such an account, attempting to demonstrate how anybody might respond, clearly presupposes some idea of what a human being is and so it is at this point that the thesis concerning the human need for recognition comes into play. If we now take this thesis together with the previous theses of liberation theory, to the effect that the oppressed are seen by themselves and their oppressors first of all as inferior but second, and more specifically, as less than 'fully' human, then it is clear that oppression works against one of the fundamental needs of the oppressed. What is described as the psychological dependence of the oppressed is only the attempt to meet this need indirectly at the same time as one accepts the basic assumption that one is a 'lesser' form of humanity. If one is denied 'full' human recognition directly, the immediate and obvious course is to try to gain this recognition derivatively from those who are seen as 'really and fully' human. This creates a strong and specific dependency on an association with the latter. The kind of association and derivative recognition sought will vary with the kind of oppression: Fanon described his own desires to immerse himself in white European culture; Freire the exaggerated respect peasants can have for the landlord (Freire 1972: 51); Firestone the superhuman effort women will put in to 'make a good catch', etc. But let's follow Firestone with the example of men and women, which is not only our immediate concern but is also one in which the dynamics are very clear, although it should be recognised that the 'pure' situation she described has significantly broken down over the last twenty-five years.

Feminists have always insisted that the need women have for men is more than the basic uncomplicated need for love, affection, companionship, etc. It is also a need for cultural legitimacy. As Firestone wrote:

> In a male-run society that defines women as an inferior and parasitical class, a woman who does not achieve male approval in some form is doomed. To legitimate her existence a woman must be more than a woman, she must continually search for an out from her inferior definition, and men are the only ones in a position to bestow upon her this state of grace. But because the woman is rarely allowed to realise herself through activity in the larger (male) society – and when she is, she is seldom granted the recognition she deserves – it becomes easier to try for the recognition of one man than of many.
>
> (Firestone 1979: 132)

Hence we have women's 'clinging behaviour' which Firestone claims is 'required by the objective social situation' (Firestone 1979: 131). She continues with her point concerning the overwhelming necessity to 'have' a man in these conditions:

> These are not trivial gossip sessions at all (as women prefer men to believe) but desperate strategies for survival. More real brilliance goes into one one-hour co-ed telephone dialogue about men than into the same co-ed's four years of college study, or for that matter, into most male political manoeuvres. It is no wonder, then, that . . . women always arrive exhausted at the starting line of any endeavour. It takes one's major energy for the best portion of one's creative years to 'make a good catch', and a good part of the rest of one's life to 'hold' that catch.
>
> (Firestone 1979: 131)

The unconscious conviction is clearly that 'having a man of one's own' will satisfy the frustrated need for recognition in two ways. First, it is to be hoped that he, as 'fully' human, will recognise you as unique, so lifting you out of the general 'less than human' status of your sex. Second, it may be that some of his 'full' human qualities will, as it were, 'rub off', for others will now see you in relation to him. It is essential to the intensity of these needs that the comparative evaluation takes the binary form, that men are not only assumed to be superior but are also assumed to be the standard of evaluation. Otherwise one would more likely seek recognition through one's achievements or in relation to whatever independent standard one believed to be operative. But when men themselves are the measure, it is only through them one can hope to come closer to full human recognition.

There is, however, a basic catch in the situation and it is this which makes it inherently unstable. For the other side of the situation which drives women to seek recognition by way of men is that men cannot so easily give it. Firestone's further point is that men cannot, without extreme ambivalence, be committed to a woman. When forced into it they assert their independence by 'ogling other women in her presence, by comparing her unfavourably to past girlfriends or movie stars, . . . by suggesting that if he were a bachelor he would be a lot better off' (Firestone 1979: 130). There are two reasons for this. Not only do they fear that women's lesser status might 'rub off' on them by way of association but, more fundamentally, it is impossible to give human recognition to, that is to take seriously, those whom one considers to be 'less' human than oneself. And this contradiction is built into the situation from the outset. Where degrees of humanity are assumed, as has traditionally been the case between men and women, then respect is impossible and it is only a lack of clarity about this which enables women to live in the perpetual hope that they will be properly loved by a man. (There is clearly more to the self-defeating character of this 'dialectic' – the dependence of women on the status of a man rather than upon the person is itself a repellent force, at the same time as it may be the kind of dependence required by men to reassure them of their status and of their control.)

The search for male recognition under these circumstances is futile, but in the first instance this only intensifies the desperation with which it is conducted. The antagonism oppressed people typically have towards each other is an aspect of this desperation, but also, as the diversion of aggression away from the powerful and onto other oppressed, it is an important mechanism for keeping relations of power in place. Its manifestations range from the absolutely tragic in the case of the colonised, that 'plunging into a fraternal blood bath . . . the suicidal behavior which proves to the settler (whose existence and domination by them is all the more justified) that these men are not reasonable human beings' (Fanon 1967b: 42), to the seemingly petty jealousies of women. It is the latter which once again following Firestone can be used to illustrate the point.

The commonplace that 'women are their own worst enemies' is the folklore recognition of the fact that women are often competitive with, and antagonistic to, each other. There is more to this phenomenon than the fact that women tacitly endorse the general cultural assumption that they are lesser and reflect this in their attitudes to each other. There is a specific dynamic involved which Firestone reveals springs from the essential futility of the

search. The problem is that so long as assumptions of men's greater importance have a hold, men cannot give – or understand – what women want.
There is, nevertheless, an uneasy and unstable resolution arrived at which
depends on the idealisation which takes place in romantic love. This idealisation, Firestone agrees, most certainly *is* an illusion, but far from it being one
of the eternal mysteries of love we can easily understand it when we see how it
works.

To begin with, idealisation is mostly something that men confer upon
women and that women want from men. Its role is asymmetric between
the two sexes: 'Women have no . . . reason to idealise men – in fact, when
one's life depends on one's ability to "psych" men out, such idealisation may
actually be dangerous' (Firestone 1979: 126). This idealisation is something
they seek for it is a form of recognition which lifts them up from an existence
'down among the women',[20] constituting them as 'special' – somewhere
between the status of men and the rest of women. Men, by way of contrast,
'must idealise one woman over the rest in order to justify his descent to a
lower caste' (Firestone 1979: 126). It is the fact that what is sought can by
definition be given to only one woman which makes the competition between
women so intense. It is more than a competition for scarce goods. It is one in
which every other woman is necessarily a threat, for the only way out of the
generalised inferiority of being a woman is to be 'unique' amongst women –
to be the only one with this midway status between women and men. The
absolute impossibility of such a competition is modified, obviously, by the
fact that most women settle for trying to get this recognition from just one
man, but the race is nevertheless desperate, especially considering that men
quickly discover that their initial idealisation was an illusion and, rather than
understand what was behind it, are very likely to locate it somewhere else.
This solution involving idealisation and intense competition is then unstable.
For one thing the idealisation sought is a lie which is continually discovered,
while for another the conditions of the competition are extremely stringent. It
is clear that the psychology produced by, and required for, relations of power
is not a particularly stable one for it only frustrates the need which gives rise
to it – the need to be regarded as fully human.

So liberation theory has given an explanation of why the way of life inherent in accepting a subordinate position is unstable. The explanation is in
terms of its assumption (itself yet to be justified) that human beings have a
basic need for 'full' recognition from others. If we now put ourselves in the
position of the heroine of liberation theory, as we might describe her, we can
start to understand how such a justification might be made. It is clear that at
the beginning of her story she would in no way accept the liberation theory
thesis that what she 'really' wants is ordinary human respect. She is convinced
that what she really wants is a man of her own. It would only be the continued experience of disappointment with the attainment of her goal, or the
overwhelming anxiety and frustration associated with trying to attain it, that
might convince her that she had in fact misidentified her need and that the

need for her own man was both a particular expression and a disguise of a deeper need. She would discover her need for ordinary human respect at the same time as she discovered the futility of her aspirations because this would be the only way to make sense of her dissatisfactions. Argued in this way, what we have here is a very curious epistemology, one which requires definite experiences not only of life, but also of suffering, to justify a basic thesis. The implications of this will be taken up in the next chapter.

The above analysis, straightforward as it may be, provides us with a reason why power is always accompanied by some form of resistance.[21] There is a fundamental need which is not satisfied and which presses forward to some other kind of resolution and so presses against the constraints of the situation. Let me then proceed to liberation theory part two and show how easy it is to explain the broad features of this resistance if one is willing to accept an argument that is conceptually simple but practically and morally very demanding.

2 The getting of wisdom

> I find myself suddenly in the world and I recognise that I have one right alone: That of demanding human behaviour from the other.
>
> (Fanon)

Liberation theory is a form of humanism. So far, though, this humanism has been apparent only in the thesis which asserts a common human need for non-comparative recognition as human (equality) and in the anticipation of the moral conclusion that this is how we should relate to each other. One of the most central humanist ideas is that of human autonomy, the idea, traditionally presented as both factual and moral, that human beings can determine their own destinies, and that they also should do so.[1] Liberation theory, too, understands human autonomy as an idea with both factual and moral dimensions although it does so rather differently from this traditional form. The difference is that autonomy is not thought to be a given fact about humans but rather something which we can attain. Nor is it regarded as fundamental, either as a value or as a fact, but in both respects it is deduced from other more basic considerations. Counter-intuitive as it might initially seem, individual autonomy becomes an objective prerequisite for the meeting of the need for recognition and is thought to be developed only in the pursuit of the satisfaction of this need. Both as a value and as a human capacity it is said to be dependent on the drive for recognition. This is counter-intuitive, because the theory therefore derives the necessity of autonomy from the necessity for love, when in everyday life we are used to opposing these to each other. But this is another dimension to the fact that the argument unconsciously recapitulates Christian themes which place the search for love at the centre of human life. (It also means that in this case there is a quick reply to those many contemporary feminists who maintain that humanism's notion of autonomy as subordination to a transhistorical, disembodied reason is part of an obsolete and oppressive Enlightenment thinking. (For one example see Flax 1990: 41.) The reply here is simply that the kind of reason which liberation theory maintains is necessary for autonomy is not transhistorical, non-embodied or whatever, since it is an aspect of the human capacity for love. It is therefore that deeply rooted kind of understanding which, as a part of the whole person, counts as wisdom and as virtue in the Socratic sense.)

It is in the course of the movement of resistance to power that the drive for respect or love becomes a drive for autonomy or self-determination. On the liberation account, resistance classically has two phases or two 'moments' which do not necessarily neatly, linearly succeed each other, although the second does emerge out of the failure of the first. The acquisition of individual autonomy is one of the important distinguishing features of the second moment, although there is a more fundamental characterisation of the difference between the two in terms of the contrast between resistance which is aimed at seizing power and that which is aimed at abolishing it. What we find, then, is that the possibility of genuine human respect (equality on this account), the possibility of autonomy and the abolition of relations of power are interdependent. The argument is that humanist ideals, that is the traditionally liberal ideals of equality and autonomy, can only be achieved with the abolition of relations of power. This runs parallel to the form of Marx's argument which can also be construed as insisting that liberal ideals are not given realities but future possibilities. Also counter-intuitive and further paralleling the general tenor of Marx's argument with respect to the positing of a new person,[2] one who has transcended antagonistic self-interest, is that these ideals of equality and autonomy are essentially linked with what liberation theory understands as the 'solidarity of the oppressed'.

Although there are certainly no humanist ideas of autonomy or equality to be found in the anti-humanist writings of deconstruction and nor are there any utopian aspirations to the abolition of power, there are nevertheless some striking parallels between its self-description as a 'double science' necessarily engaging in two phases or moments and this discussion of the two moments of resistance to power which we find in liberation theory. Both discussions are concerned with effective opposition to power, although for deconstruction this resides within 'the text' while liberation theory is concerned with its 'real life' dimensions; in both accounts each of the two moments is conceived as necessary, although one is more ultimately effective than the other; in both theories the first phase or moment is understood as essentially a moment of reversal – in liberation theory it is a reversal of who holds what powerful positions and a reversal, therefore, of whose attributes are identified as the measure of human worth, while in deconstruction it is a reversal of the respective privileging of two terms; and in both accounts the second moment is, by way of contrast, thought to strike at the relations of power themselves. These parallels, along with those I have already pointed out relating to binary oppositions, become central to my argument in the following chapters, specifically to my thesis that this aspect of deconstruction is a displacement and abstraction from the powerful and threatening truths of liberation theory.

It is in this chapter that the unconsciously Socratic themes I have been anticipating and which confer on liberation theory its very special character take shape. For if the psychological immersion in power discussed in the last chapter goes with an absence of understanding – a failure to recognise that no-one is intrinsically more 'important' than anyone else but that such a view is entirely in the eye of the beholder – then we shall see here that the movement out of determination by power can only happen with the acquisition of understanding. And if the capacity for love and the development of personal autonomy are considered as virtues then we shall be able to make sense of the idea that virtue is knowledge and that vice is only ignorance. We can, therefore, within Socrates' own terms of reference give a partial answer to his question: what is virtue? Moreover, if we do regard liberation theory in this way as a modern response to this ancient philosophic quest, the simultaneous appropriation and denial of its truths by what now passes as sophisticated 'theory' would count as the kind of ignorance parading as wisdom which Socrates understood as a part of the inevitable attempt to suppress philosophy. And although liberation theory is only broadly in the spirit of Socrates, for both the fact of actually answering the question about virtue as well as the kind of answer offered are well outside his specific philosophy, nevertheless, the parallels are clearly significant.[3]

So now let's see how wisdom – the understanding which amounts to virtue – develops. To begin with, it is forced by the failure of the first moment of resistance.

THE MOMENT OF REVERSAL

> . . . at a certain point in their existential experience the oppressed feel an irresistible attraction to the oppressor and his way of life.
>
> (Freire 1972: 49)

> . . . the native never ceases to dream of putting himself in the place of the settler.
>
> (Fanon 1967: 41)

According to the account of liberation theory I have so far given, it is most likely to be the oppressed who will initiate a change in the power situation. For even if it is supposed that everyone has a fundamental need for absolute, non-comparative recognition, mostly, though not always, the pain of being regarded as 'lesser' is harder to bear than the unease of being regarded as 'better'. This does not mean, though, that those in power cannot or do not sometimes abandon their 'up' position.[4] The processes involved in that, however, are not the focus of the theory. Let's then follow the oppressed through what liberation theory posits as their first, though doomed, attempt to find genuine human respect.

I shall proceed slowly at this point for we are on the ground where a tangle of confusions has taken root. In the 1970s it was easy enough for Freire, for example, to describe this first phase of resistance as follows: 'Many of the oppressed who participate in revolution intend . . . to make it their private revolution. The shadow of their former oppressor is still cast over them'

(Freire 1972: 31). And his readers broadly grasped what he was saying. But now, because of what I shall later show to be the conceptual slides made in deconstruction's influential discussion of substantially the same area, as well as in the 'surrational' thought which is derived from this, it is necessary to sort out more carefully the logical issues involved. We have seen that the problem for the oppressed, on the liberation theory account, is a lack of human respect and that this consists in the fact that a comparative evaluation as more or less 'important', effectively an evaluation as more or less human, is made of the two parties in a power relationship. Moreover, and this is the crucial factor in the unfolding 'logic' of the situation, the standard of evaluation is taken to be the powerful person or group themselves. Now because this latter aspect of the situation is established unconsciously and it is essential that it remain so, that is, it is essential that it looks to both parties as though the standard of evaluation is independent, this means in practice that this standard becomes identified with whatever set of attributes the powerful happen to possess. These may be maleness, whiteness, specific cultural habits or whatever. For this identification of the measure of the 'fully' human with the accidental attributes of the powerful is what enables the 'appearances' to turn the reality 'upside down', as Marx might have put it, or it is part of the fabric of the 'veil', as the more religiously minded might put it. How it *looks* is as though it is the attributes of the two groups which are measured by some independent standard and it is therefore the possession or non-possession of these which confer relative human worth on the two parties. The reality is that an evaluation is made on the basis of who is in power and this evaluation then 'latches onto' whatever attributes happen to be around; the illusion is that those in power are so because of their possession of objectively superior attributes. This illusion is essential for the smooth functioning of power and it is, I shall show, the illusion which is incorporated in much of the current discussion of binary oppositions, a discussion which associates power with the meaning of terms themselves rather than with the way in which they are evaluated.

The reason for two phases of resistance now emerges. The key distinction is that in the first phase this central illusion is as active as it is in 'pure' oppression while in the second phase it is recognised as an illusion and abandoned. This, clearly, is the difference between maintaining the essential psychological determinants of power and dispensing with them. (And when eventually it is shown that there is more virtue in the second response than in the first, then we shall also have an interpretation of the Socratic connection between understanding and morality.) So the initial attempt at resistance is characterised by the conviction that 'full' human recognition can be attained by acquiring whatever the 'privileged' set of attributes happens to be. This manifests in one of two sorts of 'reversal' of the situation which, although embodying contradictory beliefs, can and do accompany each other in practice. In the first kind of reversal the illusion engendered by oppression is fully embraced and it is believed that the possession of the very attributes which the powerful happen to have will bring with it the respect they receive. Here the oppressed person does their best to acquire these, a certain kind of education, or way of speaking, a particular taste in wine, maybe a toughness in personality, an appearance of great learning, or whatever. To some extent they may even thereby acquire the sorts of positions held by the powerful. It was, on his own account, crucial in Fanon's development that he acquired a position of status, that of a qualified psychiatrist (Fanon 1967). And there are now many examples of members of oppressed groups gaining the 'top' positions which hitherto were closed to them. What is sought and to a some extent achieved is not a change in the existence of relative power and prestige but a change in personnel, in who occupies what roles. The formerly powerful begin to lose their positions and some of the formerly oppressed step into them. This is all very familiar.

The second sort of 'reversal' is both a reversal of personnel and a reversal of values. If previously the attributes of the powerful were thought to be more 'fully' human in relation to the 'lesser' attributes of the oppressed, it is now maintained, in perhaps a slightly more daring stance than the above, that the reverse is the case. And so aggression, toughness, all the previously prized 'male' characteristics are on the way out and 'in' are the supposedly feminine qualities of sensitivity, feeling, nurturance, etc. The particular illusion that it is the attributes of the powerful which are the key ones in conferring worth is no longer maintained – except in so far, perhaps, as what we have here is an instance of Hegelian 'abstract negation' where their importance is assumed in so far as they are explicitly denied. But what is not rejected, because it is not recognised, is the underlying illusion that it is the attributes of one of the two parties being compared which so confers worth. This is the illusion which conceals the 'binary form' of the deeper illusion that the worth of people can be compared with respect to one of them as measure. And so the essential psychological requirements of power itself are perpetuated.[5]

In the classic theory as put forward by Freire and Fanon it is thought, rather too optimistically it would now appear, that this first 'moment' of resistance will give way to the second, authentic 'moment' where power as such is confronted. This first 'moment of reversal' is conceived both as a stage in the psychology of an individual and as having a political manifestation in, for example, Fanon's 'national intellectuals' who at the time of decolonisation gain the key positions, often by way of compromise and collusion with the former colonisers. And it is assumed in my central thesis that much of the successful strata of contemporary feminism can be broadly characterised as this kind of reactive movement against the fact that it is men, specifically, who have traditionally held power. The optimism of Freire and Fanon about the transience of the oppressed's aspiration for power is based on substantially the same analysis of both manifestations. For an individual the aspiration is supposed to fall away when the illusion upon which it is based has been explored to its limit and, in the way which is about to be described, found to be an illusion. The basis of support for the oppressed elite falls away when this same illusion has been abandoned by 'the people' who can then no longer see in the elite a group commanding respect for their greater education, or for their high placed associations etc. They then recognise that the elite actually hold back their hopes of a more fundamental change in order to maintain their own hold on power. In any case, neither Freire nor Fanon were too bothered in the long term about the power-seeking of the oppressed.

Fanon made it clear in the course of describing his own painful personal evolution why he thought that the illusion of the possession of certain attributes – whether those of white Europeans or the newly rediscovered ones of 'Negritude' – would ultimately lose its grip. The motive for holding to the illusion, the hope of thereby gaining human respect, he thought, made it a futile strategy which must become apparent as such. A black man could attain all the European culture in the world and he would still be seen as a black man, as 'lesser'. He could react against this and glory in the superior qualities of the Negro but to no avail. (Here Fanon describes his reaction upon reading Sartre's calm analysis of Negritude as a necessary but temporary 'moment in the dialectic: When I read that page I felt that I had been robbed of my last chance' (Fanon 1967a: 133).) What must become apparent to the oppressed person, Fanon thought, was that human respect is not in fact distributed on the basis of the possession of attributes but rather on the basis of who is in power. Even if some of the oppressed gain elite positions previously forbidden them this is not sufficient to really place them among the powerful. Possession of the superior attributes and of superior positions makes no difference if one is not of the elite group. On the classic account, the reason why the 'moment of reversal' must give way to authentic opposition to power is because the motive never was the acquisition of white culture for its own sake, or that of black culture for its sake. The motive was that these things would gain one the desired status as 'fully' human and that goal cannot be achieved in this way.

Fanon was not wrong to maintain that it is futile for the oppressed to seek respect in the above ways. To take the most immediate example, it is not the case, for the most part, that feminist academics have the genuine respect of their male colleagues and nor do they, for the most part, think that they have. Where scepticism is required is in relation to Fanon's optimism in thinking that this futility would become obvious. For he overlooked the development of movements which would become sufficiently powerful to obscure the fact that the basic need for respect was still not met. Feminist academics, to continue the example, may not have a lot of genuine respect from their colleagues but they do have the latter's very loud protestations to the contrary and what they also have is a lot of the 'goodies' acquired by moving upwards in a profession. What this creates is a strong paranoia which demands more and more of the outward manifestations of respect and status in order to keep at bay the painful realisation that one is, nevertheless, being patronised. It is a paranoia which will endure so long as the lies which maintain it continue to be told and this in turn will happen so long as the movements in question are sufficiently influential.

What is at issue is the extent to which a movement of the oppressed might achieve sufficient power to at least appear to reverse their erstwhile evaluation as lesser. For success of this kind means that power-seeking is not as futile as the early theorists believed. And although the early theorists were right in foreseeing that such movements of an elite of the oppressed would soon lose the support of their constituency – this has now happened to a considerable extent with feminism – they overlooked the possibility of these movements actually merging with the traditional power structures and bolstering themselves that way.[6]

It is necessary to be more cautious, therefore, than the early liberation theorists were about the prospects of an 'authentic' moment of resistance. Indeed, the failure of Women's Liberation and of liberation theory has been precisely the failure to achieve this transition from a self-interested political movement seeking power to one genuinely opposing it. Since I want to argue, against the times, that the latter aims are the more worthy, I shall be pursuing the line, mainly in Part III, that a deeper understanding is required of this transition although I shall treat there only of its psychological dimension. To this end, the kind of reaction against these ideas which shall be described in Part II throws light on the extent of the fears and perceived dangers involved. In any case, leaving aside the defect of a too quick optimism, there is at this point in liberation theory the outlines of an argument to the effect that an ethic of comparative evaluation of people and therefore the aspiration for power from which it stems simply will not work, at least for the oppressed. The moral argument that such behaviour is not, in any case, right is yet to come. We find it implicitly at work in the account of the second phase of resistance.

But this second phase does not only produce a moral recognition, it produces also the Socratic meta-recognition that this morality is no more than a certain self-understanding and that the corresponding immorality was only ignorance. However, quite unlike Socrates, it also tries to explain how and why the journey from ignorance to insight can be made. It is here, then, that the distinctive epistemological character of liberation theory becomes fully apparent.

SELF-DETERMINATION, SOLIDARITY AND THE BEGINNING OF WISDOM

So far, the prescriptive aspects of the oppressive situation have only been touched on in spite of the fact that these are fundamental, power being all about controlling the actions of others. Rather, it has been stressed that the psychological condition of this control is the desire to be elevated above one's kind, a desire which can lead an oppressed person to enthusiastically endorse a prescribed role in the hope of being seen to be the best amongst those who are assumed to be lesser – effectively the 'Uncle Tom' syndrome. The more basic point, however, is that this behaviour, as well as that of the 'moment of reversal', driven as it is by the anticipation of how others will react, is externally rather than internally determined. It is therefore prescribed, controlled, non-autonomous behaviour. The reason for the apparent oversight on this point is that in the 'classic' liberation account the drive for autonomy is secondary to that for recognition. Autonomy, it was anticipated, would come into play as a response to the apparent exhaustion of all the other possibilities of gaining a satisfactory kind of recognition from others. But this is precisely the point we have now reached. Our oppressed person, the heroine of liberation theory, has recognised the futility in either accepting the oppressed position or in attempting to reverse it. She has recognised the futility of behaving in accordance with the expectations of others and so she is about to become autonomous. On the understanding of liberation theory she is therefore no longer colluding with the requirements of power but is in opposition to it. We need to look more closely at the character of this newly discovered autonomy.

First, it should be noted that there are two types of determination involved and that it is the second which is the more relevant here. The first applies only to the position of the oppressed and consists in the fact that their actions are immediately controlled by the oppressor whose approval they so desperately seek. This sort of control is also challenged in the first, 'reversal' phase of resistance. But there is a broader sense in which the roles of both oppressor and oppressed are determined by the confines of the relationship of power. In this broader sense those in power are no more free to move out of their prescribed role than those they oppress, for in both cases what would have to be sacrificed is social position and this, from a place determined by power relations, appears to carry with it all the available means of finding social recognition. We have seen that the psychological key to this broader sort of determination is the acceptance, in one way or another, of the 'higher/lower' form of human evaluation made upon the basis of whatever attributes happen to be at hand. Both oppressor and oppressed are in this way determined by the prevailing mode of evaluating the worth of persons and this determination is itself held in place by the fear of losing whatever amount of human recognition one already has.

Now this brings us to the core of those demanding moral implications of liberation theory which I have suggested were the main reasons for its subsequent repression. For when our oppressed heroine is ready to give up either accepting oppression or seeking power she must risk her place in the world, that albeit unsatisfactory amount of social and personal recognition which has come her way. This means that liberation theory posits as politically necessary something like a 'dark night of the soul', a time when the only thing that is certain is that one can decide upon and live according to one's own values which here amount to the pursuit of dignity. The social risks of this transition, of rejecting the prevailing mode of human evaluation, are very high, possibly 'not less than everything'. But liberation theory, in principle optimistic, has a case that on the other side of this 'dark night' is the ability to love and the beginning of wisdom. I shall begin with wisdom.

The beginning of wisdom

Autonomy is often understood to keep company with ethical relativism. Most psychotherapy, for example, would insist that autonomy means being the source of one's own values in the sense that one is also the creator of these values. Here it is in accord with the popularity in philosophy of the Nietzschean 'superman', also the autonomous creator of values (who, like the heroine of liberation theory, is also supposed to have emerged from a 'dark night of the soul'). It is therefore a distinctive feature of the 'liberation' understanding of autonomy that it can be shown to presuppose not only a very specific moral position but also the conviction, whether tacit or not, that this moral position is objectively grounded. By 'objectively grounded' I mean that it is grounded *qua* moral position – that one arrives at a certain moral position not only on the basis that it will 'work' but also on the basis that one is convinced that it is right. (And this, surely, is no less than one would expect from 'wisdom' – that it provide us with objective criteria for recognising the 'good'.) In this context, the expression that one becomes the 'foundation' of one's own values implies only that these values are not taken directly from the surrounding social situation but are accepted on the basis of internal processes. This no more implies a relativism of values than the fact that one uses one's own mind to decide on the truth of mathematical theorems rather than accepting the authority of a teacher implies a relativism about the propositions of mathematics. The moral view in question, of course, amounts to the idea that 'respect is due to the human being as such and is not a matter of degree'. And so it is here that we shall find an argument why the 'ways of man' should be abandoned for 'God's ways'.

So far, then, I am committed to establishing that there are two necessary conditions for autonomy. The first is a commitment to the specific moral position that an unquantifiable respect from others is due to human beings and the second is the conviction (not necessarily conscious) of the objective grounding of this moral position. But since liberation theory also maintains that autonomy comes about as a consequence of genuine understanding it is also necessary to defend the thesis that the moral position is in fact objectively grounded, as well as the theory that autonomy requires that one must be convinced that it is so grounded. In other words, it is necessary to defend the idea that autonomy is not based on some kind of illusion. The result is that we shall have both an argument for a moral position and an analysis of the conditions under which such a moral position would be adopted.

This part of liberation theory is not philosophically uninteresting. To begin with, it implies that there is at least one objectively grounded moral position the acceptance of which is a resolution of conflicts which occur as a consequence of power and which are, therefore, also conflicts of modern life. We have an objective moral position which, if not 'of' modern life (as will be shown), is at least very much 'in' it. The sort of moral view which MacIntyre (1985) argued is antithetical to modernism and which others have argued is not viable at all (Williams 1991). The further significance of this moral position and its specifically modern character emerges when it is seen that it can be construed, as I have been doing, as an assertion of the value of equality, for it can then be seen to be at the heart of liberalism. This means that what liberation theory provides here is an instance of just what has been sought (rightly) by conservatives (Bloom 1987; Strauss 1953), namely an objective defence of the more valuable aspects of Western liberal traditions. For it is mostly conservatives who have argued that the prevailing cultural relativism in Western cultures, in providing the basis for respect (of a kind) for all cultures but one's own, is a movement towards cultural disintegration entailing a serious weakening of traditional ideals of democracy and tolerance. Needless to say, what I am calling liberation theory is not where they have been looking.

But the more intriguing philosophical implications of the argument which we are about to follow consist in its Socratic resonances. For the fact that it provides us with an objective grounding for the specific moral position it defends – highly significant within the terms of contemporary ethical discussion – is only an aspect of its more general Socratic character. It is the first condition on an answer to Socrates' question about the nature of virtue that it provide us with an objective way of recognising the good.[7] The second and peculiarly Socratic condition is that this analysis of the good be shown to be itself a necessary part of it. It is to be shown, in other words, that virtue is knowledge. And this, we are about to see, liberation theory does. Finally we shall see that the theory goes further than Socrates – in a quite unsocratic manner – and gives us a resolution of this paradoxical identification of virtue and knowledge by explaining why they mutually presuppose each other.[8] If the kind of understanding – wisdom – which amounts to virtue is deeper than mere intellectual assent then we have here a theory of how such understanding is acquired. To discover all these philosophical riches we must now follow our oppressed heroine as she becomes autonomous, moral, and wise instead of status-seeking and power-hungry.

Why respect is due to the person as such

First of all, then, why is it that our heroine, now that she is aware of the futility of colluding with power, turns to the morality of an irreducible human respect? What are the reasons for her choice of moral position as distinct, maybe, from the grounds upon which it might be defended *qua* moral position? The processes are rational. The significant point is that the drive for self-determination has come into play only because the world, as Marx would have said, has been turned upside down. The illusion that possession of certain attributes will bring with it respect and recognition has been revealed as an illusion and it is clear that the evaluation of human beings as of more and less worth is in fact made on the basis of how much power they have and not on their merits. We have a classic case of the 'unmasking' of a morality of the kind which Nietzsche argued applies to morality as such, or of the kind which Marx argued applies to ideology. Now from such an unmasking alone several possibilities could follow. One could, for example, follow Nietzsche in assuming that all purportedly objective morality can be so unmasked as just a disguise for a 'will-to-power' and insist, therefore, upon the acknowledged self-creation of authentic values. Alternatively one could endorse that which is so unmasked, namely power itself, as the only good in a move which goes back at least as far as the sophists.[9] The special insight of liberation theory, however, is that the illusions of power have been unmasked for a reason and this reason dictates the direction of a solution.

This reason is that our heroine has a new awareness of the character of what has been her driving need, an awareness which is incompatible with the illusions of power. The futility of her earlier behaviour became apparent with the discovery that what she had been seeking was 'full' recognition as human and that what she had previously regarded as her needs, either for a man 'of her own' or a career of her own, were in some respects superficial manifest-ations of this deeper need. It is, then, this insight into her own need upon which the whole 'unmasking' has been predicated and which leaves her with only one rational course. It means that the way forward cannot be arbitrary, a sheer exercise of will, for it must take account of this need. (Nor can this need itself be regarded as arbitrary, because her experience is precisely that it has a certain permanence. She has learned that it is a fundamental need which is behind more superficial and more changeable needs.) Nor can she adopt an ethic of power itself as the only good, for on account of the existence of the need for 'full' recognition, this has now been shown simply not to work, at least for herself as one of the oppressed. Whatever solution she adopts must deal with the way in which she is valued as a human being.

(Even with this condition it might still appear that there are two courses open. For there are two issues, that of the comparative evaluation of people *per se* and the fact that this has been revealed to be of the binary form due to one of those being compared being taken as the standard. Our heroine clearly must now reject the latter but it might seem as though it is still open whether or not she accepts the former. If she were to do so then she would have to develop a way of evaluating the relative worth of persons with respect to maybe their virtues, maybe their abilities, or achievements or whatever, a standard in any case defined independently of those to whom it is applied and so which does not generate the illusions she has now recognised – a consistent realisation of the ideology of merit. But this very hard liberal ideal does not provide a way forward. For the very experience which has led to the formula-tion of the problem has cast doubt upon the point of taking the logically unjustifiable step from an evaluation of behaviour or dispositions to an evaluation of the relative worth of the person as such. This move has a point, it has been revealed, within the 'upside down' morality which is produced by and which sustains relations of power. But it would seem to have no role outside it. Indeed, the logic of the situation is perhaps better described by saying that once it becomes clear to our heroine that she has been comparatively evaluating the worth of persons then the illegitimacy of doing so is immediately apparent. It becomes clear that a sharp distinction must be made between any ethic of excellence or desert, as MacIntyre (1988) describes the kind of recognition we might give people on the basis of their achievements or dispositions, and any judgements concerning the worth of the person as such.)[10]

So it is only a certain kind of self-knowledge which has enabled our heroine to adopt the moral position that human beings owe to each other the kind of respect which is 'not a matter of degree'. But before we bring out the full Socratic import of this result it is worth further exploring the basis of our heroine's new morality. For here we see that unknowingly she has made a lot of headway with the problem of modernity and morality described above – the 'MacIntyre' problem. She has produced an objectively based moral position which has its place in the modern world.

An objectively moral position

We have seen that our heroine has adopted a moral position on the grounds that it is workable. The question, now, is this: is this morality any more than the morality of effectiveness? Is there here no more than a pragmatic moral rationality which would show only that certain aspirations are realisable? Or can the morality itself, *qua* moral position, also be objectively grounded? Now while it could not be a part of liberation theory to insist that all the logical presuppositions and implications of what is going on here are necessarily conscious it can nevertheless be argued that there is more than the above to the reasoning processes of our heroine. Specifically it can be shown that while the moral position which asserts the irreducible worth of human beings as such is, certainly, justified with respect to its ability to satisfy a need this is not all there is to it. It can be shown that the morality as such is objectively grounded with reference to a conception of the intrinsically or essentially human. In other words, it can be shown that the idea of irreducible respect for people is not good because it is the only one which might work, but that it might work because it is morally sound. It is now time for this difficult but important idea to be unfolded.

Broadly following MacIntyre (1985, 1988) I shall take it that one of the things which is required for the objective grounding of a moral position is a conception of what it is to be human which contains a teleological component. Roughly the idea is that we can objectively ground a conception of what it is good for a human being to do with reference to a conception of a distinctively human purpose in somewhat the same way as we can objectively identify goodness in watches given once we know what is the purpose of a watch (MacIntyre 1985: 57–8).[11] It is necessary that this human telos, whatever it may more specifically be thought to be, is regarded as internal to our understanding of what it is to be human. Otherwise, considered as a mere fact about human beings rather than as something which is constitutive of 'humanness', it would be unable to provide the bridge between the 'is' and the 'ought' which is required and which MacIntyre argues was provided by the Aristotelian tradition which he seeks to revive. In contrast to the Aristotelian conception of the human telos, though, and to modify its absoluteness, MacIntyre recommends that we recognise that any such morals grounding conception of what it is to be a human being are worked out – and continually reworked – only within the context of a tradition. In other words, to some extent, we decide upon our own human 'telos'.

Two major, although almost inverse, problems have been identified with this programme. One is that it must unwittingly assume too much cultural relativity and the other is that it is not culturally relative enough. On the 'too much' cultural relativity side it is argued that we simply have no grounds for supposing that there is a common 'human nature' which is rich enough to entail the existence of a common ethical life and, moreover, if there were such grounds they would be largely empirical and to that extent beyond the scope of philosophy (Williams 1991). So MacIntyre's programme could be said to contain more cultural relativity than it can acknowledge. It must inevitably generalise to the whole human species considerations which can be appropriate only to one or to some cultures within it. (Postmodernists give a version of the objection when they insist that any conception of the human will necessarily project culturally or sexually specific characteristics as universal, so feeding into cultural imperialism and/or sexual domination by way of the repression of difference.)

The 'not enough' cultural relativity argument has already been foreshadowed. The position is that while the sort of ethics MacIntyre wants was workable in ancient and medieval societies, it cannot be made so in modern life which is antithetical to any teleological notions of humanity (MacIntyre 1985; Poole 1991; Williams 1991). This objection is endorsed by MacIntyre who deals with it by seeking to develop his programme on the basis of premodern ethical traditions which he maintains survive, marginalised, in modern society (MacIntyre 1988). Both objections are to be taken seriously. It is not my purpose, however, to discuss either the programme itself or the objections to it in general terms. All that I want to achieve here is a demonstration that liberation theory gives us one example, not taken into consideration in the discussion so far, of a moral position which is grounded with respect to an idea of what it is to be human and which meets these objections. Whether all moral positions can or should be so grounded is a larger question beyond the scope of this discussion. I shall begin by identifying the conception of a human being which is at work in liberation theory.[12]

This concept of human nature is the same as that which is thought to be discovered by the heroine of the theory herself as she struggles with existence within power relations. We have seen that the high point of the story where she decides to confront rather than conform to the everyday requirements of power is when, on the discovery of her need for 'full' recognition as human, she saw herself as having no alternative but to continue to pursue this need, only now more directly than before. If we ask why this is, since we don't necessarily pursue all those needs of which we become aware, we are brought to considerations concerning 'human nature'. For the answer which I should reconstruct liberation theory to give at this point is that this particular need is one our heroine *must* pursue because her sense of her own humanity and her ability, therefore, to live as human depends upon its satisfaction. The strength of the need, the reason why it is preferable to face the 'dark night' rather than to give up on it, is because her sense of herself as a specifically *human* being is at stake. This implies that the need in question is not only a need for human recognition but that it is also a facet of the need to experience oneself as a distinctively human being. Now the basis of this further assumption also lies in the phenomenology of the need itself. (The epistemological issues involved here will be explored below.) For at the same time as the need for human respect becomes clear to our heroine, it becomes clear as an aspect of the need to be human. The need to be recognised as 'fully' human is an aspect of the need to be able to function as fully human. There is, then, a need to be recognised as human which is itself experienced as an aspect of the need to be human. Our heroine's experience is such that she thinks being recognised as fully human, with all the reciprocity this implies, will make her human. This phenomenology accounts for the strength and apparent permanence of the need for recognition from others. It involves us in considerations of human nature, however, only if she is right in the conclusions she draws.

So is she right? Is experience, the phenomenology of a need, sufficient basis for the claim that a necessary condition of being 'fully human' is this sort of species-recognition? Provided that there are reasons to believe that her story is not just her own private story but would be anyone's then this phenomenological discovery is clearly a very strong basis for such an understanding of human nature. At this point our heroine's reflections are those of liberation theory itself, which posits her as an average–typical character. In so far as she recognises that there is nothing special about her own experiences she would naturally conclude that the need she has recently discovered in herself would belong to anyone, whether or not they had, like herself, become aware of it. This depends in turn on the validity of liberation theory itself, of which more will be said below. But for the moment we can say provisionally that our heroine is justified in her conviction that in order to live in a way we would regard as fully human we must be identified as such by others we identify in the same way.

This is a fairly minimal thesis. But there is more to the phenomenology of this newly discovered need to be human and this provides some substantial content to what can be said, or rather what cannot be said, about what it is to be human. We have seen that the character of this fundamental need only became apparent at the same time as our heroine decided that she was not prepared to earn its satisfaction – earn it, that is, in the sense of conforming to any other ideas about what the 'fully' or 'normally' human might consist in. For such conformity, she had realised, was simply to accept an illusion generated by the fact that one group of human beings had power over another group. What she wants, as we have seen, is unconditional recognition as human. The implication which now fills out our thesis is that the specification of the human as depending on the reciprocal recognition of others as human must be regarded as prior to any further specification. This does not so much add any features to the notion of the distinctively human as it forbids them. It is therefore a thesis that is well-supported by more than the phenomenology of our heroine's needs, since it is convincingly argued for by the proponents of the 'no human nature' position as described above.

(We can see here that the situation in relation to the 'too much cultural relativity' objection is complex. It is because our heroine accepts the arguments against a common human nature, especially in their postmodern version which insists that any such idea must function to establish the qualities of one group as a yardstick for the whole biological species, that she insists on the minimal conception of human nature she believes she has learned in the exploration of her own experience. She believes that her understanding of the psychological constitution of human beings is in fact a precondition for being able to refrain from any stronger conceptions of human nature, with their oppressive consequences. This clearly does not amount to a logical precondition but to a psychological precondition. More on this on pp. 48–9.)

And so it can be claimed that a necessary aspect of living as a distinctively human being is that we have unconditional recognition as human from at least some of those we recognise as human ourselves.[13] For we have a need for this recognition, which is itself a need to be human. The satisfaction of this need is therefore a human telos which is internal to the very idea of what a human being is. A human being must seek unconditional human regard from others if they are to function as a human. If this doesn't sound quite right it is because, strictly speaking, we don't have here a telos so much of already constituted human beings as of beings who are not-yet-humans. The idea, rather like that found in Hegel and Marx, is that we are still immersed in human pre-history. Or like that found in Marx and Feuerbach the idea is that our 'species' nature is yet to be realised. Nevertheless, whatever kind of humanness we do possess in this pre-human phase – potential humanness, would-be humanness or whatever – it must, for the reason just given, consist in this striving to be human. Dropping the modification we can claim simply that the general striving to be human and the more specific striving for basic respect is constitutive of our nature as human beings. We are now ready to ground our moral position that 'respect is due to the human being as such'.

However, even though we now have an idea of a specifically human telos the task is not as straightforward as may have been anticipated. Certainly, we are now in a position to claim that irreducible, non-measurable respect is a good for humans on the grounds that it is necessary for us to achieve our telos of 'full' humanity. But in what sense is it our due? Here we have to once again follow Weil (and, indeed, Locke) in recognising that such a claim concerning what amounts to our rights is more fundamentally a claim about our obligations. What is required is a justification of the claim that we are obliged to accord a respect, which is not therefore 'a matter of degree', to the human being as such. This can be done by way of a justification, first of all, of the idea that it is good to accord everyone an elementary respect as human and, second, that failure to do so is a positive wrong. But how can either of these positions which concern behaviour towards others be justified with respect to a conception of our own individual telos? Only by showing that the attainment of one person's telos is intrinsically dependent upon others attaining theirs. At this point, the necessarily social character of 'humanness' emerges. The conditions under which you will be able to accord a basic, non-measurable respect to me are only those in which you are not immersed in power where we have seen that the kind of respect you receive and give is comparative and measured. In other words, your needs for human recognition must be met in a different, non-comparative way, for it is only then that you will be able to pass through the 'dark night' to the other side of power. In so far, then, as I accord this basic respect to you I contribute both to you attaining your telos of full humanity and therefore to my own. It is therefore a good, grounded in my own telos, to give you this respect and not to do so is a positive wrong, similarly grounded. I owe it to you, or it is your due, and the objective grounding of this moral claim proceeds with reference to my own drive to become fully human.[14]

However, even putting it like this, with my own telos as the ultimate ground, has now become strange. For this particular longing for all to be accorded absolute respect as human is in itself a social longing. It is not only that any treatment of another with disregard, as unimportant, is objectively a wrong for myself in the way I have just described, because it contributes to the conditions which are negative for me, but the very point of differentiating ourselves from others in this respect no longer makes sense. The pain we now experience when someone is treated as lesser (this is no longer a source of comfort as when, immersed in power, it was a relief to find that someone else, not us, was regarded as lesser) is a direct pain, not mediated by a consideration of our individual telos. We no longer ask for whom the bell tolls, although once we did. For we have learned about our 'species' or social needs and we have seen that these essentially consist in the refusal to differentiate the worth of human beings. Our need to belong to our species is at the same time a need for our species to be worthy of belonging to. Our social needs, meaning here our needs concerning the specifically social dimension of life, the dimension where we relate not to our immediate circle but to members of the species as such, consist first of all in the need for equality as I have construed it.

The moral claim of liberation theory has now been objectively grounded with respect to this conception of human beings as necessarily striving, however little we may be aware of it, to become fully human 'species-beings', beings whose proper connection with their species is vital to them. How, then, does this morality and the idea of humanness upon which it depends stand up to the two major objections I anticipated to this kind of thinking, on the one hand that it cannot be regarded as appropriate to modern life and on the other that it will all too probably illegitimately generalise its specific idea of humanity? What relevance, first, does the morality of a respect for human beings as such which is not a matter of degree have for the modern world? Very generally it can be said that it is relevant wherever there are relations of power and very few would now deny that power operates in modern life despite the fact that modern ideals are very much to the contrary. But there is more to it, for I think it can be argued that liberation theory connects in quite a specific way to the modern world. Modern ideals can be met, it is implied, only if they are reinterpreted after the manner of liberation theory.

The argument that the kind of objectively grounded morality I have outlined can find no place in the modern world assumes that any conception of humans as having a specific telos as human is alien to the modern conception according to which the definitive feature of human beings is precisely the variability of goals amongst different individuals. The modern conception, it is pointed out, is that people pursue their own individual interests which means there is nothing in common between them which could be said to constitute a distinctively human purpose (MacIntyre 1985: 236). Strictly speaking, then, liberation theory's moral argument could not be considered to be within a completely modern frame of reference. But this is a very general argument and if we look more closely at the specific telos which liberation theory attributes to us we find that there is, after all, at least a meeting point with modernism. For, as we have seen, this telos can be presented as a version of the paradigmatically modern idea of equality. Now we have here not only a different version of what equality means (something non-measurable as opposed to something which is already measured) but a different conceptual place for it. Liberation theory replaces the classic modern conception of equality as a fact about human beings with the insistence that this is as yet only our potential. That is, it replaces the modern idea of our equality as goal seekers with the idea of equality as a goal. And it replaces the modern idea that the proper place for the recognition of human equality is the political sphere with the idea that it is a basic social value which should inform social life as such (including political life). Liberation theory is then not 'of' the modern world in so far as it insists that there is more of value than the unfettered pursuit of individual goals and that we have social needs which are overwhelmingly important. But it is very much 'in' it in so far as the implied argument is that if this social need to be valued as irreducibly human is not met then power will continue to permeate modern life very much against its own ethos. Equality can only be realised if it is extended from the political sphere to become a norm of social life more widely. Which simply recapitulates in the terms of political psychology the broad argument Marx made in terms of social theory and which was central to his later conception of socialism.[15] In any case we have an argument which is appropriate to modern life because it takes modern ideals seriously. And conversely, it could be argued that only modernism offers the possibility that this basically Christian morality could result in more than inner peace for those individuals who turn their face against the 'ways of the world'. For it is only modern life, in assuming the social importance of equality, which provides the conditions where the insistence on the irreducible value of all human beings has any social promise, in the sense of the possibility of becoming a widely accepted morality.

There is another sense in which liberation theory meets with the demands of modernism. Certainly, as left wing and communitarian theories generally do, it posits the necessity of shared human values for a viable community and insists that belonging to a community is essential for a good human life. This is the force of the insistence that we are would-be 'species-beings'. But it does so in a way that avoids the objections which liberals, in the name of the modern conception of human life, make to such programmes. The liberal insistence is that the virtue of the modern conception of people having their own individual goals is that it goes with a demand that as far as possible we be left free of any social interference to decide – and to continually revise our decisions – about what goals we think it worthwhile to pursue. The modern conception of human beings underpins a demand for the social recognition of the importance of moral autonomy and it is this demand which is politically important.[16] The corresponding liberal worry about left wing and communitarian ideas is that at a certain point the insistence on shared values for a viable community becomes an advocacy of a situation where communities impose the necessary values. But the force of the 'unconditional' in the liberation demand enables it to meet this objection, or rather it means that it is itself an articulation of the liberal demand to be left alone to decide what goals we wish to pursue. The demand for unconditional regard simply *is* the demand for this social regard not to be tied to the adoption of any specific goals. Liberation theory combines communitarian and liberal ideals. We have a moral position which is highly relevant to modern life.

Let me now turn to the 'too much cultural relativity' argument. Leaving aside the kind of objection which would insist that the very notion of an objective morality amounts to cultural imperialism, the problem identified here is this: if we ground our morality in a concept of 'human nature' then we necessarily assume that this morality is appropriate for everyone. That is, we are not only asserting that this morality is objectively right in certain circumstances or within a certain tradition as, for example, MacIntyre would have it, but that it is right with respect to human life as such. But we have no basis, either philosophical or empirical, for any such concept of human nature rich enough to support the contention of 'a common ethical life' (Williams 1991).

We should, then, inevitably be widening the scope of application of the moral position, from the culture in which it was developed and to which it is appropriate, to all cultures.

We have already seen that we are here in the rather strange situation that it is precisely because liberation theory accepts the case against any strong conception of human nature that it posits the little it does about the intrinsically human. Our intuitions that too much generalising in this respect is morally bad as well as conceptually poor arise from a psychology which the theory claims to elucidate. In other words, liberation theory takes the objection so seriously that it tries to identify the conditions in which such mistakes would no longer occur. This point, however, while relevant to the objection does not meet it.

I shall address the issue by first of all exploring the epistemology of liberation theory's use of the concept of 'human nature' and then seeing whether it can meet the 'too much cultural relativity' objection. It is here that we are confronted with the demands and peculiar epistemology of the ancient injunction to 'know thyself'. We have seen that liberation theory's concept of 'the human' is based primarily on the phenomenology of needs. According to the theory, at a certain point in the attempt to survive in power relations we are supposed to discover that one of our needs is best understood, first of all, as the need for recognition as human and second, as an aspect of the need to be human. It is this discovery of an 'inner' dimension which refers to the specifically human, that is, to our relationship with the species as a whole, which provides the primary grounds for the use of the concept. The notion of 'human nature' does not centrally derive, therefore, from philosophical considerations, nor from empirical observation of others, although the latter must be relevant.[17] On the assumptions made by liberation theory we speak of what it is to be human when we discover this dimension in ourselves. In the same way we would explore those dimensions which are discovered as individual, or as cultural, familial, etc. The point here, and this is where liberation theory's use of the concept of 'human nature' is, perhaps, distinctive, is that this provides a strong reason for formulating a concept of 'the human' – at a certain point we experience ourselves in this way or at least as having aspirations in this direction.

Clearly, however, the phenomenological discovery of a dimension of our needs and aspirations which presents itself as concerned with 'the human' is not sufficient. We must have grounds for believing that this dimension exists in others. But here our problem is that just as we did not ourselves grasp this dimension in ourselves previously, so it is likely that others will not now grasp it in themselves. For we discovered the nature of our own need only as the resolution of serious and prolonged conflict in our lives. It is not the sort of need which is immediately open to either empirical observation or to phenomenological inspection. Nor can the conditions for its 'inner' or 'outer' observation be simply reproduced by formula in the way desired by modern science, for its discovery presupposes the messiness of life itself. It is for this reason that I should maintain that what is going on here in liberation theory satisfies the requirements of 'knowing thyself' more than it does any contemporary notion of what is epistemologically acceptable. For the conception of human beings assumes that our 'nature' is such that it can only be understood in the actual living of it. A condition of wisdom is having wrestled with life itself, for self-knowledge can only be won.

So if we are here supposing an understanding which, although accessible to everyone, would not at any particular moment be adhered to by everyone, how can we confirm that what we have discovered as the dimension of 'the human' also exists in others? The reason we have for thinking that others may have the sorts of needs we discovered in ourselves is given by the analysis of the distorting effects of power in liberation theory, in so far as this fits with our observations of the behaviour of others in situations of power. Which I submit it does – the power of the theory is precisely that it makes explicable so many of the seemingly petty distortions which we observe in everyday behaviour. But the necessary supposition, as we have seen, is the existence of the distinctively 'human' needs which have been described. The epistemology consists, then, of a phenomenological discovery confirmed by those observations which would confirm the analysis of power itself. The emphasis, however, is on the phenomenological discovery, the 'inner' knowledge, and the fact that it is a discovery and not just a report of an act of introspection. The point here is that it therefore presupposes life experiences and the resolution of the conflict embedded in them.[18]

On this basis we can now consider the objection that in using a conception of 'the human', liberation theory exceeds the scope of the available evidence, and would project as universal what must be only a specific morality. It is undeniable that in positing a human need to be specifically human, liberation theory does make claims about everyone and not just about those who are engaged in relations of power and who provide the confirmation of its hypothesis. MacIntyre is correct, therefore, to argue that such claims of 'the human' are relative to particular traditions in the sense that they arise from these traditions and are appropriately used only within them. But this relativity cannot be argued – and nor would MacIntyre do so – with respect to the content of such claims. A claim about what we think is essential to being human has to be a claim about all human beings. The question now is just how dangerous this excess of content actually is. For what I have tried to give is a justification for liberation theory proceeding as it does in exploring the phenomenology of our needs. Not to proceed in this way would be to ignore an important dimension of our experience of ourselves and the understanding to which it gives rise. That we articulate this experience by going beyond the available evidence is built into the character of the experience. Provided we remain aware, as MacIntyre would insist that we must, of the provisional nature of our articulation of 'the human' and the fact that it is based very much on a certain set of experiences it is, I maintain, more important to explore this intrinsically social facet of life than to be rigid about the evidence requirements.

So liberation theory has produced one example of an objectively grounded moral position which is appropriate to social contexts constituted by power relations and which is specifically appropriate to modern life with its aspiration to equality. I said above that significant as this is in terms of the contemporary discussion, it is one facet of the Socratic nature of liberation theory which also consists in the further fact that the understanding of the objective grounding of this moral position is shown to be necessary for the position to be adopted. However, it has been the fact of this objective grounding which has been difficult to establish. The further Socratic resonances now become readily apparent.

The idea upon which the Socratic identification of wisdom and virtue depends is that everyone always seeks the good. In other words, no-one deliberately does evil.[19] The qualification here of course is that we seek the good within the understanding that we have of it. Once this thesis is accepted then it follows immediately that differences in virtue consist only in differences in understanding. Now if we consider the foregoing account of liberation theory it is implied that (and implicitly explained why) at every stage of her story our heroine is seeking what she perceives to be the good, in the sense that she is pursuing satisfaction of her needs. So in her initial 'unreconstructed' stage she understands the respect she needs to consist in the social status of 'having a man of her own'. Later this gives way to the search for a 'career of her own' and finally she understands that the deeper need was in fact for simple and unquantifiable human respect. At every stage it is the way she understands her needs which is the crucial determinant of her behaviour, for at every stage she pursues her need (the good) as she understands it. So this compassionate understanding to the effect that in some sense everyone does their best is the underpinning both of the Socratic notion of virtue and that of liberation theory.

But there is more both to Socrates' moral position and to the understanding which is at least implied in liberation theory. Socrates is most famous for his attempt to persuade us that the only worthwhile thing in life is the cultivation of our own soul, or the acquisition of virtue.[20] He wants us not only to seek the good – which we do anyway – but in seeking it consciously to act only on the basis that it is the good. (The difference is between desiring something which is good and desiring it because it is good, that is, in desiring both it, itself, and its goodness.) We are about to find the same basic idea in liberation theory. Not only does our heroine, through her searches, arrive at the morality that 'respect is due to the human being as such and is not a matter of degree', not only does she (maybe tacitly) discern the objective grounding of this morality, but she recognises that it is the fact that it is an objectively moral position which has now become the basis of her action. What we are about to see is that the fact that she thinks her new demand is for something objectively moral is essential for it to enable her to move beyond the psychological grip of power. It is essential, therefore, to the very possibility of developing an alternative to power. The kind of moral stance that Socrates thought to be incompatible with the political life, our heroine (and liberation theory which articulates her thoughts) regards as the only possible basis for resistance to domination.

Radical needs as moral needs

Remember that we are still accompanying our heroine through her 'dark night of the soul'. She has abandoned the prevailing values on the grounds that they will not yield the kind of human respect she needs and so she is no longer dominated by the need for recognition from others in the sense that this need determines her behaviour. For that reason she is autonomous. But this in no way implies that the need for recognition has been overcome, only that the search for its satisfaction is internally rather than externally directed. Despite the popular sayings to the contrary – 'don't worry about what people think' etc. – autonomy does not make us unaffected by the behaviour of others or release us from the need for their recognition. Indeed, the very contrary is the case. Because the need is recognised its satisfaction can be consciously and deliberately pursued. But because the recognition of her need comes with the recognition that it cannot be satisfied within the status quo it now becomes a driving force which will transform her relations with others. It is now a need in which she is 'rich', a 'radical' need.[21]

But at this point liberation theory goes beyond the standard critical theory notion of 'radical needs', for what is radical about our heroine's recently recognised need is not only that it is about to disrupt the old relations which sustained comparative evaluations of the worth of human beings but that the way in which this demand is made can only result in a different kind of relationship. This difference, we are about to see, consists in the fact that the moral principles within the terms of which the new relationship is advocated must constitute the actual basis of the relationship. The contrast is with the dominant social relations whose moral expression can be shown to be a rationalisation for someone's self-interest (as, say, where a morality of self-reliance can be shown to rationalise the inequalities of capitalism). So these relationships our heroine is determined to bring into being will be, albeit on a vastly smaller scale, of the kind which Marx hankered after, being both consciously constructed and transparent. But they will be both of these things *because* they are moral. Let me explain why.

We have seen that our heroine will adopt the morality of respect being due to the human being as such because it is the only potentially workable morality. We have seen, also, that this moral position can be objectively grounded with respect to an understanding of 'the human'. What we haven't yet seen is that our heroine also is necessarily convinced that there is an objective grounding of her moral position, for this is the crucial ingredient in her ability to bring new kinds of relationships into being. If we look at why our heroine, upon discovering her need for human respect, believes that it is right that this need be met we see at the same time why she must assume that this 'rightness' is objective. The belief in the moral nature of her need arises when she realises that it cannot be met with the available resources and so the question of why it should be pursued emerges. The question is made more forceful by the perception that the pursuit of this need jeopardises the satisfaction of those many other needs which depend on her social place. Previously, her needs were themselves morally unquestioned and in the modern way she had been able to identify the good simply with their satisfaction. Needs had been the basis for moral justification and not themselves in need of it. But now she has to choose between social conformity and the many needs it satisfies and the further pursuit of this need for basic human respect. And this choice between needs or ends, since it is not made pragmatically in terms of which ones are realisable, can only be made in moral terms. There is no other basis. (The ultimate choice is whether we justify the good in terms of what we want or whether we justify what we want in terms of the good.) Moreover this moral choice can only be made in objective terms. One reason for this is that subjectivism in morals is ruled out by the refusal to make needs or ends themselves the ultimate criterion of goodness.

Some of these moral objective grounds we already know. We have seen that the need for irreducible human recognition presents itself as an aspect of the need to function as human and so, although it is unlikely in most cases that our heroine would herself be fully articulate about the issues, she has a sense at least that it follows from this that her 'goodness' *qua* specifically human being depends upon the satisfaction of this need. But there is also the further question of why the need to be human should itself be pursued. This, too, presents itself as morally right. For while it could be said that this is simply a stronger need than the competing needs for social conformity, the reason it is so (and this once again refers to the phenomenology of the situation) is because it carries with it the promise of a moral fulfilment as an aspect of human fulfilment. If the need for recognition presents itself as an aspect of the need to be human then a concomitant of this is that it also presents itself as a need for morality and therefore as itself a moral need. We only ever embark upon our 'dark night' with powerfully moral instincts.

Now if there is any substantial (i.e. non-conventional) distinction between the notion of rights and that of wants, goals or needs then it can only be that rights are those needs which are such that it is morally right that they be met. And so the need of our oppressed person comes to be identified by them as a right. It is, as well, a 'natural right' in the traditional sense meaning a right which is based in what it is to be human, in 'human nature'.[22] So why is this so important?

The demand for Simone Weil's 'respect which is due to us as human' cannot be met by the 'ways of man' in the social world as it is, permeated by power. This idea is at the heart of liberation theory. But what this means is that there is no basis upon which this demand can be made of others, other than that purely moral one which is also one's grounds for pursuing it and which, being objective, is also distinct from it. There clearly cannot be any direct appeal to self-interest, or any appeal to efficiency, viability, or whatever since the meeting of this demand puts one in opposition to the social order. As well, it is a part of the demand itself that it be met for moral reasons alone, on the grounds that it is a just demand. For our heroine has suffered, and knows that she has, and as a result she needs now not just elementary respect itself, but respect which is understood to be her due. So we have here a demand whose satisfaction cannot, in its nature, be engineered or manipulated. It is a demand which is such that there is no gap between means and ends for it is a moral demand, pursued for moral reasons, upon a moral basis and can only be met in these terms. It can only be met by a new kind of human relationship, one which is transparent, conscious and moral. It is the solution to the riddle of life and knows itself as such.[23] It is precisely *not* a strategy.

The search for respect for her humanness as such has forced our heroine to become autonomous. But this autonomy was itself only acquired by way of the acceptance of a definite moral position with an objective basis and by way of the resulting demand for new kinds of relations with others. Let us now accompany our heroine to the other side of her 'dark night' to find out more about these new relations. Here we find that if her quest was Socratic its end is Christian – in the very broad sense.

The solidarity of the oppressed or the ability to love

The 'dark night' of the soul gives us an autonomous person. But in liberation theory this autonomous person is still very much a needy person, their autonomy consisting in the recognition rather than the overcoming of their dependency on the proper recognition and respect of others. We have, then, the long awaited synthesis of the supposedly dependent 'related' feminine personality and the supposedly autonomous, 'non-related' masculine personality.[24] More importantly, we have a person who is now able to relate to others in terms of the others' needs as well as their own. Why such an ability to relate openly should develop in terms of the specific political principle of the 'solidarity of the oppressed' we shall see shortly. But first let's look more closely at this new capacity which makes possible the discovery of others.

Two things change when we are released from our commitment to power. First, we develop a capacity to listen to others, a capacity which we did not have before, despite what we may have thought. Simone Weil insisted on the rarity of this capacity when she maintained that, despite the fact that what people need, above all, is understanding, in the 'fallen' earthly condition it was next to impossible for people to really listen to each other and that the capacity for such understanding was possible only as the result of a deeply transforming religious experience (McLellan 1989: 284). Perhaps so, but religious transformation is itself quite worldly within the terms of reference of liberation theory which would see this transformation into people who can listen in the following way: in the context of oppression the needs of the oppressed are both strictly unintelligible and strictly unsatisfiable. This is because the basic need for human respect has been fused with the desire for status or position and if either of these are explicitly recognised it will be only the latter. But the things which should, then, apparently satisfy the needs, such as 'a man of one's own', fail to do so and consequently they appear to be both limitless and undefined. We are naturally repelled by such needs both in ourselves and in others. From the perspective of liberation theory the situation is simple. The need for status is not the more powerful of the needs in action, it is rather a misidentification of the more basic need which is both easy to understand and to satisfy when we are no longer ourselves immersed in the 'higher/lower' variety of human recognition. But this readiness to accord others basic respect as human also results in the ability to listen. For once the principle is grasped, as it is here, that human needs are neither insoluble nor crazy then it is easy to extend it to other life problems. The needs of others are no longer so disconcerting. More fundamentally, what unconditional respect as human amounts to, as well as a non-comparative recognition of human worth, is precisely the recognition that people both must and can themselves identify their problems and attempt solutions. In which case what is required from others is not a solution to problems but an understanding of this process. Understanding from others is necessary for it to become a distinctively human process, in much the same way as we have seen that recognition as human is necessary to experience oneself as human. Our story, our attempt to become human, must eventually be told and also be heard before the process can be complete. After our 'dark night', freed from the grip of power, we can, if we care for them, now offer this understanding to others. But do we care for them?

The second thing which changes when we refuse to collude with power is that it is in the nature of our aspirations that we now care for the welfare of others as we do for our own. We have broken the link which binds us to others only to seek confirmation of our own position and so we have achieved that openness to the 'other' which contemporary French feminisms have thought to be so extremely difficult to theoretically identify or to change in practice.[25] For precisely what it is that we seek is that no one's life be thought to be intrinsically more valuable than anyone else's. It follows from this that we shall regard others primarily as ends rather than as means, that is, that we shall have a genuine concern for them which was not possible when we were either in competition with them or were overwhelmingly dependent on their social position. For then others were means, the primary motive for relating to them being to receive confirmation of a specific social standing, either as a 'good woman' or as a success story. Satisfaction of the need for social recognition remains, of course, one motive for relating to others, but since this need is now confronted directly it leaves us free to relate to them also for their own sake. This does not mean that we are not more involved with some more than others, that we don't have our likes or dislikes, that at times we may not choose isolation and self-immersion, or that we are not in all likelihood more involved with our own life than anyone else's. The form any relationship will take will depend on the circumstances. All that is implied is the development of relations with others for their sake as well as ours.[26] So how does this capacity for apparently universal love become the specific principle of the 'solidarity of the oppressed'?

Quite simply because this 'other relatedness' implies opposition to power. Treating all with undifferentiated respect means flying in the face of the power and its insistence that some are more important than others. Listening to others on the assumption that they can, with a little help from their friends, identify and solve their own problems is to assume their potential for autonomy and allow for the possibility that they might depart from the prescribed order. And not as a point of principle, but as a point of fact, those who are in active opposition to power and who are most likely to be developing these non-instrumental relations will be those who have been oppressed. The point is the political one – that such genuinely human relations are the alternative to power relations; that they can only be developed in opposition to power and for the most part with those who, from the point of view of the status quo, are 'lesser'. It does not mean, as it has been taken to mean, that 'the oppressed' as a group share those natural virtues which by themselves are sufficient to bring about a new and better order.[27]

I have set out to show that there is a moral position in liberation theory which strikes deep chords in us. We have seen that the theory contains a 'story line' which is in broad terms that of Christianity.[28] Pursuing one's needs for love ('seek and ye shall find') the scenario proceeds from immersion in the 'ways of the world', through a 'dark night of the soul' where one rejects these ways and is on one's own, from there to the 'blessedness of the persecution' which is courted when one is in 'solidarity with the oppressed' and finally home to the position where one can give and receive love, so 'inheriting the earth'. For whatever reason and however we respond, such a story calls on a morality with which we already familiar at some deep level. What liberation theory does is to give it a political and psychological shape. In the next chapter I want to show that contemporary feminist thought also calls upon this morality and that it does this by invoking this shape – the schema of oppression – which liberation theory gave it. The morality is not, however, directly expressed but is displaced in a way which allows for its more demanding implications to be sidestepped and which in turn allows for a highly advantageous compromise with power.

Postscript to Part I

By the late 1970s liberation theory had all but disappeared from academic feminism. At the same time the women's studies movement began to flourish. The initial victory consisted in no more than being welcome at universities, in becoming just an accepted part of the curriculum. Then more and more appointments were gained and it soon became an entrenched part of university establishments, able to bureaucratically impose feminist courses, criteria for appointments, non-sexist language and the like.[1] I shall argue that there is a connection between these two phenomena – the disappearance of the early 'liberationist' ideas and the emergence of a powerful and bureaucratically connected women's studies movement. The first indication of this connection is to be found in the manner of the disappearance of liberation theory, in the fact that it was not, as such, rejected but rather radically misdescribed. The consequence of this is that what was explicitly rejected was a quite different, indeed opposed, set of ideas, ones which were in fact seldom held. Liberation theory itself was written out of history in the way I described in the Introduction. The second indication is in the character of the kind of feminist theory, the feminism of 'difference', which largely replaced it. The clue is not so much in what is asserted, for on the surface this appears radical enough, but in the combined effect of quite appalling methods of reasoning with a sophisticated, scholarly appearance. Shortly I shall argue that these latter features, amounting to what I earlier described as 'surrationalism', enable this sort of feminist theory to function as a means for acquiring power which is appropriate to a movement whose moral credibility depends on the perception that it opposes power. This suggests that liberation theory had to go both because what it said it was antithetical and unintelligible to the emerging aspirations for intellectual prestige and the formal status which accompanies this, and because of the unpretentious way in which it said it. However, it also suggests that it had to stay because it alone was able to strike the moral chords necessary to legitimise the radical pretensions of the new movement. So that it could continue to function covertly its existence had to be ignored overtly.

The second of these considerations, then, leads on to a relatively complicated trail which is the subject of Part II. But the first, consisting of a straightforward matter of fact, is the clearest pointer to the fact that something is wrong. The major misrepresentation involved is at the heart of one of the central orthodoxies of current academic feminist thought. The orthodoxy is this: feminism in the 1960s and early 1970s was a philosophy and politics of 'equality' or 'sameness'.[2] Since then, the movement has developed and the aim is no longer for women to be 'like men' but rather to insist on our distinctive differences. These differences are not adequately defined, in the way that they have been for millennia, with reference to men, that is, as an absence of, or complement to, male qualities. Rather they must be defined autonomously. They are 'positive' rather than 'negative' differences. The feminism of 'equality' or 'sameness' tacitly assumed that the only alternatives are sameness or 'negative' difference, thereby itself participating in the repression of positive differences. It was therefore unable to radically subvert the status quo which is itself built upon 'the logic of the same'. Only a feminism of difference can be truly subversive.

It is clear that the point of this false contrast between early and later feminist thought and politics is to convey the sense of an advance having occurred. That this is so is not affected by the fact that it did not take long for it to be recognised that the assumed dichotomy between 'equality' or 'sameness' and 'difference' itself provided the predictable scope for further academic publications advocating its 'displacement' or 'deconstruction'.[3] But the historical account is false and the dichotomy between the politics of 'sameness' and of 'difference', deconstructed or otherwise, exists only as a construct of the politics of difference itself. The sense of an advance is an illusion which conceals the fact that what actually occurred was a retreat. In stressing the factual incorrectness of this orthodoxy I am leaving aside for the moment its theoretical weaknesses. These consist mainly in the confusion of equality and sameness and in the assumption that the fundamental problem to be addressed by feminism is that of the sorts of attributes women are either seen to have or aspire to have. Both issues have been addressed in Part I but in the last chapter of Part II I shall offer, also, an explanation of the error. At issue at the moment, though, is the political function of the false attributions rather than their theoretical poverty.

My claim of a substantial misdescription of early second wave thinking hinges on the argument of Part I that it was liberation theory (albeit in a number of versions) which was crucial to the emergence of the 'second wave' of feminism. It can now be seen that liberation theory was a 'politics of equality' only in the sense of asserting the irreducible, immeasurable value of all human beings. In no way is this idea of equality appropriately contrasted with that of 'difference' unless difference is meant to imply that we should differentially evaluate human beings. In so far as the argument was that equality so understood must become an aspect of everyday life, it functioned much more as a critique than an endorsement of liberal theories which would limit the idea to that of equality before the law. (I am assuming here that the attribution of a politics of equality is intended to be also an attribution of basically liberal ideas.) As for the imputation that liberation theory was a politics of 'sameness' aiming for women to be 'like men', the criticism of the limitations and ultimate futility of such an aspiration was the explicit point of the theory. It is true, of course, that liberation theory was not a theory of sexual difference – although it is clearly a theory of individual difference – but the thesis that it is therefore a theory of 'sameness' could be maintained only on the assumption that the assertion of 'sameness' and the assertion of 'difference' must function in the manner of a 'binary opposition' – an opposition which divides a field both exclusively and exhaustively. (More on binary oppositions in Chapter 4.)

This is not to say that a straightforward liberal feminism, a genuine 'politics of equality' in the sense probably intended by the orthodox description, was not around in the late 1960s and early 1970s. This kind of 'equality' feminism has always been a part of the women's movement in Western countries. Nor is it to say that there was not the occasional (although never uncontroversial) advocacy of androgyny (Morgan 1970; Tanner 1970). It is to say that these were not sufficiently powerful currents to justify the orthodox account's sweeping dismissal of earlier feminism as the 'politics of sameness'. It is also to say that the overlooking of what was a much more powerful current suggests the question: why was liberation theory written out of history?

Part II

Dualisms and confusions

To say that the class character of science resides in the defence of the interests of a given class is only a pamphleteer's argument or a falsification pure and simple. In reality, science may be bourgeois or proletarian in its very 'nature', notably in its origins, its conceptions, its methods of study and exposition. In this fundamental sense, all the sciences, social or otherwise, including mathematics and logic, can have and really do have a class character.

(A.A. Bogdanov)

Many feminists working within the sciences can accept that the various social apparatuses, institutions and practices surrounding science – the funding and administration of scientific projects, the hiring of staff, practical applications of science, the development of technologies etc. – are bound up with social values and power relations; but some consider it more difficult to criticise science itself. 'Pure science' is usually considered immune to these sociological/political 'issues'. . . . While this kind of analysis is important it only addresses the most superficial level of the problem . . . we examine some deeper, structural investments and patriarchal commitments in science, including their implicit assumptions, their preferred, validated methods (methodological claims) and the criteria by which sciences are evaluated (epistemic claims).

(Elizabeth Grosz and Marie de Lepervanche)

Flashback
The infamous history of the 'two sciences' thesis

Obscurantism is known to be a frequent companion of radical authoritarian movements. Seeking to justify the unjustifiable – their own aspirations and/or power – such movements typically develop theories which have an appearance of profundity, often of breaking with centuries, even millennia, of 'strait-jacketed' thought, but which actually work by means of the most elementary logical slides and confusions. We readily recognise this in such cases as that of the degenerate medieval Aristotelianism which Hobbes ridicules; in the 'official' dialectical materialism of the old Communist Parties; in the 'eternal ice' theory of the German Nazis, etc. In retrospect, the modes of reasoning are laughably poor and the natural link between authoritarianism and intellectual confusion is clear.

Things are not so clear, of course, when the authoritarian movement is currently powerful. Then the intellectual pretension really looks like profundity, the political aspirations appear to be no more than are just and long overdue and somehow the proclamation of a new dawning of human thought doesn't seem at all like fanaticism. The logical mistakes which permeate this pseudo-intellectual life are not identified as such but rather seem to suggest new and sophisticated ways of thinking – ways which have broken free of the old restrictions. Only the crass, those imprisoned in the old forms, could so miss the subtlety of what is going on to think them straightforward mistakes. Power – or fear – has the effect of numbing the mind.

Because hindsight does make some things easier to recognise I shall, in this second part of my argument, make use of analogies which can be drawn between influential strands of contemporary academic feminist thought and a set of theories which, being very much a part of the history of ideas, are now widely regarded as paradigmatic of obscurantist reasoning in authoritarian interests. (Why they were not so universally regarded in their own time and why many otherwise competent intellectuals should have, apparently sincerely, tried to defend them is something that close observers of our own times might be able to understand.) I am referring to 'the Lysenko Affair' of the former Soviet Union where for some three decades, between the 1930s and the 1960s, the 'crank' theories of the Ukrainian plant breeder, T.D. Lysenko, were imposed by the state on the study of biology.[1]

Before giving a brief account of this affair, which is now largely forgotten, let me forestall some anticipated objections to this procedure. Using historical examples to throw light on a current situation does not imply that all the features of the former are being said to be analogous to all the features of the latter. The comparisons I would draw are between a kind of argumentation which is found often in contemporary feminist thought and that which was characteristic of 'Lysenkoism'. These comparisons between ways of thinking do not imply either that the social conditions in which these occur are directly analogous or that feminists would wish them to be. What I mean is that it is not implied that our own social conditions are anything like as politically repressive as those of this period of Soviet history and nor is it implied that academic feminists are Stalinists where this epithet usually connotes a willingness to make ready use of extensive state powers. The relationship between social conditions and kinds of thought is not that close.

That having been said, it would be disingenuous to deny that the point of demonstrating the analogies is to emphasise the anti-intellectual character of the way of thought and related to this, its usefulness for authoritarian purposes. While, then, there is a range of socio-political climates in which such thinking might flourish, it can nevertheless be shown that they would have in common the dominance (and not just the inevitable presence) of those who value status and power more highly than, and at the expense of, the life of the mind. Gulag or not, it is cause for alarm if such a climate has reached our universities.

In any case, I do not pretend to establish anything by way of analogy. The actual analysis of the mode of thought is contained in the following chapters. The point of the analogy is, as I have just suggested, to make the conclusions of that analysis easier to digest. Here, then, is a brief reminder of 'the Lysenko Affair'.

THE LYSENKO AFFAIR

The essential facts are these. In the 1920s, shortly after the Revolution and despite being in terrible economic circumstances, the Soviet Union was one of the world leaders in research in genetics.[2] At that time, however, the practical applications of genetics were minimal and the advanced research did little to improve the backward state of Soviet agriculture. Lenin's conviction that science would enable the transformation of the economy was, in agriculture at least, a commitment to the long term. It was against this background that in the 1930s Lysenko began to get Communist Party support for his planting techniques ('vernalisation', treatment of the seed before planting) and subsequently for the theories ('Michurinism') with which he explained the purported success of these techniques.[3] The two central factors in gaining this support were the promise of enormous practical successes and the presentation of the theories, in line with Communist Party ideology, as being variously 'dialectical', 'arising from practice' and 'proletarian'. Increasingly, Lysenko and his followers attacked genetics as a scholastic, bourgeois, idealist theory with the result that the state support they enjoyed began to extend to the repression of genetics and geneticists.

The conflict culminated in 1948 when research into and teaching of genetics was officially banned and 'Michurinism' became the only permitted approach in biology. Laboratories and research institutes were closed down, textbooks were rewritten and geneticists who did not recant were dismissed, arrested and not infrequently shot (all of which had been happening, although less systematically, since the late 1930s).[4]

Predictably, the eventual downfall of Lysenkoism was brought about by its very political success. With the scapegoat for the backwardness of Soviet agriculture, the 'bourgeois' geneticists, no longer on the scene Lysenkoism began to unravel. For now it was unable either to deliver the promised spectacular successes in agriculture or to avoid responsibility for disastrous experiments. It was not, however, until 1965 that genetics was officially reinstated. The destructive effects on Soviet genetics research and on Soviet agriculture were long lasting (Joravsky 1970: 271–305; Lecourt (1977: 129–34).

I am not going to argue that it is a 'bad thing' to repress scientists and scientific inquiry (because I assume it is not necessary). And others have demonstrated the baselessness of Lysenko's theses in fact.[5] What is instructive in the immediate context is the manner in which these theses were typically argued, for it is here that we can see the distortions which an aspiration for power, presented as the liberation of the oppressed, can produce on intellectual inquiry when it is allowed to enter that domain.

THE 'TWO SCIENCES' THESIS

At the heart of the argument of Lysenkoism was the 'two sciences' thesis – the claim that there is 'proletarian science' and there is 'bourgeois science'. What made this thesis deeply controversial was the fact that it is not primarily about the applications of science, nor about the class character of those who might engage in it, for it is not about 'external' aspects of the way in which science is practised at all. The proponents of this thesis were clear that this allegedly political character of science was thought to affect its very conceptualisation, that is, the content of scientific propositions and the way in which they were argued (Joravsky 1970: 68).

Now it is with respect to the 'two sciences' thesis that the most striking analogy can be drawn with contemporary academic feminism. The analogy is specifically with those feminisms of difference which, in maintaining that 'sexual difference' must 'make its mark on thought', conclude that there are two kinds of thought – 'feminist' or 'feminine' versus 'patriarchal' or 'masculine thought'. For it was the parallel insistence that class differences between groups of people must translate into an intellectual (but equally political) difference between kinds of thought which was behind the 'two sciences' thesis.[6]

(A somewhat weaker analogy can also be drawn – and on occasion I shall do so – between both of the above 'two sciences' conceptions and the opposition between 'Aryan' and 'Jewish' physics (and science more generally) insisted upon by some scientists who supported the German Nazi Party in the 1930s.[7] The 'Aryan' science movement, however, was a much more short-lived phenomenon than that for 'proletarian' science and never developed the same kind of complexity of argument.)

However, the mere presence of a 'two sciences' thesis in two different theoretical contexts provides only a superficial analogy unless in each case it can be shown to be involved in similar modes of reasoning. Let me then, as a basis for later comparison, display the essential features of the way in which arguments for Lysenkoism worked. In particular we might now see why it was that in order to describe these arguments, Joravsky introduced the concept 'surrationalism', with its stress on the show of rationality concealing irrationality (see my Introduction, p. 10).

LEAPING LEVELS OF ABSTRACTION

The central arguments for Lysenkoism were geared to defending the fundamental thesis upon which the claim for the possibility of spectacular agricultural results was based – a thesis antithetical to genetics,[8] namely that acquired characteristics of organisms can be inherited. The core of the reasoning was this: 'Morganism/Mendelism/Weismannism' (as the Lysenkoists referred to genetics after its founding theorists) is mistaken when it divides the 'germ substance' (that which is active in inheritance – effectively the gene) from the rest of an organism and maintains that, unlike the organism itself, it is unaffected by the environment (and hence that characteristics acquired by the organism cannot be inherited). The mistake consists in the fact that whereas the germ substance is said to determine the nature of the organism, it is supposed, itself, to remain unaffected by the latter and so by any environmental changed induced in it. The reason why this is a mistake is because something unchangeable cannot be thought to be the origin of change. And this mistake is just the mistake of (variously) atomistic, linear, metaphysical, idealist, mechanistic thinking of which genetics is therefore an instance.[9]

Michurinism, by way of contrast, maintains that there is no division in the organism between the part which is involved in inheritance and the rest, that the whole of the organism contributes to the 'germ substance', that the whole of the organism interacts with its environment and that characteristics acquired in this interaction can, therefore, be inherited. Michurinism has no difficulty in explaining the fact of change and is thus an instance of that materialist and dialectical thinking which would grasp phenomena in their interaction.

The argument incorporates the 'two sciences' thesis when it goes on to identify idealist etc. thinking with a bourgeois outlook and dialectical thinking with a proletarian one. The key role of this thesis in bearing much of the real weight of the argument, though, is not apparent at this stage. It will become so shortly when we have looked further into the above reasoning.

The first point to note is that the argument misses its target. The attributions of idealism, metaphysics, etc., although made in Marxist jargon which may now sound crude and heavy handed, would not be without substance if it really were the case that geneticists insisted that the gene was an unchanging substance which nevertheless caused the processes involved in heredity. For in that case their position would share in the weaknesses of traditional metaphysical and idealist arguments (going back to Plato) which explain the world with reference to the uncaused and unchanging (God, the forms, or whatever). The difficulty with such explanations has been shown to be that of bridging the gap between the unchanging and the changing in such a way that the former can be said to be the cause or origin of the latter.

But the concept of the gene was not such as to justify the ascription of idealist metaphysics understood in this sense, for two reasons. First, the gene was not thought to be unchanging in any absolute sense nor, second, was it thought to be the sole or even the main agent in producing life. With respect to the first point, the gene was regarded as a material entity and so was assumed to be capable of all sorts of interactions with other material entities (resulting, obviously, in changes to itself amongst other things), although most of these were not yet understood. Indeed, to discover just what these were was regarded as part of the programme of genetics and of biology. Genetics denied the existence only of one specific kind of causal interaction, namely those in which changes produced in an organism would normally transmit to the genetic substance.[10] With respect to the second point, all that was maintained was that the gene was crucially involved in whatever the mechanisms were which transmitted characters between generations. The conception was of a relatively durable substance, the involvement of which in the relevant interactions functioned as a kind of blueprint for the transmission of characters. There is nothing idealist, metaphysical or philosophically improper in positing the presence of a durable substance as an aspect of crucial mechanisms. It is only if the necessary presence of these mechanisms were overlooked and the gene alone was thought to have agency that the Lysenkoist point would have had substance.[11]

These two points are related. It was because the gene was not assumed to be absolutely unchanging but was thought, rather, to be capable of physical interactions that it was also thought to be only involved in the mechanisms of reproduction and was not completely identified with them, so assuming sole agency. The metaphysical mistake of which genetics was wrongly accused occurs when, on the one hand, ordinary causal powers are withdrawn from something (God, the forms, etc.) with one hand and then absolute agency is attributed with the other to make good the deficiency (and the making good then has to fail because there is no longer any medium in which the agency can operate). The more basic mistake in Lysenkoism, then, relates to the first point – it was the interpretation of genetics as implying that the gene was absolutely unchanging, that is, as effectively denying its possible involvement in any ordinary causal mechanisms. This was the substantive content of the accusation that the gene was only a metaphysical entity.

But now the nature of the mistake begins to emerge. It is a mistake which depends on conflating a thesis denying a specific causal interaction of a gene (the thesis actually maintained in genetic theory) with one denying its causal interaction as such. It is the mistake of confusing levels of abstraction, of moving from the assertion of specifics to the assertion of generalities. Moreover, in this case, where the confusions concern the application of the category of causality, the mistake is one which transmutes scientific questions into philosophical ones. For the assertion and denial of specific causalities is the substance of science, whereas questions concerning the category of causality as such (for example, whether anything can be said to be both unchanging and yet have causal agency) are philosophical.[12] (In the same way, much contemporary postmodern thought confuses the assertion of specific 'samenesses' with a favouring of the category of 'sameness' and then with a whole philosophy of 'the same'. I shall show this in the next chapter.)

POLITICS AND TRUTH

Now that it is clear that there is minimal rational substance to the Lysenkoist argument, the question becomes one of why it was successful, of why it was accepted by so many for so long. If the appeal was not to reason, how did the argument work? This is something about which I shall have a lot more to say but the main point can now be made.

We have seen that the substantive content of the Lysenkoist argument consisted in the attribution of idealism to genetics. However, since the grounds of this attribution were fundamentally confused the argument required something more, something which would conceal the confusions. This was the function of the 'two sciences' thesis. To the rational content of the Lysenkoist argument, the identification of idealism with bourgeois science and of dialectics with proletarian science clearly adds nothing. (And this is so whether or not there is any substance to these identifications of philosophical positions with class positions. The thesis adds nothing to the description of the causality of the gene which is the issue.) However, without the addition of the 'two sciences' thesis, the question would have been lurking: why were they (the geneticists) so stupid? Had no answer been supplied to this question, the fact that they were not so stupid after all may have quickly become apparent. But when idealist metaphysics was said to be bourgeois an answer was already supplied to the threatening question, which therefore did not have to be asked. It was, admittedly, an answer only for the committed, for those who already saw themselves as being in opposition to the bourgeoisie and who were therefore very ready to believe in the intellectual limitations of the latter but it is the reasoning of the committed (of a certain kind of the committed, I should say) which is at issue. Although, then, the 'two sciences' thesis had no role in the content of the argument it had a crucial role in its persuasiveness.

This point could be generalised. If political loyalty was sufficient to prevent this line of questioning, it was probably also sufficient to prevent other kinds of critical questioning from being pushed very far. On the other hand, it is important not to exaggerate the claim and imply that the only thing at stake was blind fanaticism. It is necessary to understand how bad reasoning can actually have a grip on people and this means acknowledging that an amount of genuine reasoning is usually involved. (My interest here, as in the case of contemporary feminism, is in those who really were impressed by the reasoning and not in those who were either completely cynical or completely intimidated.) Indeed, when one reads the better advocates of Lysenkoism one can get the impression of intelligent and informed people stretching their intellectual capacities to make the argument respectable, to make it square with what were the known facts, and to make it internally consistent.

My analysis suggests, nevertheless, that the rational considerations in Lysenkoism were minimal and that most of the weight of the argument was carried by the 'two sciences' thesis in virtue of the political commitments which it evoked. If so, the 'two sciences' thesis was not just a descriptive, allegedly factual thesis about kinds of thinking and class outlooks but had become as well a way of deciding which theories are right and which are wrong. Since it functioned in argument mainly by appeal to political considerations, then it was the means whereby politics could start determining theoretical issues. It is time to return to the central subject, contemporary academic feminism, and see how it deals with the idea that there are two kinds of thought.

3 Feminist theory as 'power/knowledge'

The 'two sciences' thesis revisited

The history of Lysenko is finished. The history of the causes of Lysenkoism continues. One history is at an end. Is the other endless?

(Louis Althusser)

Liberation ideas did not completely disappear from feminist thought in the mid-1970s. Instead, they went underground. They are tacitly expressed in what is possibly the most popular theme in the feminism of 'difference', namely the criticism of binary oppositions, dichotomies, or dualisms as they are variously described.[1] The function of the underground presence of liberation ideas is to confer moral credibility on the later ideas which are, I shall show, more appropriate to an authoritarian exercise of power than to any confrontation with it. There is, then, an ambivalence about power behind the interest in this theme. While both sides of this ambivalence need to be shown, I shall begin by demonstrating the connections the theme of binary oppositions has with unjustified power for it is such connections which explain the repression of liberation ideas rather than vice versa. The continued presence of liberation theory and its direct oppositional stance will be demonstrated in the next chapter once the reason why it must remain covert has been established.

It is clear that the contradictory stance towards power must not become obvious if the ideas in question are to find acceptance. But it is not the oppositional stance which is concealed – rather, this is exaggerated. The critique of binary oppositions is presented as a radical way of thinking which is in opposition to the most entrenched power structures of Western civilisation. What is concealed, therefore, is the fact that this theme so readily lends itself to authoritarian uses that it can only be understood as a function of an aspiration for power. In arguing this I will, then, necessarily be exposing some of the conceptual slides and built-in incoherencies which are the means of its concealment. I will be revealing the 'surrationalist' character of this kind of feminist thinking. (To remind the reader: 'surrational' is a term I borrowed from David Joravsky, who defined it as 'a show of rational discourse, camouflaging a basic refusal to meet the tests of genuine reason' (see Introduction: p. 10).)

I shall look at the discussion of binary oppositions or dualisms mainly as it is often found in the growing number of feminist textbooks, readers, anthologies, conference reports – the sorts of writings which help constitute 'women's studies' as a movement, either by means of an introductory presentation of ideas for students or other newcomers or by means of the statement of an assumed common orientation. I shall be reconstructing a very typical argument and so it should be noted that the individual instances of this will naturally vary slightly. This argument often goes under the name of 'deconstruction'.[2] However, there is also a 'serious', more intellectually legitimate kind of deconstruction which is found less often than that which I reconstruct here and the analysis of which I have reserved for Part III. But it is the many 'surrational' versions of deconstruction that I shall now argue are intellectually incoherent, serve a political function and do the latter by means of the former.

The argument I would expose in the first instance contains four major moves: the assertion that Western thought is determined by a dualistic form; the apparent inference that this form is political, involving the domination of one of two terms by the other (often this is at the same time the inference that it is patriarchal); the inference that a 'moment of reversal' in the alleged position of dominance is necessary but not sufficient to confront the politics involved; finally the conclusion that a new form of thought (variously, feminist theory, feminine writing, writing as a woman, feminist deconstruction) is required.[3] In this chapter, because I am discussing the argument only in so far as it indicates an aspiration for power, I shall gloss over the third move which has its main role in the expression of the contradictory commitment to opposing power and so will be discussed in the next chapter. Here I want to reveal that the above argument runs parallel both in its 'logic' and in the kinds of uses to which it lends itself to those moves which were once made from 'bourgeois formal logic', to 'proletarian dialectical logic' and, to a lesser extent, to those made from the idea of 'Jewish' world physics to 'Aryan' physics.[4]

DUALISMS

The crucial step, I shall show, is the first one – the assertion that Western thinking is determined by binary oppositions or dualisms. We are told often, for example, of 'the dualistic oppositions which determine our ways of thinking' (Jardine 1985: 24), of 'the straitjacket of patriarchal binary thought' (Toril Moi 1989: 194) and that 'The real problem is that our thinking is framed by dualism and polarity, concepts that permeate western culture' (Haste 1994).[5] The 'thought' in question is here only vaguely defined if at all, being referred to variously as Western metaphysics, language, and/or philosophy, and/or theory (including science).[6] The significant point, though, is the fact that these dualistic oppositions are thought to be not so much established as the result of a certain way of thinking as they are determining of the way we think. This will turn out to be the necessary ideological move because it will enable ideas to be rejected ('dismantled') without any critical discussion which even pretends to meet them in their own terms. This is because once such a thesis is accepted it is no longer the content of ideas which is at issue but their form, the content now being thought of as either determined by, or at least secondary to, the form. It is then only necessary to take the second step described above and identify this form of ideas as intellectually and politically pernicious and we have at hand an easy means for rejecting and denouncing ideas, one which requires no demanding critical engagement at all, at the same time as it could, to those new to theoretical discussion, have the appearance of theoretical sophistication. What we would have, then, because it is a means of rejecting ideas without good reason, is a tool of authoritarianism in the domain of the intellect. But it also clearly constitutes the requisite intellectual procedures of a cruder form of power where academics of a certain kind are eliminated from institutions allowing others, more politically desirable, to take their place.[7] This is why a diversion from the content to the form of ideas is a time-honoured strategy in authoritarian political movements which aim to destroy the intellectual traditions of their opponents.[8] But this is to run ahead.

The starting position of this kind of thinking is the thesis that the dualistic form is constitutive of 'our thought'. Whether or not this is an ideological manoeuvre of the kind anticipated depends upon the grounds upon which the claim is made. Indeed, the difference between what I am calling the 'serious' and the 'surrational' treatment of the subject depends on whether this thesis generates questions or answers. The more serious account both asks and attempts to answer the question why dualisms can be said to be determining of Western thought as well as the question how they do so. (I shall discuss this account in Part III.) Although the answers are such that they easily lend themselves to the ideological move I am about to describe, the point is that the question is asked and the answers are discussable. Moreover, since they are not assumed to be definitive answers, much of this 'serious' discussion is an attempt to develop and explore the concepts involved, those of 'différance', the 'unitary subject', the 'semiotic', the 'female imaginary', etc. In this more 'serious' kind of thinking the claim concerning dualisms in Western thought is a starting position in the sense that it generates questions or, if you like, a research programme. The contrasting move which is found more frequently (if indeed there is a move at all and the claim is not baldly asserted)[9] is to produce a list of the said oppositions in place of an explanation of the thesis that such dualisms determine our thinking.[10] Because this procedure quite profoundly begs the question, it is able (in conjunction with the assertion of the political nature of dualisms) to found the desired answers that almost all Western thought has been male and repressive. If one were, then, to draw on Louis Althusser's concept of ideology, the 'surrational' feminist account of binary oppositions could be said to be ideological in the sense of being geared to the production of pregiven answers about their alleged patriarchal character.[11] To follow how this is done we have to see first just how the necessary question comes to be begged.

It is undeniably true that many (but not all) of the central problems of philosophy, in particular, are formulated in terms of pairs of contrasting terms: God/world; mind/matter; soul/body, etc. It is therefore not at all difficult to produce a list of the oppositions or antinomies of Western philosophical thought. But the question which is at issue is that of the extent to which these oppositions arise from the character of the problem under consideration versus the extent to which the problem is created by the contrasts which could then be said to have been produced for other reasons. On the answer to this question hangs the intellectual worth of the Western philosophical tradition. It is not answered by pointing to the existence of the oppositions because their existence is not controversial – it is their intellectual legitimacy which is in question. What we have, then, in the move from the production of the list of contrasts to the thesis that these have determined Western thought is the assumption that the philosophical tradition has no intrinsic intellectual worth and that philosophical problems are not genuine problems. The move, therefore, constitutes a diversion away from the content of philosophical problems.

The reason it is a diversion is not because such a position cannot be argued or because it should be assumed that the answer to the question of the legitimacy of the problems of philosophy is necessarily always in philosophy's favour. Wittgenstein, for example, argued in an intellectually legitimate fashion that many philosophical problems are pseudo problems. The crucial issue is whether the conclusions are reached by way of an engagement with the problems as such. The feminist move in question avoids such an engagement in a way that Wittgenstein did not by asserting/assuming at the outset that the dualisms determine the problems. It is, therefore, only a diversion and without intellectual merit. But the political achievement is significant, for once the move is accepted the focus is upon the form of ideas and this will turn out to have enormously fruitful results of an ideological kind.

That this is the situation is not affected by the presence of a further move which is often made and by virtue of which the 'theory' of binary oppositions can become specifically feminist. This further move consists in the claim that these dichotomies are in some fundamental way informed, if not determined by the male/female dichotomy.[12] For here we simply have the continuation of the assumption that the dualisms are not formulated in response to genuine problems but require a different explanation. And so a 'fundamental' dualism is posited to do the job.[13]

HIERARCHIES

'Surrational' deconstructionist feminism begins with the thesis that the binary oppositional form determines Western thought and avoids showing that this is the case. Ideological convenience has been bought at the cost of intellectual worth, and the only way forward now is to make more exchanges of this kind. For when, accepting the premise that dualisms determine Western thought, we move on to ask what exactly is wrong with this, conceptual difficulties arise which can be dealt with only by creating confusion. The problem is that the obvious and most promising line of explanation is excluded by the requirements of the opening move. The likely explanation of what might be wrong with dualisms would be in terms of the specific ways in which they are used. For example, they could be seen to be typically used in the attempt to impose false alternatives on people (Tapper (1990), unpublished). Or one could argue in company with J.L. Austin amongst others that a tendency towards dichotomous thinking is one of the major ways in which philosophical reasoning, in particular, can go wrong. Or again, as we saw above in the discussion of liberation theory, a dualistic allocation of personal attributes can be used to give content to the evaluation, necessary for the establishment of power relations, that one person is better than another. But these sorts of argument imply that dualisms sometimes, even often, involve errors in reasoning and the very fact of making such an argument further implies that such errors can be corrected within and by 'Western thought' itself. They are thought to typically occur as mistakes in Western reasoning rather than to be constitutive of it. But we are here discussing the position which maintains that dichotomies dominate our thinking rather than, at times, being more simply an instance of it going wrong. Those who would maintain this position, therefore, have no alternative but to show that the fault lies in the binary form itself and not in specific uses of it.

The problem is that this is impossible from the outset. It is agreed that a dualism, binary opposition, or dichotomy is a purely logical relation which can hold between a pair of terms, the relation consisting in the fact that the terms are both exhaustive and exclusive of the relevant domain.[14] That is, everything under consideration is described by either one or the other of the terms but not both. So, for example, where 'male/female' functions as a binary opposition every person (or animal/plant etc. if relevant) will be considered to be either one or the other but not both. The definition is clear and unexceptionable. But as such, as the pure form of a contrast, considered independently of the content of the terms being so contrasted, and therefore independently also of the way it might be used (i.e. as terms perhaps mistakenly being thought to be of this form, or the contrast made perhaps being thought to be inadequate to the complexities of the situation or some such) there *can* be nothing wrong with the binary form of the kind which these feminists are seeking. It is just a logical form which may or may not hold between two terms.

This difficulty is rarely confronted head on.[15] (However, in a moment I shall look at one of the rare accounts which reaches the above point and bravely faces up to the conclusions where others prefer obfuscation.) Nevertheless, the supposition that there is something very wrong with the binary form *qua* pure logical form is most definitely made, first of all in the manner of its descriptions – 'the patriarchal binary straitjacket' etc. More import-antly, it is made in the way much feminist argument proceeds, where it is often thought sufficient to identify a dichotomous form in order to refute the con-tent of the idea whose form it is. And it is implied, I have tried to show, in the assertion that this form dominates our thinking together with the assumption that there is something wrong with our thinking therefore. But in none of these situations is the precise content of the supposition made explicit and consequently its absurdity does not become apparent. What happens, I should imagine, is that one or more of the explanations which are excluded by the insistence on the determining character of dualisms but which are never-theless very persuasive accounts of what can go wrong with dichotomies are tacitly referred to (in the minds of those accepting the idea) in order to supply the missing answer to the question of what is wrong. For the experience of the various misuses of dichotomies is a common one, and so, in the absence of clarity about the fact that the charge is *not* one of misuse, we are likely to assume that this is just what it is. But this tacit appeal is clearly not sufficient and the question must be more explicitly addressed. This is where its second major thesis comes into play – the assertion of the hierarchical, repressive character of the binary form. However, what we get here, it will shortly emerge, is another unexplained and (within the terms of reference estab-lished) inexplicable assertion. Nevertheless it does the job of identifying the binary form as both conceptually and politically undesirable and so answer-ing the question of what is wrong with it.

This next move then is to simply assert the hierarchical and therefore polit-ical character of these binary oppositions. We are dealing with 'a structured set of oppositions that serve to privilege particular terms and concepts, and to repress others' (Shiach 1989: 156) and 'every opposition entails, repression, violence, death' (Moi 1989: 194). If the assumption involved in the assertion of the first thesis concerning the dominance of dualisms was that they are intellectually poor, that which is introduced at this point is that they have also an oppressive political dimension. This assumption is conveyed by the highly politicised language. We are told that terms, concepts and signifiers 'domin-ate', 'debase', and 'repress' each other. And although it is this language which I shall insist can only operate metaphorically, it nevertheless very effectively implies that there is something politically 'off' about the binary form. I say it is an assumption which is introduced here because the claim of a hierarchy necessarily associated with dualisms, whether this claim is made in political language or not, can have no sound theoretical basis, for the dichotomous form itself carries no such privileging or hierarchisation. The reason is as before – we are considering a logical relation between two terms and any evaluation which may be made either of the terms or of the relationship between them is logically distinct from this.

There is, however, a lot of empirical evidence for a different claim with which this claim now becomes confused. When the lists of oppositions are given – day/night; light/dark; man/woman; mind/body; nature/culture; cause/

effect, etc., etc. and it is claimed that the first term is valued more than the second, this strikes one as probably largely true. But the position I am attacking is not that people often value one term of a dichotomy more than they do the other term – the claim is that this evaluation is implicit in the binary form itself, that it is the opposition itself which entails violence and repression. The 'hierarchy' or 'privileging' is not attributed to an evaluative act which is its only possible basis but is located in the form itself.

The recognition that the attributed hierarchy of terms cannot arise from the binary form itself is at least implicit in the more 'serious' feminist deconstructions and in Derrida's own writings, where the aim is to show in the operations of a particular text just how this 'privileging' is established. Such a manner of proceeding assumes that the fact that one term is regarded as more important than its contrast is not established by the distinction itself but rather by other parts of the text which refer to it. It is something which has to be shown in each case.[16] (Donna Haraway's influential 'manifesto for cyborgs' is, I think, somewhere between the 'surrational' attack on binary oppositions I am describing and a serious argument but I shall discuss it in a footnote.[17])

As an aside at this stage the differences with the argument in liberation theory could be noted. In liberation theory the troublesome act of evaluation – the idea that one person is better or worse than another – is considered to be logically distinct from whatever pairs of attributes are latched onto to give it content. More importantly, the evaluation is seen to be historically prior to the binary allocation of attributes and the reverse assumption was shown to be an illusion, although a powerful one. That is, it is argued that the reason why male attributes are seen to be superior to female ones is not because such an evaluation arises from a perception of the attributes themselves but because it follows from a prior evaluation. It is a consequence of the evaluation that men are better than women. The illusion which is exposed, and which to some extent we now find recapitulated in this kind of feminist 'deconstruction', is that the evaluation somehow naturally follows from the character of the attributes themselves – although it must be admitted that feminist 'deconstruction' locates the evaluation in the formal rather than the substantive character of the attributes. In liberation theory, then, there is no difficulty in explaining what is wrong with attributes allocated in the form of binary oppositions, such as masculinity/femininity etc. Those in question are the result of the prior evaluative act of people and it is the latter, itself fully explicable, which is the problem.

GRASPING THE NETTLE

I have claimed that in most of the cases I am considering, the theoretical issues involved in locating hierachisation and political incorrectness in the binary form itself are avoided in the manner described above. Elizabeth Grosz, however, does fully bring out the implications of locating deep political and intellectual problems in the binary form as such. Since her account has been very well received I take it that many believe she does manage to articulate here an important position.[18] (Grosz is also widely regarded as Australia's leading feminist theorist.) Since she actually spells out what I am trying to establish is implicit in the looser discussion of dualisms I shall briefly discuss her account before I go on to examine the uses to which this feminist conception of the politically oppressive nature of theoretical form has been put.

To begin with, let us note – and this is not contentious – that there are two ways in which two terms can divide a domain exclusively and exhaustively and so constitute a binary opposition. First, such a division can be due to the manner of the definition of the terms in question and a simple question of logic. Any two terms of the form 'A' and 'not A' (i.e. such that they are defined as the negation of each other) will necessarily divide a domain exhaustively and exclusively, such that any of its elements will be described by one or other of these terms but not both. Second, it can be due to contingent facts about the elements of the domain. So, for example, the terms 'male/ female' might be thought to exclusively and exhaustively divide the domain of human beings but if this is so it depends on the contingency of the existence of two biological sexes which is not a question of logic but of fact. In this case, the two terms may be said to be of the 'A/B' form since they are not defined in terms of each other.

Grosz's argument that there is an 'implicit hierarchical structure in binary oppositions, which accord positive value to the primary term and regard the secondary term as its debased counterpart' (Grosz 1988: 101) proceeds with reference to the first of these binary forms: 'Dichotomous structures take the form of A and not-A relations, in which one term is positively defined and the other is defined only as the negative of the first' (Grosz 1989: xvi). So definitions of the 'A/not A' form are taken to imply that the 'A' term is prioritised over the 'not A' term, which is said to be its 'debased counterpart' (Grosz 1988: 101). And: 'The binary oppositional grid establishes a privileged model of theoretical inquiry where the identity of a privileged term is guaranteed only by the elaboration and expulsion of its opposite and other' (Grosz 1988: 99). We are provided with examples: 'Reason is surreptitiously defined by claiming it is not corporeal, not based on passion, nor madness, nor emotions rather than described in positive or substantive terms' (Grosz 1988: 101). The hierarchical character of binary oppositions, soon to be identified as 'the structure which separates subject and object, teacher and pupil, truth and falsity' (Grosz 1990:168) has now become identified with definitions of the 'A/not A' form.

Given that if one term is defined as the negation of another it follows immediately that the latter can be similarly defined as the negation of the former, this is exceedingly thin ground upon which to infer that one of the two terms is somehow favoured over the other. An argument may of course be made out in terms of considerations external to the binary form itself, but this is at best equivocation, for the point, which this writer makes particularly clear, is to locate the sins within the binary form. Now I would agree that when women are defined as 'not men' in the way Aristotle did and in the way Freud's understanding of femininity as castration is also thought to do, then there is a problem. But this problem lies in the inadequacy of the content of the definition and in the fact that the logic of its use is restricted so that the implication which does follow from the form, namely that men are 'not women', is disallowed. There is no problem with the mere logical possibility that two terms be defined as the negation of each other.

The further, equally serious, problem if we adopt this line of argument is that the empirical grounds upon which the whole case concerning binary oppositions tacitly rested is now undermined. For the binary oppositions that do seem to recur in Western thought are mostly not of the 'A/not A' form but are more often of the second kind described above. They are usually of the 'A/B' form and are thought to contingently, not logically, exhaust their domain. Reason, for example, is not defined – surreptitiously or otherwise – as 'not' emotion, passion, madness, etc., although, in conjunction with an account of the emotions etc., these things may be thought to be implied. It is more often defined in substantive terms such as proceeding in accordance with certain rules or methods or as an innate capacity.

The significance of the position just described is that I think it is the only way a line of argument which would locate political and intellectual problems in the binary form can be pursued. The fact that it is widely and approvingly referred to confirms this. But whether or not the critique of 'hierarchical dualisms' is developed with this sort of clarity – to what I take to be the point of absurdity – it nevertheless is able to function in the way I have described. The focus on the alleged form of 'mainstream' ('malestream') thought provides a quick and easy way to dismiss ideas both politically and intellectually in the one move without having to meet an opposing position or to know anything very much about it.[19] At the same time, the ability to make sweeping claims about whole movements of thought gives the appearance of enormous learning. We now have the basic intellectual tools required for the exercise of power in the domain of theory.[20]

Many feminist opponents of dualisms are content with this much theoretical armoury. These feminist theorists understand their task to be primarily that of exposing the patriarchal character of traditional theories.[21] But there is an obvious further step, the culmination of the above manoeuvrings, which is now waiting to be taken. It is necessary to stress that this next step is most certainly not taken by anything like a majority of academic feminists. But it is taken by a very influential minority who to a large extent have managed to set the terms of debate and it is treated by other academic feminists as though it were an intellectually reputable position.[22] Since it is a step which highlights the thoroughly alarming character of much of what passes for 'radical' theory it warrants what is now a long overdue exposure as a move which is both intellectually disreputable and politically coercive. It consists in going from the identification I have been describing of one theoretical or logical form as 'patriarchal' and bad to the identification of an alternative theoretical or logical form as 'feminist' and good. If we take this step we become advocates of 'feminist' theorising and 'feminist' science in the strong sense where what is at issue is allegedly a radically different form of thinking from 'mainstream' or 'malestream' thought. It puts us straight back into the land of 'bourgeois formal logic' versus 'proletarian dialectical logic', which is also the land of 'bourgeois' and 'proletarian science' – only of course the names have changed to 'the patriarchal logic of sameness' versus 'the feminist logic of difference' and 'patriarchal' versus 'feminist' science. Ironically, the battle still centres upon the subject of biology.

PATRIARCHAL VERSUS FEMINIST THEORY

First, a qualification: the kind of result I am anticipating from the identification of 'feminist' and 'patriarchal' theoretical forms can clearly be achieved by fixing not only upon the form of ideas but on any two sets of allegedly competing theoretical characteristics. All that is required is that there is some aspect of theories which can be picked on as a basis upon which one theory can be promoted and another dismissed and which is external to any actual theoretical conflict which may be at issue. (To be drawn into a genuine debate is alien to this sort of theoretical strategy, both because it leaves the answers open and because it requires sufficient knowledge to actually engage with the subject. It therefore implies a respect for one's protagonists which is incompatible with their easy denunciation.) Moreover, there could only be an advantage in the ability to shift ground by having a number of contrasts available. So we find that while those engaged in debating Lysenkoism complained repeatedly that scientific issues were settled on philosophical grounds, the latter in fact covered a fairly wide range, moving from the insistence on dialectics, to the importance of practice, to the materialist/idealist conflict etc.[23] Similarly, the distinction between 'feminist' as opposed to 'male' theory or science is not always made in terms of patriarchal binary logic versus a logic of difference, that is, in terms of theoretical form. Very often, we find it made also, for example, between feminist 'situated' knowledges and patriarchal 'perspectiveless' theories, or between theories (male) which assume the subject/object distinction and those (feminist) which reject it, or between theories (male again) which endorse the idea of objectivity and those (feminist) which do not, etc. And sometimes we are given a whole list of contrasting features by which feminist and patriarchal theory may be distinguished.[24] To repeat, all that is necessary is that the contrast in question, like all of the above, has nothing to do with any substantive theoretical question. (In the same way some fundamentalist religions educate their followers into recognising the marks of the devil but not into thinking about the problem of evil.) My argument can, then, be readily generalised to include all such attempts to distinguish 'feminist' from 'male' or 'patriarchal' theories, although I shall centre on those which work by contrasting the allegedly competing forms of the two sorts of theories, because these are at the heart of my analysis of the fate of liberation theory. (Anticipating that analysis, I would note here that once an identification of a 'feminist' versus a 'male' or 'patriarchal' theoretical form has been made, the essential elements are in place for the projection of a real life political conflict onto an abstract domain. It is now different and irreconcilable theoretical *forms* which are in conflict and real people, as postmodernists will say quite explicitly, are no longer at issue.)

My specific claim, then, is that having argued in the way described above against the alleged dualistic form of mainstream theories some feminist theorists proceed to take the further step of identifying an alternative theoretical form as intrinsically or distinctively feminist. What results is a new version of the 'two sciences' thesis with markedly similar forms of argumentation. There are two different ways in which the transition is made from the idea of the 'maleness' of dualisms or dichotomies to the advocacy of an alternative feminist theoretical form. The first proceeds from the argument discussed above to the effect that there is something oppressive about the A/not A contrast and moves on to identify contrasts of the A/B form as somehow liberatory and feminist. Accordingly, it might be suggested that feminist theory would focus on 'differences' rather than 'samenesses' since the former, it is maintained, take this A/B form. The second intimates that the 'unsettling' of dichotomies is itself intrinsically feminist, where what it is to so unsettle is left suitably vague.[25] For the most part these moves, like the earlier ones purportedly against dualisms, are insinuated rather than argued, the reader being lead along by the apparent logic of the situation whereby if one form of thought is bad and oppressive it seems to follow that there is an alternative one which is good and liberatory.[26] Very often such moves are made as introductory comments to articles on some more specific subject where their introductory character is assumed to release the writer from the obligation to argue the position. Sometimes we find instead an acknowledgement to the many feminist scholars (often unreferenced) who have supposedly already established the case. But we do also find this line of thinking as the theoretical substance of feminist writings. In the case studies below I shall demonstrate how this unargued transition from the identification of an alleged 'male' or oppressive theoretical form to an alleged feminist or liberatory one constitutes the core argument of the two influential writings considered. My hope is that the strategies exposed in these case studies will be identifiable by the reader as varieties of similar strategies commonly found in current feminist literature. For it is in the nature of my case, which would reconstruct a typical argument or strategy, that not every instance can be discussed. First, however, there is an epistemological argument which needs to be addressed.

A SCANDALOUS POSITION

The acceptance or rejection of theories upon the basis of features which do not bear directly on the theoretical issues presupposes a definite epistemo-logical position. Since this position is central to the kind of argument I am reconstructing here and since it is also, I think, a scandalous position which merits independent exposure, I will divert from the main line of my argument to consider it.

The position in question is that theory choice is political. This position is not limited to the insistence that theory choice is in fact often made on political grounds – it is the position that it also ought to be. It is required by the kind of argument I am reconstructing here for this would choose between theories on the basis of theoretical characteristics which are thought to be in some sense political. (Were there an argument that theories with these allegedly feminine/feminist characteristics were better *qua* theories, what follows would not apply. Very often, there is not.[27]) However, it is not only the case that this epistemological assumption operates, possibly unnoticed, in these more ideological instances of feminist theory, but it is also present in a significant amount of feminist philosophy which is explicitly addressed to epistemological issues and not all of which could be described as ideological or 'surrational'. The latter discussion provides the background, sometimes acknowledged and sometimes not, which supports the former. (Often the two discussions occur in the same piece of writing as in the two case studies below.) I will address my argument, then, both to this directly epistemological discussion as well as to some of the cases which advocate feminist .versus patriarchal thought forms with which I am more centrally concerned. My efforts here will be directed mainly to showing that the assumption that the-ory choice is political is being made. This is because I don't regard it as intellectually reputable and I maintain therefore that once its existence has been exposed very little needs to be done to reveal its illegitimacy. The task, then, is mainly one of unravelling the confusions which either conceal what is going on or conceal the full import of what is going on. Because of these confusions I shall begin by specifying precisely what it is about this epistemological position which is disreputable.

I do not think that it is at all unacceptable to attempt to argue that different kinds of socialisation or psychological construction or whatever affect the way in which we conceptualise and that in this sense we may be able to distinguish 'male' and 'female' ways of theorising, or of engaging in science. This is Evelyn Fox Keller's project and both the arguments and evidence she has assembled for this proposition are worthy of serious critical discussion (Fox Keller 1983, 1985). Nor is it illegitimate to go even further, as Margaret Whitford understands Luce Irigaray to be doing (Whitford 1991), and argue that our sexual identity affects the very categories within which we organise our perception and understanding of the world and to maintain, therefore, that significant changes in the one may well effect significant changes in the other. Nor again is it out of court to consider the proposition that different theories may be enmeshed with different kinds of political and practical interests and that much contemporary research may in different ways serve male interests. There are no considerations which from the outset make any such projects or theses untenable. Whether or not they are worth pursuing depends very much on the arguments and the evidence which are put forward. As well, it would be quite proper to make allowances for the fact that if the problem runs as deep as is it claimed then it may take time for an understanding even to be articulated, let alone adequately defended. Attempts such as these to identify 'male' and 'feminist' thought are worthy of discussion.

The position which I maintain *is* illegitimate from the outset is the one whose existence I have set out to expose. It is quite different from any of the above but it is almost always put forward so that it is confused or run together with at least one of them. It is quite different because it concerns the truth or acceptability of theories whereas the above all concern either their conditions or their effects. (I shall discuss shortly the way these two distinct sorts of issues are often confused in feminist theory.) It is the position which asserts, first, that male and female theories (or patriarchal and feminist theories) are incommensurable in the sense that no shared theoretical criteria of validity can be established and second, that because of this incommensurability the issue is therefore to be decided on political grounds. To repeat: it is not the position that theories often *are* chosen on political grounds; it is the position that they *ought* to be so chosen.[28] This 'truth is political' thesis goes further than relativism in so far as it takes the extra step of insisting that if questions of truth cannot be decided on intellectual grounds then they *can* be decided politically. It lacks, therefore, the consistency of a relativism which accepts the consequences of its own argument and lives with no particular commitment to any set of ideas. It is not an intellectually reputable proposition because it amounts to the claim that politics alone decides what is true, or if we back away now from the notion of truth, it becomes the claim that politics decides what we should think. If politics alone decides then power alone decides and it also follows immediately that there is no basis upon which power itself can be criticised. We are no longer on serious intellectual ground.

THE RELATIVIST BACKGROUND

Contemporary feminist theorists quite explicitly occupy the authoritarian and anti-intellectual ground just described when they first of all argue/ assume that there are no shared criteria of validity (conception of what counts as proof) between what they would classify as 'male' and 'feminist' theories but nevertheless move on to advocate that theories be chosen on feminist political grounds.[29] (In this respect they are more candid than the proponents of 'proletarian science' who maintained that the best political choice was also the most scientifically objective choice.[30]) They come very close to occupying this ground, although often unintentionally, when they insist, as they almost all do, on the impossibility of objectivity (the 'God's eye view', they say) and then proceed to advocate a commitment to 'feminist' theory. For here they are faced with the difficulty of finding grounds for their choice of theory which do not eventually collapse into purely political ones. (Note 31 develops this point with reference to the arguments of Helen Longino and Donna Haraway.[31]) The question is how this scandalous position that truth is political has managed to intrude into contemporary epistemology.

It has done so against a definite philosophical background, broader than feminist theory itself, which has developed over the last few decades and which is itself very questionable. This background consists in the widespread rejection of any kind of foundationalist epistemology and in the associated rise in popularity of relativism. (Although it should be noted, against the common assumption to the contrary, that the one does not follow from the other, for the rejection of one kind of account of truth in no way entails the rejection of all accounts.) It is in this context that the 'truth is political' idea has been smuggled in and its full import concealed. The smuggling operation is revealed when we realise that the arguments for 'feminist science' as opposed to 'male science' are very often in fact no more than the popular arguments for relativism. (This description is often resisted.[32]) In this way the two epistemological positions, one a traditional and reputable position, the other completely disreputable, are run together. However, even if we leave aside the decisive fact that these arguments for relativism don't establish the desired conclusion that truth is political, they are worthy of a brief examination in their own right. I shall take up the two most common.

The first proceeds from the thesis, now widely accepted as a result of the rejection of foundationalism, that there is no universal scientific method: 'If there is no single, transcendental standard for deciding between competing knowledge claims, then it can be said that there are only local historical ones, each valid in its own lights but having no claims against others' (Harding 1993: 61).[33] In other words, there is no single scientific method and so there are no shared criteria of theoretical validity between any two competing theories.[34] The latter must be incommensurable. This argument depends on a misunderstanding and an unjustified inference.

The standard argument (in this context) is that whose origin is usually attributed to Gaston Bachelard.[35] It is an argument against a single or universal scientific method, against 'shared criteria of validity' in that sense, but in no way does it imply that in theoretical disputes no common meeting ground can be found. It is not implied, in other words, that such disputes cannot be settled by theoretical considerations. It is not an anti-rationalist argument. Rather, it is implied that the criteria upon which different disputes are settled both within and between different sciences will be different in each case because they will be established by the science in question. In Bachelard's terminology they will be 'internal' to the science under consideration. So far from it being denied, say, that biological arguments can be countered in terms of considerations from biology it is insisted that this is precisely where they must be met. Appeal must be made to concrete considerations from the science in question rather than to universal, philosophically established, criteria. (This is the kind of argument which was implicit in the case of those scientists who argued so strenuously against Lysenkoism. Their repeated insistence was that at stake were scientific issues which could be settled only on scientific grounds, by which they meant the arguments and evidence from biology itself. Abstract philosophical considerations, 'dialect-ical' or otherwise, applied grid-like to all and any science, were inherently unable to decide such questions as the reality of the gene.[36])

The 'feminist science' proponents appear to be unaware of the rationalist character of the argument which informs their own theoretical background. They would not otherwise so easily slide from the idea that there is an absence of 'shared' criteria of truth or 'adequacy', in the sense of an absence of universal and therefore 'external' criteria, to the idea that there is an absence of shared criteria in the sense of any common theoretical meeting ground between two competing (or would-be competing) positions.[37]

The second argument, perhaps even more frequently advanced than the first, is related to it but takes up the question from a different angle, that of the 'subjects' or 'knowers' of theories. The argument depends upon an equivocation between what I shall label its 'strong' and 'weak' versions. (The equivocation works so that when one version begins to become obviously untenable the weight of the argument is shifted to the other.) This equivoca-tion effects the running together of questions concerning the conditions, causes and effects of knowledge with questions concerning its validity which I claim can conceal the presence of the 'truth is political' thesis.

The strong version begins with the thesis that the notion of objectivity and therefore also of rational theory choice implies that all knowers are 'the same'. Alternatively, but to the same effect, it is said that the notion of object-ivity and the traditional epistemology which defends it both rely on a concep-tion of individuals as 'perspectiveless', 'disembodied', 'contextless', 'floating free' of any social context.[38] The premise accepted, the rest of the argument is straightforward. 'Knowers' are not all the same, they are 'situated', meaning that they undertake their 'knowing' from a particular perspective for particu-lar reasons, against a specific social/psychological background. And they have bodies ('are embodied'), and in all these respects they are different. Therefore, it is concluded, there is no objectivity.

Now my main argument is that this 'strong' version is tacitly relied upon in the discussion of the 'sameness' and 'difference' of knowers. But it must also be said that it is, not so uncommonly, put just like that.[39] So before consider-ing the more plausible 'weak' version of the 'knowers are different' argument let's be clear why this 'strong' version is unacceptable. This is on account of its first and major premise which is obviously false. Neither the thesis of objectivity nor 'traditional' epistemology have denied (or tacitly relied upon the denial of the idea) that people live in social contexts, that they have different sorts of motives for doing theory, that they have bodies, and particu-lar perspectives and that these are all different sorts of conditions for doing theory. What is claimed is that these things, while clearly conditions of theory, do not themselves always – particularly in the case of 'objective' theory – fully determine the theoretical content and research techniques, etc. For if they did, then it should only be by the luckiest of accidents that we could ever have true or even partially true theories. (Nor could the proposition that the 'situatedness' of theories determines ideas itself be confidently asserted – although this is just to repeat ancient arguments.) Objective theorising, it is claimed, is partly determined by the character of its object as well as by that of its subject. The 'strong' version of the 'knowers are different' argument, then, begins with the transparently incorrect claim that traditional epistemology and/or objectivism maintain that 'embodiment' is neither a necessary nor a sufficient condition for knowledge.

The 'weak' version, however, maintains that objectivism requires only that 'embodiment' etc. are not sufficient conditions for objective knowledge and this premise is correct. The 'weak' version is sometimes put by claiming that 'objectivists' recognise the relevance of 'embodiment' or the 'differences of knowers' to the context of discovery but not to the context of justification.[40] But in what respect does this much weaker thesis imply that 'all knowers are the same' or that they 'float free of social context'? Only in the weakest of respects, if at all. That in so far as we are able to theorise objectively we are able to do something which is not fully determined by our 'situatedness' and therefore by our differences – that the 'objectivity' of knowledge is something to which the differences of its knowers are irrelevant except as necessary causal conditions for its possibility. The more objective knowledge is, the less determining is the subjectivity of the knower. So the assumption is not that objective knowers somehow operate independently of social context – 'the dislocated, disinterested observer' (Code 1993: 21) – but only that as objective knowers they are not fully determined by the context. It is indeed 'irrelevant to the "goodness" of results of research whether researchers are Japanese or British, white or black, Catholic or Jewish' (Harding 1991: 32, describing and rejecting the oppressive 'universalist' assumptions of science). It is irrelevant, that is, to what the 'goodness' consists in, although it may or may not be relevant to the fact that good results were produced. It is important to distinguish the two claims.[41]

But if this plausible but much weaker thesis of the requirements of objectivity on knowers is the premise of the 'weak' argument, then a correspondingly stronger second premise concerning the differences of 'knowers' is required to yield the desired relativist conclusion. In this version of the argument, what must be claimed is not the very obvious thesis that knowers live in social situations which make them different and that these situations might determine whether they become 'knowers' and what kind of 'knowers' they become, but the much more dubious proposition that these differences are always determining of what they think. In maintaining or assuming this position feminist epistemologists find themselves – where they would not at all wish to be – back with the crudest of Marxist epiphenomenalisms according to which ideas simply reflect social situations. And this thesis, as James

Harris has argued, is just the one which has *not* been demonstrated in the enormous amount of literature on feminist epistemology which has been produced in the last two decades (Harris 1992: 173–95). What has been shown, certainly, are strong political influences in relation to the funding of science, its choice of projects, on who becomes a scientist and such like. What has also been shown is the existence of deep sexist prejudices which have been responsible for all sorts of mistakes and sloppy research, in other words for departures from accepted scientific procedures. But the full determination of what we take to be 'objective' ideas by 'situatedness' has not.

The argument almost always moves from the former sustainable claims concerning the relevance of situatedness to aspects of the practice of science to the latter unsustained ones concerning its internal determination.[42] Or it conceals by the kind of equivocation I am about to describe that it is the latter which is at issue. For given that this essential premise (of the full determination of the internal procedures of science by situation, perspective, and so by 'difference') is unsubstantiated (as well as having resonances which are distasteful to most) the argument that objectivity is impossible can only work now by tacitly appealing to the 'strong version' which does not require this premise.

A nice example of the equivocation between the two positions is the argument, attributed to Luce Irigaray, and strikingly close to the arguments made in the 1930s for 'bourgeois' and 'proletarian' science, to the effect that 'traditional' epistemology assumes that the processes of theoretical production 'leave no trace' upon the product.[43] At first glance it appears that the 'strong' but absurd claim above could not be what is at stake in this formulation because it seems to be clearly implied that everyone, even traditional epistemologists, in recognising that ideas are a 'product' must also recognise that 'socially situated' agents are a necessary condition for their production process. All that appears to be denied is that the traditionals recognise the 'trace' on the product. But when we think about what it might be 'to leave a trace upon the theoretical product' we find that we must move from one of the above accounts to the other to retain plausibility. For on the one hand it must be that the processes of production are more than necessary conditions for knowledge. They must also constitute a sufficient condition for 'the trace which is left on the product' or else there is no point of difference with what seems to be now sensibly acknowledged as the position of traditional epistemology. However, the appearance of crude determinism must also be avojded, hence the nice formulation about 'traces' on the product. The impression is that there is still some range of free play for ideas – it is only a 'trace' which is left on the product. But if so, we would be right back with traditional epistemology and its alleged illusions. If there is more to knowledge than this 'trace', then this more has the 'situatedness' of the knower as a necessary but not sufficient condition. If there is not, and the 'trace' is the entire knowledge product, then we are right back to the crude and unpopular thesis that knowledge is determined by social conditions. But it must be one or the another, unless the 'fluidity' and 'ambiguity' which are supposed to characterise 'feminine' knowing means having it both ways at once.

In sum, what has been established in the argument about the 'difference of knowers' is the uncontentious idea, which feminist epistemology has pursued at great length, that knowledge has conditions. What is contentious and remains unestablished and almost unargued is that these conditions so determine the content of knowledge that objectivity is impossible. The necessary slide is from arguable and argued theses concerning the effect of politics on the conditions and effects of ideas to unargued theses concerning their content. In a significant amount of feminist epistemology the case for 'the sameness and disembodiedness' of the 'objective' knower, I am suggesting, oscillates between the strong version above, which is formally valid but absurd in its original premise, to the less absurd weaker version. But the weaker version, more plausible in its understanding of the requirements of objectivity, has an unsubstantiated, if often suppressed, premise concerning the full deterministic effects of 'situatedness'. The argument can work only by sliding between the two versions.

There is a possible line of defence of this argument which I shall briefly entertain. It might be, in ignorance of the philosophical possibilities of defining the notion of 'objectivity' primarily as a function of the object, that what is being assumed in this argument about the 'sameness of the objective knower' is the very specific, but strangely idealist and subjectivist neo-Kantian account, according to which 'objective' phenomena are those in which 'everyone has an interest' and are distinguished by this from 'cultural' or 'value' phenomena in which the interests are held to be more specific. (The assumption being that the 'real object' as noumena cannot be known and that the phenomena which can be are constructed by human subjects as a result of their values or interests.) This kind of account became a part of mainstream social sciences mainly through the influence of Max Weber and it was a central aspect of what he saw to be the problem in attempting to define and to defend the idea of a 'value free' social science (Weber 1949). In this context, the charge that 'objectivity' implies that 'all knowers are the same' might have something more to it than I have allowed above, in so far as it is implied that alongside all our cultural and other differences there is a common interest in the 'objective'. But if this is the account to which this kind of feminist epistemology refers, and if we leave aside that it is a very debatable one, then what would need to be addressed at the very least are Weber's own arguments. For in denying objectivity as 'value freedom' feminist epistemologists point out no more about the role of values in social theory than was fully accepted by Weber in his argument for value freedom. Weber insisted that values determined the choice of problems in social theory, the manner in which a phenomenon was construed, the choice of research and expository methods, and of course, much of the actual subject matter. He argued, however, that the specificity of the values at stake in all these respects did not affect the 'proper' treatment of the evidence (however this was gathered) in the attempt to establish those relationships necessary for social scientific explanation. In this area alone, he insisted, the values of the researcher should be kept to the minimum. The requirement excludes such things as the arbitrary interpretation of texts, the arbitrary exclusion of relevant evidence, biased samples and such like, the sorts of things to which most feminist epistemologists themselves rightly take exception.

I have discussed two arguments for relativism which are commonly made in recent feminist epistemology. They fail to establish relativist conclusions. Even less, then, do they establish the further conclusion, brought in on the basis of relativism, that theory choice or truth is rightly a political question. This assumption that what we think both can and should be decided on political grounds is both required by and to some extent is the point of the procedure I am reconstructing whereby theories are judged on the basis of their theoretical form or some other characteristic. For what I have been describing as the investment in power of this kind of argument consists in its capacity to be used to dismiss and denounce some theories and to promote others without having to engage in the theoretical issues. The operative assumption is that political considerations are decisive. But as well, the continued practice of this form of argument promotes the idea that this is the proper basis of theory choice. For the most part this crucial idea is implicit in the form of argumentation I am discussing, but what I have tried to show here is that even when it is argued more explicitly there are no strong intellectual grounds advanced for it and it is smuggled in with arguments for relativism which are not themselves very good.

I shall now resume my discussion of the 'surrational' mode of argument, often presented as feminist, which would locate intellectual and political inadequacies in theoretical form and, by way of posing two alternative forms, one patriarchal and intellectually limited, the other feminist and intellectually fruitful, would provide an easy but illegitimate form of deciding theoretical questions. There are difficulties in the nature of what I am attempting to establish. It is necessary, if I am right, to show that this form of argument is widespread in the literature and that it is typical of a certain kind of stance. The importance of the point consists in the fact that it is not an isolated occurrence but is a kind of thinking which is generated when certain kinds of political situations develop in intellectual contexts. However, in each individual case in which this kind of thinking occurs, the terms in which it is presented will be slightly different. Sometimes all the moves I have reconstructed as typical are made, sometimes only some of them are. The language and context of the discussion vary in different instances. And while I hope that I have established the widespread presence of this mode of argumentation, I think it would be fruitful to pursue the discussion with reference to case studies, to show how it operates in specific cases where its presence may not be obvious. The two case studies I have chosen are of papers which attempt to dismiss the subject of biology on philosophical/political grounds. They are both written by academic feminists who, in Australia at least, are very influential and are regarded as leading intellectuals. Both papers, in line with the particular case I want to present, would locate the politics and the adequacy of the theories they discuss in their theoretical form.

FIRST CASE STUDY: GENETICS BECOMES FEMINIST ETHICS

In 'A "Genethics" that makes sense', Ros Diprose (Diprose and Ferrell 1991) argues her concern that genetic theory is 'involved in the production of difference in terms of sameness' (ibid.: 71). She is perfectly clear that her aim is to criticise genetic theory itself, *qua* theory, as distinct from its applications and so there is here no equivocation on this point of the kind I have just described. After sympathising with the concern of David Suzuki and Peter Knudsen in their book *Genethics* that the theory of genetics may lend itself to 'misguided attempts to normalise and/or isolate individuals considered to be inferior' (ibid.: 70) she takes them to task for locating the problem only in the application and not in the content of genetic theory. The problem, she maintains, is not only the 'contamination of science by the ideology governing these other (more efficient) means of regulation' (ibid.: 70) for

> We may be sympathetic with the call to responsibility being made by the custodians of science towards the geneticist. But if the formative activity of applied genetics is informed by a similar distribution of difference at the level of theory then perhaps this 'finger pointing' is slightly misplaced.
>
> (Diprose and Ferrell 1991: 71)

While the argument that follows is not made out as one for 'feminist science', as opposed to 'male science' it is put explicitly in terms of the desirability of an ethical evaluation of the content of genetic theory, which is very close if not equivalent to arguing for a political evaluation. Equally explicit is the fact that the basis for this ethical evaluation is the alleged theoretical form of the fundamental concepts of genetics – a notion of 'difference as complementarity' (ibid.: 72).

This directness about the presence of the kind of position I am attempting to establish is one reason I have chosen to discuss this paper. But this does not make my task as easy as it might be thought. For what is gained by the absence of equivocation is lost in the elusiveness of the language in which the paper is written. So another reason for discussing this paper is to identify and challenge, as far as possible, just what is actually being claimed behind this daunting obscurity.

The argument departs from some general philosophical propositions on the nature of science: 'Genetic theory takes place in a mode of existence which assumes a distinction between the subject and the object of knowledge. . . . As a branch of science, genetics promises absolute knowledge or the Truth of Being' (ibid.: 71). At this stage the position is relatively carefully put and there is no suggestion that philosophical considerations might be used to legislate upon the content of genetics – it is the 'mode of existence' of genetics as a science and not what it specifically asserts which appears to be at issue. On Heideggerian sorts of grounds it is suggested that science and other of 'the objectifying practices which represent our being . . . are secondary modes of "understanding"' (ibid.: 68). The primary mode, it would appear, is that which recognises that 'our "being" and the "world". are constituted by the relation "in"' (ibid.: 66). Whatever one might think of such an argument, it would remain safely upon the terrain of philosophy if it stopped there. That is, if the 'secondariness' of science were asserted and it was then left alone to pursue its secondary path in the way intended by most philosophers who make this sort of claim.

Here, however, there is a point to these philosophical preliminaries, which is to undercut any claim that genetics *qua* theory should not be subjected to ethical/political criticism. For this alleged secondariness of the scientific mode is assumed to undercut any claims for the autonomy of genetics. The reasoning seems to be as follows. First, it is asserted about genetics that 'its authority is derived from the claim to know the origin of the expression of difference outside its "social meaning"' (Diprose and Ferrell 1991: 70). Leaving aside the convoluted description of the gene – a description which itself begins to beg the question of the importance of a notion of difference in genetics – the point which I believe Diprose is trying to make is that the authority of genetics to determine its own concepts and procedures derives from a straightforward acceptance of the subject/object distinction or its variants, or in other words from the idea that the 'object' (the gene) is independent of its construction by the subject (its 'social meaning'). The implication is that the recognition of the 'secondariness' of this 'objectifying' mode – in other words, of the fact that what it depends upon is not a true, but only a made distinction – has undermined this authority. And so the argument proceeds to establish a different kind of authority, that of a certain kind of ethics – 'an ethics of bodily specificity' (ibid.: 66) – to make judgements about the concepts of genetics. If genetics is not, as it is presented, about understanding real objects called genes then (along with other sciences) it is itself 'a particular mode of existence' (ibid.: 68) and it 'has a role in the constitution of our being' (ibid.: 68). More crudely put, the thesis is that genetics has a social role and this makes it fit for ethical judgement. The point is the now popular one that discourses produce their objects – 'genetics is one particularly dominant mode of an infinite number of discourses which makes differences real' (ibid.: 75) – but Diprose has extended it to the further idea that they do so in a way which is sufficiently socially significant to warrant ethical intervention. Genetics is no longer only a 'secondary mode of understanding' but one which can be interfered with by an understanding of the 'primary' mode.

This, I think, is the core of the argument. Once the legitimacy of the role of ethics (politics) is established in relation to genetics the rest is plain sailing. So is there anything wrong to this point? Isn't it obvious that sciences including genetics do have a social role and does it not follow from this that it is appropriate to judge them ethically/politically? Such a position may appear to be reasonable until one reflects upon the implications. It is important to remember that Diprose is very explicitly not talking about the social role of the uses of genetics but about the social role of the theory itself. So what is implied in the insistence that ethical considerations are appropriate is that genetic theory could somehow develop differently were such considerations kept in mind. For without realistic alternatives ethical judgements are not appropriate. It is, then, as though the geneticist, on noticing the offensive connotations in the concepts of the structure of the gene could somehow have taken a different path and conceptualised it differently. It is as though the experimental results and other requirements of the theory are not constraining. (In the same way, in the Soviet Union of the 1930s, the argument of the Lysenkoists seemed to assume that the geneticist should have realised that positing the reality of the gene as a mechanism was not in accord with the required amount of political optimism concerning the possibilities for change and so proceeded differently (see note 13 to the previous section, 'Flashback').) The notion that ethics is appropriate in considerations internal to the theory of genetics requires the assumption of a kind of scientific voluntarism.[44]

This is, I think, absurd. But the logical point is that it simply does not follow from the fact that an activity is social or is 'a particular mode of existence' that ethical considerations are relevant to it internally. Chess is also a 'particular mode of existence' but it does not follow that its rules should be reconsidered on ethical grounds. Indeed, the most developed of human activities are those whose 'goods' are internally defined in MacIntyre's sense (MacIntyre 1985: 190). Such activities are pursued for their own sake and ethical considerations are relevant only externally, to questions concerning the social conditions which make them possible and their impact on other social practices.

Moreover, the denial of autonomy to scientific activity which is assumed here – in the implicit demand that its conceptualisation itself conform to ethical/political requirements – does not necessarily follow from the rejection of the subject/object distinction or from the characterisation of science as secondary. Most non-realists have been able to consistently recognise that all intellectual activity, despite the fact that it is a social activity or a 'mode of existence' is in its nature autonomous in the sense that only intellectually relevant considerations can weigh, otherwise one is not intellectually engaged but is doing something else like art or story telling. They have also often recognised the dangers of repression in denying this. They have recognised, in other words, that intellectual activity is constituted internally. Diprose, like many contemporary academics, goes much further than the philosophical background upon which she draws and appears to be unaware either that she is doing so or of the powerful sorts of considerations which have lead the vast majority of philosophers to draw back from her sort of position.

It may be objected (possibly correctly) that what Diprose is maintaining is that genetics and other sciences do nothing else than 'constitute our being', that is, that they have only a social role. She would be then explicitly denying that these discourses constitute their objects internally and would be demanding that they be responsive at all times to external social/ethical considerations. This is in fact the only position which she can consistently maintain, but since it amounts to the explicit abandonment of intellectual life I can debate it no further.

To proceed with the argument. After the right of ethics to legislate on issues in genetics has been insisted upon there is a discussion of genetic theory although, as we shall see, this focuses mainly upon the formal characteristics of what is taken to be its central conception of difference and not upon substantive issues. First, it is brought to our attention that the DNA double helix is conceptualised as a 'neat coupling' (Diprose and Ferrell 1991: 72) reminiscent of 'the way in which we map sexual difference at the level of the social – as opposition and complementarity, where the negative is the other side of a favoured image' (ibid.: 72). There is here the suggestion of Diprose's central thesis that there is something ideologically/politically wrong with the conception of the DNA, but rather than proceed immediately with this we find instead a discussion of the causal properties of the gene. This discussion, the point of which shortly becomes clear, deserves a special mention on account of its remarkably cavalier treatment of scientific results, a fact which is obscured beneath the appearance of profundity. Diprose expresses surprise at the fact that the geneticist does not take the above similarity in the formal features of the conception of the DNA and of sexual difference to suggest that 'the microscopic distribution of differences [in genetics] mimics sexual difference' (ibid.: 72) and remarks that for the geneticist 'it is the other way around: difference as complementarity at the macro-level is an expression of and stops with the genetic code' (ibid.: 72). The argument, in plainer terms, appears to be that the understanding of the relations between the sexes as complementary is taken by genetics as the basis of the genetic code and that one would expect (within this framework) for it to be the other way around. 'Sexual difference' here seems to be a mix – deliberate, I assume – of 'the way in which we map sexual difference at the level of the social' (ibid.: 72), which I take it refers to a general ideological yin/yangish sort of understanding of the relations between men and women, and the fact that 'the man and woman each contribute half the complement of chromosomes to be found in the cells of their offspring' (ibid.: 72). Either way, the claim is astonishing. The psycho/social understanding of sexual differences as complementarity is simply not part of the subject matter of genetics and even if geneticists and others wish to draw such unsubstantiated speculative conclusions they have nothing to do with the theory of genetics as such. And the suggestion that there is something arbitrary about the geneticist positing the gene as more causally fundamental than the behaviour of fully developed bodies implies that the attempt to identify causes and mechanisms is irrelevant to scientific activity. Given formal similarities between two concepts,

Diprose seems to think that in principle it is open which one is posited as fundamental, that it is a question only of what 'mimics' what, rather than a question of establishing, in accord with the evidence, causal mechanisms which have a specific direction. Her more important aim here, however, is to take genetics to task for allegedly believing it has found 'the origin of difference' (ibid.: 72) in the gene. The reason for this latter concern emerges with the next move.

From the fact that the gene is considered causally fundamental it follows according to Diprose – and this really *is* the claim – that 'the gene is proposed as the origin of meaning' (ibid.: 72). The purpose of this move is clear, its basis is not. Its purpose, as we shall see, is to place genetic theory on the terrain of a theory of meaning where it can be much more readily discussed in terms of the conceptualisation of differences. That is, assuming, as Diprose obviously does, broad Saussurian/Derridean assumptions about meaning as difference. And the insistence on the charge that genetics is concerned with 'origins' and that the gene is conceived as 'the origin of difference' now makes some kind of sense given Derrida's account of the misguided metaphysical search for 'origins' of meaning – which has nothing to do with genetics. (I will not follow any further the argument about the futility of the alleged search for origins in genetics, except to mention that it involves the claim that the incompleteness of genetic theory is a result of this philosophical inadequacy – 'The effect of attempting to contain difference within a notion of complementarity also manifests in the inability of genetics to explain adequately the process of DNA transcription and translation without reference to other "outsides"' (ibid.: 73).) As to the basis of this mixing of genetic theory with a theory of meaning, it is not clear whether Diprose believes that it is justified by the use of the notion of a 'code' in genetic theory or whether it is somehow derived from fusing philosophical claims about the lack of a neat separation between the subject and the object with the content of genetic theory. The former, the more respectable of the two, would depend on taking the notion of a genetic code literally in the sense of something which transmits meaning. Whereas in genetics the notion of a code is clearly metaphorical and is intended to convey only that the DNA is '*like* a code' in so far as its mechanisms are like those of a code (see Olding 1992: 10). But the DNA code does not transmit meaning – it is just a mechanism.

To this point we have the suggestion that genetics works upon the same notion of difference which informs prevailing notions of sexual difference and a neat manoeuvre whereby the distinction between genetic theory and a theory of meaning has been dissolved. Most of the work has been done. All that is required now to reveal the political/intellectual errors of genetic theory is to develop the former thesis, drawing upon the popularity of the Derridean critique in order to emphasise its problematic character (Diprose and Ferrell 1991: 74). This is not at all difficult and developing the earlier considerations insinuating the decisive role of sexist thought in the positing of the DNA as a 'neat coupling' we soon find the core of the offensive notion in the fact that 'the order of nucleotide base pairs along the DNA double strand' (ibid.: 72) is a 'sequence [which] must first be replicated or "transcribed" into the form of a mirror image of itself' (ibid.: 72). The problem here is not due to the fact that positing of the replication of the DNA sequence in that of the RNA fails to cope with the experimental results of genetic theory. Nor is it thought to be due to any internal inconsistency in the arguments of genetic theory. Rather it resides in formal features of the conception, in the fact that this replication can only explain 'sameness from repetition, not difference' (ibid.: 73) or, in other words, that it is an attempt 'to contain difference within a notion of complementarity' (ibid.: 73) which is an alternative language to that of binary oppositions. The argument is following the format of the ideological deconstruction described above. A scientific theory is being found wanting, not on any grounds relevant to its content, but because some of its conceptions have a certain form which is thought to be objectionable.

The theme is developed with reference to the understanding of the expression of the genetic code until it is concluded that in genetics 'diversity, which is the rule rather than the exception, tends to be understood in terms of disruption, breakdown or mutation in the process of transmission' (ibid.: 73). (Ignored here is the fact that the mixing of genes in two chromosomes – the basis of individual difference according to genetics and with no connotations of breakdown or disruption – could also be seen as an understanding of 'difference' or 'diversity' if we are to view such abstractions as though they were a part of the content of genetic theory.) What is by now supposed to have been shown is that at the very heart of genetic theory there is a conception of difference as deviation from normality. And because we have already been informed of 'the complicity of genetics in the *production*, rather than the indifferent description of this spacing' (ibid.: 71), we can infer from this that the uses of genetics which concern Suzuki and others follow from the theory itself – they are not so much abuses as proper uses: 'It is therefore not surprising that difference in "applied" genetics is understood in the same terms' (ibid.: 73).

Behind the obscurity and apparent sophistication of the way it is expressed, the argument reduces to the following moves: first, on the basis of the rejection of philosophical realism, the authority of genetics to proceed autonomously is undermined and in its place the authority of ethics is insinuated. Second, by way of a misreading of the idea of a genetic code, we are subtly led onto the terrain of a theory of meaning where it might seem Derridean-style arguments can be used appropriately. Third, there is the identification of a pernicious notion of difference in the conception of DNA and RNA. The moves involved, the quasi-philosophical 'refutation' of a scientific theory and the location of concepts with 'politically incorrect' formal features are rather too similar to those which sixty years ago were used to accuse genetic theory of a failure to grasp reality dialectically. It is to be hoped that those arguing in this way never again attain influence within the science itself.

For that to be so, text book introductions to the problem of women and science of the following kind may have to be countered.

SECOND CASE STUDY: A FEMINIST INTRODUCTION TO SCIENCE[45]

'Feminism and Science' by Elizabeth Grosz and Marie de Lepervanche (1988) is presented as 'an overview of feminist interventions into science' (Grosz and de Lepervanche 1988: 4). Although it therefore purports to be descriptive of a number of feminist arguments, the positions described are arranged in order from the weaker to the stronger and it is clear that it is the strongest position which is advocated.[46] This strongest position is that which maintains the possibility of two kinds of science, science as we know it with its 'patriarchal commitments' (ibid.: 5) and 'feminist science' (ibid.: 25) of which, aside from its 'representing women's positions and interests' (ibid.: 24), all we can know at the moment are its most general features. But there is no doubt about which of the two kinds of science women at least should prefer to develop. In the case of this paper I am saved from mere speculation that behind the advocacy of 'feminist science' (as was also the case with that of 'proletarian science') is the more immediately political aim of taking over the relevant institutions because the authors themselves clearly state that this is the case. The entrenchment of women (as feminist scientists) in public institutions, they insist, must proceed even before this kind of science has anything but vague philosophical considerations to recommend it: 'Only when they are firmly entrenched can women actively produce methods and discoveries that depart from male norms to produce different kinds of knowledges, and only then will the male domination of science be overcome' (ibid.: 27).

The main thing which I want to show about the paper is that it is constructed to lead the reader into accepting, although not by any process of sound reasoning, the idea that questions of truth (or of theory choice) are ultimately political, ultimately questions of feminism. This is the idea which I have maintained is intellectually disreputable but which lends itself to an easy dismissal of ideas convenient for the exercise of power. That this *is* the position central to this paper has to be shown. For, although there is no other position which is consistent with what else is said (for example, the repeated warnings against the continuing belief 'that science itself, its method, data, and forms of proof are not discriminatory' (ibid.: 16) and the opposition to the fact that ' "Pure science" is usually considered immune to these sociological/political "issues" ' (ibid.: 5)) there is nevertheless much equivocation whenever the argument comes to the point of showing how the method and forms of proof of science are discriminatory. Here there is usually a reversion to more discussable positions concerning either the conditions of 'the production of knowledges' (ibid.: 25) or instead to claims made about science. (The fact that the 'truth is political' position is implied by their paper does not necessarily mean that it is the author's intention to advance this position. My guess is that they, also, are unclear about just what it is they are saying, although statements like those which I chose as the second epigraph to this Part II make me hesitant in this judgement.)

Grosz and de Lepervanche begin their substantive discussion by addressing first 'the most superficial level of the problem' (ibid.: 5), that of sexual discrimination faced by women scientists or would-be scientists. This section covers some of the statistical material on women scientists. The paper then proceeds, under the heading of 'Women as objects of scientific investigation' (ibid.: 10) to mention some of the sexist claims that have been made about women in biology, sociobiology and branches of medical research. This part of the paper concludes with the case study of Rosalind Franklin whose unhappy role in the discovery of the structure of the DNA is intended to illustrate the difficulties women face as a result of both sorts of problems. (The discussion of this case is so selective that I must comment even though the issues raised are not central to my argument. I refer the reader to note 47 to this chapter.[47]) Now if we take the author's own description of this first section none of the considerations raised in it would be such as to touch upon the deeper claims they will soon make that science is, itself, in 'its internal functioning' (ibid.: 7) masculine or patriarchal. For neither the fact that biology has often contained unbased and prejudiced conceptions of women nor even, if true, their claim that the psychological drive of Watson and Crick in the search for the DNA structure (one which would not extend to Franklin) was that of 'the quest of the gods for the key to womanless reproduction!' (ibid.: 15) touch upon, respectively, the theory of natural selection or the claim that the DNA has the structure of a double helix. One should expect the argument for such stronger claims to be reserved for the later sections. The ground, however, is already being laid. To take one example:

> Granted that Darwin is a progenitor of the modern biological sciences, it remains a largely unexplored question as to how much the problematic notions of sexual difference form an essential part of the theory of evolution and the doctrine of the survival of the fittest. Clearly a large number of contemporary biologists would wish to distance themselves from his pronouncements about women while accepting his understanding of evolution; the degree of dependence of the latter on the former needs to be addressed.
>
> (Grosz and de Lepervanche 1988: 11)

The point here, as Alan Olding (1991) has argued in his discussion of this paper, is that the reason why the connection between Darwin's views on women and his theory of natural selection 'remains an unexplored question' is because it is as much in need of such exploration as, to modify the popular graffiti, a fish is in need of a bicycle. The degree of the dependence of the latter on the former does not need to be addressed because a moment's reflection reveals that there is no connection. The one theory posits minute variations in reproduction, the other a certain conception of sexual relations.

In any case, now that the idea that 'problematic notions of sexual difference' might essentially distort scientific theories has been suggested we can move onto the second part of the paper where this idea is explicitly maintained. This part begins with an appeal to the idea that binary oppositions function in a politically undesirable way. At least there is no other reason given for the advice to be wary of some basic distinctions:

> First, we must regard a number of distinctions and oppositions circulating within the sciences with great suspicion. Among the more problematic oppositions used to defend science against any external criticism, including those used by feminists, are the following: the distinction between scientific 'facts' and theories . . . between pure and applied sciences . . . and between science on the one hand and its abuses on the other. Although problematic in their own terms and increasingly criticised within the sciences, these oppositions have nevertheless functioned as devices for placing science above any mode of political or non-scientific involvement, let alone criticism. Second, we must be wary of a familiar defensive tactic used to undermine any serious questioning of science: the strategy of distinguishing between different sciences, accepting criticism of the less secure versions while presuming that the more secure forms are immune from these criticisms.
>
> (Grosz and de Lepervanche 1988: 6)

The strategy here, I think, is this: the assumed onus of proof is reversed so that the 'science-is-patriarchal' thesis is presented not as one which requires a lot of argument but rather as one whose own obviousness is undermined by what are 'devices' and 'defensive tactics' used to give unwarranted support to the contrary thesis. The 'feminist science' thesis, far from being the sort of thesis about which we have good reason to be very wary, is assumed from the outset to be in the victim position and the well supported ideal that truth cannot be decided politically is presented as the illegitimate aggressor whose position can only be maintained by these 'devices' and 'defensive tactics'. So it is insinuated at the beginning of the argument that not to support 'feminist science' is to fall prey to the 'binary' tactics of male domination.

But the fact is that it is the 'feminist science' position which requires to be argued and the distinctions which are referred to here (leaving aside the fact/ theory distinction which is the subject of its own massive debate) are the very distinctions which normally would be made until, perhaps, it is shown that there are connections between the terms distinguished. Unless it can be demonstrated that what many would accept are the abuses of science are a necessary result of the content of science then the distinction between the two is appropriate. If one assumes, as we are asked to in this paper, that the misuses of science against women are a direct function of its theoretical results, there is virtually no case to argue. Similarly, if one wants to criticise the sciences, one clearly should initially distinguish between them, for a criticism of one does not spill over into a criticism of another unless, again, the connections can be shown. By describing these elementary but perfectly proper distinctions as devices and defensive strategies and advising us to be wary of them Grosz and de Lepervanche seek to relieve themselves of the burden of proof of an indefensible position.

Having begun by dispensing with the elementary distinctions which would be necessary to argue a counter-position, the paper proceeds with the case for 'feminist science'. This is developed from an account of a different, weaker position described as that of 'gendered science' and with which it will be confused at crucial moments. The question which is taken up under this heading of 'gendered science' is that of the different psychological positions available to men and women who engage in science and the thesis is that the psychological position of women in science is not tenable in the way that the position of men scientists is. (Science is said to 'privilege the masculine knower' (Grosz and de Lepervanche 1988: 19).) This general position which concerns the conditions in which science is developed and does not touch upon its truth conditions is, I think, both sustainable and important. For if the psychological conditions are such as to exclude women from science then it is likely that both women and science suffer as a result. But this case has been well argued elsewhere and my aim is to show how the move is made from this discussable position to the position that feminist interests should decide what is true.

It is made very clear that the 'feminist science' thesis provides 'the most radical, far-reaching feminist analyses' (Grosz and de Lepervanche 1988: 24) and is therefore stronger in its claims than that made by the proponents of 'gendered science'. So what does the 'feminist science' thesis contain that the 'gendered science' thesis does not? The argument for 'gendered science' is based on two sorts of considerations: the thesis that the different kinds of psychological formations of men and women result in different kinds of thinkers and different kinds of concept formation and the thesis that the metaphors predominantly used to describe scientific activity – metaphors of mastery, conquest, etc. – are such as to give men scientists an identity which is thereby denied to women scientists. These are the broad components of Evelyn Fox Keller's well-known feminist writings. What more, then, does 'feminist science' involve?

We are told that it would require the rejection of the idea that 'science could, if reformed, become gender neutral' (Grosz and de Lepervanche 1988: 24) and that instead its advocates 'wholeheartedly affirm the sexual specificity of science and its representation of masculine positions and perspectives' (ibid.: 24). This could mean either that the truth of science (its forms of proof, criteria of acceptability) as well as the way in which it is done is gender determined or it could mean that it is important to maintain both 'masculine' and 'feminine' ways of doing science as different modes which nevertheless confront gender neutral truth conditions. But since the 'gendered science' thesis incorporates the latter idea, it must be inferred that it is the former which is intended. Or that the vagueness functions as equivocation, allowing a fall back to a defensible position if the indefensible one is challenged.

But if so, if we are intended to accept that what we take to be true is a function of whether our concern is with men's or women's interests, then the basis upon which we are asked to accept this idea is only the suggestion quoted above (p. 96) that this is 'the most radical, far-reaching' position. For when Grosz and de Lepervanche go on to describe 'feminist science' they fall back on arguments about the kinds of things that might be said about science, the kind of considerations they have just allocated to the weaker 'gendered science' position and they do not refer to the internal workings of science. So, summing up the 'feminist science' argument with reference to the writings of Luce Irigaray, whom they take as its central exponent:

> Irigaray suggests that man effaces his masculinity and particularity to proclaim instead the global relevance and *perspectivelessness* of his construct. Thus the claims that science makes about its own truthful, objective, neutral position are in fact attempts to resist recognising its masculinity.
>
> (Grosz and de Lepervanche 1988: 25)

But this support for 'feminist science' is only *ad hominem*. Even if when men spoke of truth they were effacing their masculinity, the question would remain whether there is nevertheless any good (intellectual) reason for so speaking.

The only other discernible argument for 'feminist science' follows the general form described in the substance of this chapter. It proceeds from the alleged identification of 'binary oppositions' in orthodox male science (contrasts of the A/–A form) and again the supposed identification of the non-binary form (the A/B form) in what is taken as a partial example of 'feminist science', namely the work in biology of Barbara McClintock:

> McClintock anticipates many of the insights developed by feminists working in the humanities and social sciences about the problems of binary polarisations and oppositions. . . . According to Fox Keller, [whose work on McClintock is the basis of this discussion] she regards a non-oppositional relation of difference (the A/B model not the A/–A model) as crucial to understanding how the sciences could work. Where polarisation and division sever the connections and impose distance, McClintock's recognition of difference 'provides a starting point for relatedness'.
>
> (Grosz and de Lepervanche 1988: 23)

The question we should want to ask at this point concerns the reasons for the virtues of McClintock's approach. Is it because it embodies a better conception of the relation of difference or is it because this conception accords with experimental evidence? We might be relieved to read on: 'Fox Keller emphasises that McClintock's unconventional approach to her work, her attempt to rethink her data and entertain quite different conceptions from her colleagues, nevertheless provided testable, repeatable results' (ibid.: 23). The relief, though, is temporary because we soon find out that this respect for experimental results is more of a limitation than a strength. For in the final section on 'feminist science' we find that Irigaray, in an argument which I take to be endorsed by Grosz and de Lepervanche, is described as identifying as problematic 'the presumption that proof, repeatability are criteria of objectivity when this assumes the identity or sameness of two experimenters' (ibid.: 25). Nevertheless, McClintock is clearly credited with developing a superior model of the DNA:

> In discovering that genetic sequences are not fixed, given that genetic transpositions have occurred, McClintock's work problematised the prevailing understanding of the DNA as 'the central actor in the cell, the executive governor of cellular organisation, itself remaining impervious to influence from the subordinate agents to which it dictates' (Fox Keller, 1985: 169. Cf. Sayre, 1975: 189) – a clearly anthropocentric and androcentric metaphor (reflecting the hierarchised system of social stratification in our culture). Instead of presuming that nature functions as a modern corporation, she regarded it as an environmental system in which signals external to the cell account for reorganisation of the DNA molecules. DNA could thus be regarded not simply as a genetic transmitter of biological information, but also as a receiver, and thus as a communicational circuit.
>
> (Grosz and de Lepervanche 1988: 24)

The conclusion, then, can only be that the superiority of McClintock's conception consists in the fact that it contains a 'better' conception of difference as well as in the superiority of communicational politics over hierarchical corporation politics. Whether or not the DNA is in fact structured so that it is impervious to outside influences does not figure – it is the political connotations of the metaphors that may sometimes be used to describe the alternatives which are assumed to be decisive. The facts of the matter, having been deemed irrelevant in the beginning with the rejection of the fact/theory distinction, do not count. This is, then, another case of the kind of argument I am trying to expose. A feature or features external to the scientific issues at stake (the logical form of the conception of difference, the political correctness of the metaphors used to describe the workings of the genetic code) are taken as the criteria upon which theories should be accepted or rejected and issues concerning the actual workings of the gene can be safely by-passed.

This case study completes the demonstration of the associations with authoritarian power of a popular strand of current feminist thinking. These associations consist in the fact that the central, if not the only possible use, of the mode of argument is to enable the kinds of intellectual practices which until recently were the prevailing ones in educational and research institutions to be rejected without argument at the same time as they are denounced politically. I have tried to unravel some of the confusions on which the procedure depends.

It is this authoritarian character of the theory which explains why, if there is still an appeal to the old liberationist conception of power, it would have to operate covertly. A clear analysis of the workings of power informed by an unequivocal opposition to it would be too threatening to the actual operations of this sort of theory. As well, the motivational base of the latter simply could not support the in-depth exploration of the former. The most which this kind of power-seeking feminism can sustain is a gesture of opposition. Moreover, if, as I have argued, the necessary basis upon which feminism has gained power in universities has been its pretensions to radicalism, then such a gesture must be made. I shall now move on to show that, in the case of this 'surrational' deconstructionist feminism, this radical gesturing is contained in the tacit expression of the earlier liberation ideas.

4 Radical pretensions

... the bourgeois lumpen intelligentsia: aspirant intellectuals whose ama-
teurish intellectual preparation disarms them before manifest absurdities
and elementary philosophical blunders, and whose innocence in intellectual practice leaves them paralysed in the first web of scholastic argument which they encounter; and bourgeois, because while many of them
would like to be 'revolutionaries', they are themselves the products of a
particular 'conjuncture' which has broken the circuits between intellectual-
ity and practical experience (both in real political movements, and in the
actual segregation imposed by contemporary structures) and hence they
are able to perform imaginary revolutionary psycho-dramas (in which
each outbids the other in adopting ferocious verbal postures) while in fact
falling back on a very old tradition of bourgeois elitism.

(E.P. Thompson)

As I have reconstructed it, what I am describing as the 'surrational' or ideological feminist treatment of dualisms contains four basic moves. The first
two, the assertion of the determining presence of binary oppositions in Western thought and the inference of their necessarily hierarchical character, were
discussed in the previous chapter in the course of attempting to reveal the
strong connection between this kind of thought and an easy (because
unargued) and flexible mode of political denunciation. They are moves without intellectual basis which, because of their ultimate reliance only on the
authority of a certain political position, mean that this theoretical approach
finds appropriate expression only in the exercise of power. In the last two
moves, which assert the necessity and the insufficiency of a 'moment of
reversal', we find very striking parallels with the structure of liberation
theory. These, I shall now show, indicate the covert expression of feminist
liberation theory and therefore, also, of an appeal to oppose such arbitrary
authority or power.

Once this has been demonstrated, my argument concerning this kind of
postmodern feminist deconstructionist theory will be drawing to a close. For
I shall then have shown that it is directed towards fundamentally opposed
aspirations and is based, therefore, on a contradiction. The contradiction is

between its use, which can only be authoritarian, and its content, which will now be seen to imply a radical anti-authoritarianism. The existence of this contradiction, together with the obviously essential requirement that it remain concealed, must constitute a good part of the answer to the question with which I began concerning the apparently systematic and functional character of intellectual confusion in this kind of academic feminist thought. What I shall have done is to have identified the broad objective constraints or 'discursive rules' which constitute this 'discourse'.

Such an analysis can, as I have mentioned before, be readily extended to apply to the more general (not specifically feminist) kinds of deconstruction. Here we should see the covert presence of the more general form of liberation theory in contradiction with an implicit appeal to the authority of a theoretical form which allegedly transcends the domination of the binary structure. We should see a more general contradiction between the radical pretensions of this theoretical orientation and its essentially authoritarian use. While this more general analysis is not my immediate aim, it does enable my account to be placed within the context of the strange history of the ex-1960s and 1970s student radicals, a history which is now just beginning to be understood. So I shall conclude this chapter with what I think is a small contribution to that understanding.

The argument which follows will not be the completion of all that needs to be said about the combined presence and avoidance of the basic ideas of liberation theory in contemporary postmodern/deconstructionist thought. For the two theses concerning the 'moment of reversal' on which this part of the argument is based belong also to the 'serious' deconstructionist treatment of dualisms, which differs from its ideological, surrational counterpart with respect to the treatment of the first two of the above theses. Since this difference does not hold when we come to the last two theses, both kinds of deconstruction come within the scope of the analysis I am beginning to develop here a projection of the ideas of liberation theory onto the 'safer' terrain of metaphysics and/or the relations of signifiers. With 'serious' deconstruction this constitutes the beginning rather then the end of my analysis which I shall continue in Part III. The main difference between my analyses of the two sorts of thinking concerns the extent of the incoherence generated by contradictory aspirations. The more intellectually legitimate versions of feminist deconstruction, we shall see, are characterised by a more or less coherent conservative argument which is in contradiction only with the fact that it is presented as a radical argument. With the less sound derivatives we have a much stronger contradiction between an intellectually incoherent mode of argument which can only operate coercively and its self-presentation as 'truly' radical. Nevertheless, both kinds of this popular form of academic feminist thought can be shown to derive their radical appeal and moral legitimacy from the covert expression of liberation ideas.

THE PARALLELS

Consider the parallels between liberation theory's analysis of how people evaluate each other's worth and the analysis of signifiers in all kinds of deconstruction. The basic structure of liberation theory, we have seen, is as follows: first, there is the assertion of a discrepancy between, or more strongly an inversion of, the appearance of independence of two terms and their actual relationship of dependence. The idea merits some repetition in the present context. What appears to be independent, it is claimed, are first of all the respective evaluations made of a pair of attributes (for example, 'masculine' and 'feminine' attributes). In other words, it looks as though the former attributes just *are* better than the latter. (That is, that the comparison is made after the respective evaluations.) What also appears to be independent are the evaluations which seem to follow from this, namely the evaluations of the relative 'amounts' of human worth of those who have these differing pairs of attributes. So it also appears, for example, that men just *are* better than women.

However, upon analysis we discover a deeper relation of dependency which reveals that these two sets of apparently independent evaluations are in fact interdependent. This deeper relation of dependency is identified as the practical relationship of power between the two groups of people with the respective sets of attributes. This relation of power is said to make interdependent, first of all, the evaluations of the 'amounts' of human worth of the members of the respective groups. In other words, these evaluations are in fact (though not in logic) such that one group will be regarded as fully human only because the other is regarded as less than human. As a consequence of this, the evaluations of the respective sets of attributes belonging to the members of the groups are also rendered interdependent. For these evaluations are now seen to be a result of the evaluations of the respective 'amounts' of humanity of the two groups. For example, the idea that masculine attributes are better than feminine ones can now be seen to be in fact derived from the idea that men are better than women. (The appearance is the reverse – it is the evaluations of the pairs of attributes which are assumed to be the basis of the evaluation of the people involved.) The liberating insight in all this is that the powerful person derives their power from their relationship with the powerless and not, as it appears, from their own qualities. But the main point for the moment is that liberation theory begins by arguing the presence of a hidden relation of dependency which gives rise to an illusion of independence of some of our judgements.

Second, liberation theory asserts that this real dependence of the two groups necessarily leads to a 'moment of reversal' in which the apparent and illusory independence of the evaluations of the pairs of attributes is maintained but there is an attempt at reversal either with respect to which set of attributes is thought to be superior or with respect to who is thought to have them. This 'moment of reversal' is understood as the result of the oppressed group striving for dominance over the oppressing group.

Third, it is the failure of this moment of reversal in at least some respects which is said to reveal that the deeper problem consists in the hitherto hidden assumption of relative degrees of humanness, resulting from the hitherto hidden relationship of power.

Fourth, it is maintained that the important aim must be to challenge and break both of these deeper hidden relationships in a movement of 'authentic' resistance.

Compare this with the basic theses of deconstruction. First, it is asserted, although here the assertion is of a pair of signifiers or terms rather than of people and their qualities, that there is a surface independence concealing a deeper dependence. The intended or represented meaning of the text which, it is maintained, asserts the straightforward superiority or priority of one term over another is thought to be at odds with the (unrepresented) way its meaning is in fact generated, such that the respective terms are inter-defined. Parallel to the first thesis above of liberation theory, the point here is that, contrary to appearances, the 'superior' term derives its superiority only by way of its relation to the 'inferior' term. Further parallel is the idea that this relation of superiority and inferiority between signifiers is a relation of power or domination, for the opposition has a 'conflictual and subordinating structure' (see quotation which follows).

Second, a 'moment of reversal' is said to be necessary both in order to begin to reveal this interdependence and to initiate opposition to the 'violent hierarchy' in which it consists. Derrida's own well-known account makes this clear:

> On the one hand we must traverse a phase of overturning. To do justice to this necessity is to recognise that in a classical philosophical opposition we are not dealing with the peaceful coexistence of a vis-a-vis, but rather with a violent hierarchy. One of the two terms governs the other (axiologically, logically, etc.), or has the upper hand. To deconstruct the opposition, first of all, is to overturn the hierarchy at a given moment. To overlook this phase of overturning is to forget the conflictual and subordinating structure of the opposition.
>
> (Derrida 1972: 41)

There is an often-recited list of examples to illustrate what this phase of overturning might look like. Possibly the best known is the reversal of the alleged 'prioritising' of speech over writing which purports to show that the former is dependent upon and derivative from the latter. But it includes also the reversal of the alleged priority of cause over effect, of presence over absence, of mind over body, of truth over falsity, and so on.

Third, the standard account of deconstruction would hold that this phase of reversal is insufficient to undermine the 'power' relations which inter-define the two terms because it only reverses the hierarchy, thereby perpetuating the binary relationship on which it depends:

> If one simply reverses philosophical/political dichotomies, placing the subordinate term – absence, writing, difference, woman – into the dominant position previously occupied by presence, speech, identity, man, a (reverse) logocentrism still operates. Moreover the force and violence that gave the dominant term its primacy is in effect ignored.
>
> (Grosz 1990: 96).

Fourth, the point then becomes to challenge this whole 'subordinating structure' by means of a second phase, often described as a 'displacement' of the binary relation,[1] and consisting in the insertion of 'marks' which, never 'constituting a third term' because of their inability to be included within the relevant binary opposition, are referred to as 'undecideables' (Derrida 1972: 43): 'we must also mark the interval between inversion, which brings high what was low, and the irruptive emergence of a new "concept", a concept that can no longer be and never could be, included in the previous regime' (ibid.: 42). The point here clearly is, despite its lack of clarity, to in some sense break, challenge, subvert or whatever, the binary opposition rather than remaining confined within it. This means that like liberation theory, deconstruction insists on the necessity of each of the phases of reversal and displacement. (However, it should be noted that whereas liberation theory sees both of the two 'moments' of opposition as historical and therefore as temporary, in deconstruction, for reasons which will emerge, the necessity of both phases are understood to be structural and eternal as 'the necessity of interminable analysis' (ibid.: 42).[2] Deconstruction therefore has to understand itself as consisting in both movements simultaneously and so it describes itself as a 'double science' (Derrida 1972: 41, and 1991: 108).)

As it stands, this account of the second phase of deconstruction, although no less clear than many of those found in more enthusiastic expositions of the subject, is not very intelligible. On the whole I do not think that the position can be made much more intelligible, although I shall give an account of what the argument behind it appears to be in Part III.[3] More immediately, though, I want to draw out the implications of the above very strong parallels between 'liberationist' feminism on the one hand and both kinds of feminist deconstruction on the other.

THE DOMINANCE OF THE SIGNIFIER

I suggested earlier, using instances of psychotic thinking as an analogy, that the fact of two views running parallel to each other where only one of the two is actually expressed (and where the other one would also be relevant) could be thought to amount to the covert expression of the one by means of the other if it could be shown first, that the expressed view is inappropriate or in some other way inadequate while the other is sound and second, that there is good reason for both the expression and the avoidance of the more sound view. The incoherence of the first view could then be explained in terms of the fact that it partially expressed the second view.

Now I take myself to have already met the second of these two requirements in the case of the parallel views of liberation theory and deconstruction as described above. For I have argued that a powerful reason for such a double attitude towards the ideas of liberation theory would consist in the simultaneous perception of the frightening consequences of a clear cut, unequivocal confrontation with power together with the recognition that it ought, morally, to be opposed. I also suggested that in the right circumstances, if the opposition to a certain form of power gains wide support and *itself* offers the opportunity for power, this ambivalence can develop into a more cynical mode where the appearance of being 'truly radical' disguises a new form of the exertion of power. One can then successfully present oneself and one's movement as victims of injustice while at the same time using this perception to gain positions of influence. There are, then, these two sorts of reasons – fear and opportunism – for referring to, while avoiding the full implications of, liberation theory. So my question now is with respect to the first of the two above considerations. Can it be shown that the ideas of both kinds of feminist deconstruction are less coherent than those of liberation theory?

It is clearly crazy to seriously assert the existence of political relations of dominance and repression between signifiers, that is between linguistic, conceptual items. If this is what is being asserted I have barely a case to answer. The insanity of such a view might then well be explained with reference to the fact that it partially alludes to a saner view to which it is structurally similar. So, is this what is being asserted? At the risk of posing a false dichotomy I would suggest that there really are here only two alternatives – either such an assertion operates as metaphor (more strictly metonymy) and what is really being asserted is that relations of political domination between people give rise to the positing of certain relations between terms (the latter being used in the metaphor to stand for the former), or it is meant more literally. (Or we oscillate between these two positions in the politically useful but intellectually illegitimate mode of equivocation.) In the first case we are back on the terrain of liberation theory, in the second we are somewhere else.

However, that it is the second literal meaning which is at stake is very strongly implied by the following: first, it follows from the repeated explicit claims made in this context to the effect that it is the subject which is structured by language and not vice versa. These claims imply that the primary relations of domination are within language. Second, it is also implicit in the fact that the deconstructionist analysis never leads back into a discussion of relations between people but remains at the level of 'the text'; and third, it is clear from the fact that the solution to the political violence is not thought to lie in changing relations between people but rather in the mysterious insertion of the 'undecidable' into the chain of signifiers. (Fourth, it is also what is actually said (written) – that one signifier in a binary opposition dominates the other.) So the claim, I think, has to be construed literally to mean that signifiers, that is linguistic, conceptual items, dominate each other or, if you like, that relations between concepts can be relations of political domination.

But the absurdity involved here is so obvious that we must consider the alternative possibility. (Others who maintain that this is indeed the absurd position have discussed why it is absurd in more detail (Callinicos 1989; Ellis 1989).) As well, we can note the uneasiness in those advancing the idea when Derrida, in the quote on p. 103, qualifies his assertion that 'one of the two terms governs the other' with a parenthesis purportedly explaining how – 'axiologically, logically etc.'[4] Suppose, then, that we try to interpret these theses of deconstruction metaphorically. Such an interpretation must, once again, refer us to the use of the allegedly politically dominating signifiers. For what the metaphor must consist in is the substitution of relations between people with relations between signifiers. However, once we are on the terrain of relations between people we are back in the ordinary world of people using concepts in definite ways. And once we are back there the metaphorical attribution of political characteristics to signifiers is going to be, once again, context dependent. But this means two things. First, that we cannot claim that binary oppositions as such can metaphorically stand in for human relations of power, for only particular binary oppositions arising in particular contexts will be a consequence of those relations. Second, and more fundamentally, the focus of the deconstructionist strategy would have to be directed against these practical relations of power between people rather than against the concepts which result from them. The metaphorical interpretation of the claim that there are political relationships between signifiers seems then to be against the whole thrust of deconstruction. (As well, when in Part III I examine the deeper, philosophical arguments advanced by the more serious deconstructionists, it emerges that the claim, based on a mixture of Lacanian psychoanalysis and Fichtean notions of the self as constituted in its division from its objects, really is that the basic distinction between self and other is, in itself, violent and one of domination.) At most we can say that there is an equivocation between the literal and the metaphorical interpretation but in any case the deconstructionist view emerges as inadequate and bizarre.

What I am arguing here then is that the three considerations – the parallel structure of this 'deconstructionist' discussion of dualisms and liberation theory, the implausibility of the former view and the recognition that there are effective reasons for partially avoiding the latter – strongly suggest that there is a covert expression of, or tacit appeal to, the liberation conception of power relations between people in the deconstructionist view of relations between terms or signifiers. The function of this covert expression is to insinuate a genuine radicalism by means of conjuring up the basic ideas of the earlier radical theory.

There is here an obvious objection, although it is also one which can be easily met. My account may have some plausibility in a situation where the earlier 'liberation' ideas were known but it seems less likely now that they have almost completely disappeared from the intellectual scene. Fanon's theories were well known in France at the time when deconstruction was becoming popular amongst intellectuals. (There is in this a tragic irony for what I am suggesting implies that his ideas were first of all distorted and then successfully appropriated by that very strata of French intellectuals he was known to despise.) And as well, a looser form of these ideas were still circulating amongst feminists when feminist deconstruction began to take off as 'the' approach. But how does it work after that when the ideas of liberation theory had disappeared from all contexts? There are two relevant considerations. First, it is the initial development and reasons for acceptance of this kind of thinking which is the harder phenomenon to explain. It is less difficult to understand why, once entrenched in the institutions of higher education, it should have reproduced itself. But second, the essential ideas of liberation theory can be grasped very readily without any developed theoretical structure in so far as they amount to quite basic moral perceptions. In this context, the ideas appealed to are, first, that notions of superiority are only an illusion generated by a hidden relationship and, second, that a genuine confrontation with power cannot proceed only by way of trying to grasp it. These ideas are almost elementary moral notions. My thesis is that deconstruction relies on an appeal to this common morality but gives it the appearance of extra profundity by transposing it onto the counter-intuitive terrain of 'the signifier'.

We have seen, then, the second side of the contradiction which renders the more surrational kind of feminist deconstruction as confused and obscurantist. If, as I showed in the previous chapter, in its use it is authoritarian, then it now emerges that in its content it suggests a principled radicalism, that is a genuine opposition to power, by tacitly alluding to the very ideas it displaced. If this combination of opposed factors explains why the ideas so produced will depend on logical slides, equivocations and a lack of clarity, it also explains the feminist 'amnesia' I set out to understand, the strange but remarkable 'forgetting' by organised second wave feminism of its own origins. If the old ideas were still around and being articulated, even only in terms of the history of feminist thought, this would have the effect of revealing the real basis of the radical appeal of deconstructionism. It would undercut the latter's claims to originality and it would expose the absurdity in the idea that political confrontations can be made at the level of the signifier. More profoundly, perhaps, liberation ideas are ones which (as I argued in Chapter 2) can only encourage the activity of thinking for oneself and relying upon one's own judgement. And that kind of thing would be lethal to a theoretical programme which appeals without argument to political sympathies and loyalties, relying upon the assumption that ideas must be good and/or true because they are feminine, female, non-patriarchal or whatever.

There is one more question to be addressed before the analysis of this less respectable but more dominant kind of feminist theory can be concluded. The above considerations, I hope, throw some light on the constraints upon the production of this sort of theory which result in an almost necessary confusion. But they do not throw light upon how such a theory could be generated intellectually. That is, while this sort of feminist deconstruction may be largely explained by the fact that it is a compromise between radical pretensions and an authoritarian practice, this does not explain how this compromise – the theory of the 'patriarchal binary straitjacket' – was derived. This latter question is of interest because one presumes that the theory was not deliberately designed as such a compromise and that its practitioners do not see it that way. It must have appeared originally (before it was either a trend or a virtually compulsory part of the syllabus) to recommend itself on something like intellectual grounds. Questions of this kind, referring as they do to subjective processes of the mind, are not very fashionable at the moment but this one is nevertheless intriguing. For if I am right that there is little of intellectual worth in this approach then it is both bewildering and fascinating why anyone ever could have thought otherwise. What then remains to be done is to trace the intellectual manoeuvring which makes this way of thinking possible. This task, that of unravelling the mystery of how the more surrational kind of feminist deconstruction could be generated, I shall undertake in the following chapter.

5 The mystery of speculative feminist deconstruction

> If from real apples, pears, strawberries and almonds I form the general idea '*Fruit*', if I go further and *imagine* that my abstract idea '*Fruit*', derived from real fruit, is an entity existing outside me, is indeed the *true* essence of the pear, the apple, etc., then – in the *language* of *speculative* philosophy – I am declaring that '*Fruit*' is the '*Substance*' of the pear, the apple, the almond, etc. I am saying, therefore, that to be a pear is not essential to the pear, that to be an apple is not essential to the apple; that what is essential to these things is not their real existence, perceptible to the senses, but the essence I have abstracted from them and then foisted on them, the essence of my idea – '*Fruit*'. I therefore declare apples, pears, almonds, etc., to be mere forms of existence, *modi*, of '*Fruit*'.
>
> (Karl Marx and Frederick Engels, 'The mystery of speculative construction')

How then does this displacement occur? How do the straightforward, accessible and coherent ideas of liberation theory become transformed into a theory of the patriarchal character of signifiers? The result, I have argued, is such as to allow for the combination of authoritarian practice with an appearance of radicalism, but this does not explain how this result is derived. I shall get into this question by slightly altering tack and picking up again the issue of humanism. In trying to show that liberation theory is tacitly expressed in the feminist deconstruction I have been analysing the fact has to be taken into account that the former is a humanist theory of a more or less classic mould while the latter is one of the most popular forms in which the prevailing anti-humanist, postmodern mood is articulated. I shall begin, then, by showing why it is that the humanist element of the theory disappears in the hands of these feminist academics (and like minded postmodernists).

Now liberation theory in all its versions (feminist, anti-racist, pedagogical, etc.) must be counted as classically humanist, first, because, it assumes the possibility of human self-determination. It is also humanist on account of its own specific recasting of the traditional humanist ethics of equality in terms of an insistence upon an immeasurable and irreducible value of human beings for each other. As well, these days, it might often be counted as humanist in the weaker sense that it refers generally to human beings rather than to specific races, sexes or classes, although this sense of humanism has its point of contrast only with the politics and philosophy of 'difference' or 'heterogeneity'.

On all three counts, the humanism of liberation theory comes into conflict with the theme of the patriarchal nature of binary oppositions, but the argument with the last two is more central here. This is because the rejection of the first sense of humanism, consisting in the denial of human self-determination on the grounds that it is an aspect of the illusory desire for 'Mastery', is derived from the structuralist aspect of 'deconstruction' which would see human actions as an effect, not a cause, of 'the text' or 'the signifier'.

But my interest is in the more political argument, which is directed against any serious use of the concept of 'the human' and so applies more to the last two senses in virtue of which the theory is humanist. This is the argument, which is also that found in postmodern thought more generally, that humanism is inherently oppressive because the concept of 'the human' cannot be used without the concept of 'the Other' or 'Others', the 'less-than-human'. The reason for this, it is maintained, is that the concept of 'the human' is always defined in terms of the specific attributes of whatever the dominant group happens to be. This implies that whenever we use the concept of 'the human' we are assuming that the attributes of those not in the dominant group are 'less-than-human', or in other words we are assuming that they are 'Other'. (In its specifically feminist version the argument maintains that the first and fundamental 'Other' is 'woman' and that the concept of 'the human' therefore really refers only to men.) To support this thesis, both general and specific, the oppressive history of political movements with humanist ideals is brought in evidence.[1] The solution is to abandon the notion of 'the human' and, rather than to use a concept which purports to refer to all of us while in fact referring only to some of us, to focus instead on our differences.

Now there is, on the face of it, more of a puzzle about the postmodern deconstructive argument than there is about the humanist approach of liberation theory. Granted that humanist thought has often been used to mystify the character of oppressive politics and granted that this has occurred in the manner in which it is alleged, such that the specific attributes of dominant groups are identified as the distinctively human attributes, so constituting others as 'Others', the puzzle is why it is assumed that it is impossible to redefine what it is to be human in a way which does not do this. Why is the only solution to abandon, rather than to reform, our idea of humanity? The latter would appear to be the more obvious direction. It was, for example, the direction taken by the early socialists who attempted to undercut the tacit identification made by some liberals of 'the human' with the bourgeois property owner and who redefined the idea so that it clearly applied to workers. And it is the direction taken by liberation theory which wants to claim human status for those to whom this has been denied. Why not continue along these lines and insist on eliminating any hidden assumptions in the use of the concept which would confine its reference, say, to males? Why not, in other words, criticise humanism for its failure to realise its own ideals but retain these ideals and show how they may actually be achieved? In the absence of any argument that this cannot be done it seems rather hasty to insist on throwing out the whole programme.

I am not aware that any variety of postmodern thought has articulated an argument for the necessary oppressiveness of humanism, as distinct from the case that it historically has been so. (And I *have* searched for such an argument.) But there is an implicit or assumed argument which can be reconstructed and the nature of this argument, as well as needing to be addressed in its own terms, throws some light on the question I am asking here about the processes of thinking which result in the feminist notion that binary oppositions are, as such, patriarchal. I shall proceed by way of a comparison with the argument of liberation theory.

HUMANISM AND FORM

It is significant that liberation theory and 'deconstruction's' rejection of humanism identify the same problem. Both perceive and take exception to the fact that dominant groups operate not only by believing themselves to be better than others but more fundamentally by aspiring to the status of 'fully' human. Moreover, the central discovery in both theories is that, very much contrary to the way it appears, one group is identified as 'normal' or 'fully human' only because another group is identified as 'lesser' or 'Other'. Both theories insist, also, that this identification occurs by way of 'the human' being defined in terms of the attributes of the former group alone. (Neither theory would assume that this is a conscious phenomenon.) According to both theories, the problem is with how people understand their own humanity.

The difference which results in one approach attempting to strengthen the humanist position and in the other abandoning it consists in their respective explanations of this problem. Liberation theory (at least in my reconstructed version) identifies as crucial to all three of the above features of oppression a peculiar and distorted way of evaluating people which it maintains arises in the context of power relations. The fact that power is a struggle over degrees of 'humanness' rather than some other kind of status is accounted for by the fact that it is the evaluation of the worth of people as such, that is *as human*, which is operative. Second, the fact that human attributes are defined as those of the dominant group is explained as the result of this deeper assumption involving the comparative judgements of the worth of human beings. The explanation, which I expounded fully in Chapter 1, is that the evaluation of a set of attributes as better or more fully human than another set is derived, in fact though not in appearance, from a prior evaluation of the worth, as human beings, of the people who have these attributes. Finally, the fact that this evaluation of the worth of human beings, for reasons I also developed in Chapter 1, in practice always takes the infamous binary form explains the fact that the evaluation of one attribute as 'fully' human depends upon the evaluation of the other as 'lesser'. According to liberation theory, the interdependence of these evaluations of attributes is explicable in the first instance in terms of the interdependence of the deeper, and generating assumptions of the worth of human beings. (The background and completely unconscious assumption is that there are, as it were, two places, each of which must be occupied, and two groups to occupy them. Which place – that of the 'fully' or 'lesser' human – one group occupies is, against this background, logically related to which place the other takes. The crucial assumption of the differential worth of people is then in fact only made in the form of a binary opposition because it is always implied that when one group is identified as 'fully' human, 'normal' or whatever, other, different groups automatically become 'lesser'. The terms 'fully human' and 'less than human' are here exclusive and exhaustive of the field of humans.) What this amounts to is that in order to explain the situation of oppression as described above, liberation theory identifies one very specific binary opposition at work, one which concerns the evaluation of persons as such. I shall return to the question of the adequacy of this move but first let's consider the alternative approach of the surrational kind of feminist deconstruction.

We have already seen that this argument identifies humanism itself with the situation of oppression. The explanation for the problematic assumptions, all of which concern 'humanness', is thought to lie in the nature of the very concept of 'the human'. But, as I have said, there is a puzzle why this is so, why it is assumed that 'humanness' can *only* be defined in terms of the attributes of a particular and dominant group. For what liberation theory identified as a specific usage in a specific context of the concept of 'the human' is here assumed to extend to *any* use. The distorted and unconscious usage of the idea of 'the human' we find in oppressive situations is therefore assumed to be its general use, and humanism is thought to be unable to free itself from an association with oppression. My solution to the puzzle would identify another assumption, which I suggest *must* be operative in this deconstructionist explanation.

The consequence of 'the human' being defined in terms of the attributes of a dominant group certainly is, as this kind of postmodern feminist argument insists, that it is always found in the context of a binary opposition, paired with some form of the concept of 'the Other', the latter concept capturing those so left out of the reference of 'the human'. If, then, the claim is that 'the human' must be so defined, the assumption has to be that the binary form in which it is found in this context is somehow necessary or essential to the concept itself.

At this point I want to take up the question which is my main concern in this chapter – how this deconstructionist mode of thought is generated – and make the suggestion that this last assumption, which I have just derived by tracing the argument backwards, is heuristically primary. If this is so, then it means that the focus of attention of the feminist deconstructionist is not on the content of offensive assumptions concerning the 'fully' and 'less than' human but rather it is on their logical form, on the fact that they are binary oppositions. This would explain the strange assumption that the concept cannot be redefined in a way which avoids a binary pairing with the 'Other'. For if the content of any offensive definition of humanness were to be considered then it would be clear that it can be argued with. It can be asserted that 'humanness' is not a matter of degree and that it does not consist in the attributes of special groups and so on. To regard the form of the concept as unalterable, it would seem to be necessary to have first disregarded its content, to have excluded this from one's focus. Conversely, if the content is disregarded then the form *will* appear to be unalterable. My hypothesis is that this mode of thinking has apprehended the idea which people in oppressive situations have about 'the human' only through its form, only through the fact that it is in a binary opposition with a concept of 'Others'.

This hypothesis is strengthened if we look further into the explanation of oppression given by this feminist deconstruction, for nowhere do we find that it turns to a consideration of the content of the oppressive assumptions about 'humanness', despite the fact that it quickly gets into deep water by failing to do so. It is as though there is an 'epistemological obstacle' to any such consideration. To emphasise this point let's look first at how straightforward the explanation is when, with liberation theory, we focus on the content of the oppressive ideas. The presence of the assumption of degrees of human worth (identified, obviously, by its content), is itself explicable and can also help explain the problem liberation theory set out to solve. The recognition that evaluations can be made on the assumption of 'degrees' of human worth, in a context which ensures that the respective 'higher/lower' evaluation will be of the binary form explains, as we have just seen, why the attributes of the dominant group become 'the' human attributes. But it also explains why we so frequently find that human beings will refer to different human attributes in the form of binary oppositions within which one set of attributes is valued over another. We can explain, in other words, why pairs of terms – 'male/female', 'white/black', 'rational/emotional', etc. – are so often found in this particular kind of binary form. They are all generated by the assumption of degrees of human worth, which we have seen itself takes the binary form and is the common assumption in different specific oppressive situations. This is not all. Together with the insistence that people have an overpowering need for recognition as human, we can explain what is painful about oppression. Finally, the assumption of degrees of humanness and its binary form is itself explicable, as was shown in Part I, as a result of power relations. For it is the crucial assumption which both justifies differential treatment and, when it is the only known way in which human respect is distributed, makes people very dependent on the situation which produces it.

Now consider the explanatory situation when the focus is on the form of the oppressive assumptions about 'humanness', specifically when it is on the binary form of the pairs of concepts 'fully' and 'less' human, 'Human' and 'Others', 'Self' and 'Other', etc. The difficulty immediately arises that without some consideration of its content, the identification of this form alone cannot explain why many other pairs of attributes, male/female, black/white, heterosexual/homosexual also usually take the binary form, nor can it explain why one term is systematically valued more highly than the other.[2] All that can be said is that there are other pairs of concepts which also seem to take the binary form. This is just what is maintained in this kind of thinking – the instances of 'binary oppositions' are multiplied and we find the long lists of them mentioned before. But the question of where they come from remains unanswered as also is the question of what is wrong with them. (It is different with 'serious' deconstruction which I discuss in Part III.) The reason is that if the attention remains focused on the form alone, if the content of the ideas is ignored, and with their content the context in which they are used, then all possibilities of explanation appear to be closed.

If we continue to explore how the explanation would go according to my hypothesis, we find that it is just how it does go in surrational feminist deconstruction. Having reached the above point, where all there is at hand is a list of offensive binaries, a way of pretending to come up with an explanation – or more accurately of concealing from oneself and others that there is none – presents itself. This is to generalise from the situation and then return and present this same situation (the fact of many binary oppositions in human thought – that which requires explanation) as an instance of the generalisation so derived. The situation so generalised, it is no longer a case of there being lots of binary oppositions about, but rather a case of the binary form being the logic of the whole of Western culture, Western metaphysics or whatever. In this way could be 'explained' the presence of so many binary oppositions and the necessity of the concept 'human' to establish its 'Other'. It follows from the fact that this is 'the' logic of the 'whole' culture. Such a 'strategy' follows precisely the logic described by Marx in the quotation which heads this chapter. Moreover it is, as I have both argued and argued against, precisely the course that is taken.

This strategy, though, is not sufficient to make the account look respectable and the problem of explanation now grows even further out of hand, in my hypothetical version and the actual surrational version alike. For the above move has only introduced something else to be explained, namely the logic of the whole of Western culture. This cannot be done and so whenever the question seems to press in, the only recourse available is to reverse the above manoeuvre and to present what was originally supposed to be explained as though it were an explanation (of what was supposed to explain it).[3] That is, in the way described in Chapter 3, we now present our list of the many instances of binary oppositions in place of an explanation of why Western metaphysics has the binary form. (And here we are extremely lucky that we find that there are a few more binary oppositions to be found in metaphysics itself.) By this time it has been long forgotten that the original concern was with the fact that people try to diminish each other in the way that they do.

And there is more. Even if we get away with this, our problems as post-modern feminists are not over. Still the question raises its head of what, in any case, is wrong with the binary form? We have long ago left behind the possibility of considering the content of the 'more human'/'less human' opposition, something which might have provided a clue – although only at the cost of referring back to the people who have these ideas and the contexts in which they have them. All there is now to reflect upon is the form of the problematic ideas and generalisations from this to the 'whole' of Western culture. We know, nevertheless, that something is wrong, for the perception of this was our starting point. Where else to look, then, but to the binary form itself? And it is precisely here that we rediscover the oppression we set out to explain. Except that, of course, it is no longer human beings who dominate and oppress each other for it is no longer known where one would find them. In the binary form itself we find a 'hierarchy', such that one term dominates the other and has 'the upper hand'. The fact that this discovery is entirely inexplicable in terms of considerations of the conceptual form alone, for reasons which have been argued, is concealed by the manoeuvre we have now used on the two earlier occasions when things got difficult. When the question seems to press forward we simply present a list of cases of 'hierarchical' oppositions either overlooking or equivocating on the fact that this hierarchy can only be identified outside of the binary form itself in the context in which the concepts are used.

The situation amounts to this: there is in operation in 'real life', produced in situations of domination, a particular binary opposition which would treat human respect as though it were of scarce and measurable quantity and which allocates people, then, to positions of 'full' and 'lesser' human worth. Obnoxious as it is, we can understand both how it comes about and what it does. This is the understanding of oppression of liberation theory. It is the perception of this specific binary opposition which is also the core of sense in the deconstructionist insistence that binary oppositions are themselves the key to human oppression. But what has happened in the latter analysis is that the purely formal aspect – the fact that it is a binary opposition – has been emphasised and the content of the opposition, which enables it to function as it does, is ignored. It is this which makes possible the curious identification of the entire humanist tradition in which the definition of 'the human' is in principle open, with the context of oppression where it is a concept which operates only within definite constraints. The intellectual issue between liberation theory and the feminist critique of binary oppositions, then, is whether our problem is the 'logic' of binary oppositions whose existence and operations are mysterious or whether it is the realities of domination and the validity of aspirations to be accorded basic human respect which 'is not a matter of degree'.

FORM AND FUNCTION

If it is a focus on the form at the expense of the content of ideas which explains the *ad hoc* manoeuvring which this feminist deconstruction presents as explanation then the question is what accounts for such a focus. The answer is that it is this focus on form which enables contradictory aspirations to be reconciled. Moreover, the character of the reconciliation is, unlike that of the genuinely psychotic thinking to which I have earlier compared it, such that it allows for apparently normal, even successful social functioning. This is because it produces what on the surface looks like legitimate, even pro- found, explanation. This kind of surrational intellectual phenomenon is therefore to be explained neither as intellectual stupidity (although a certain lack of intellectual training is essential for its survival) nor, despite protest- ations to the contrary, as a deliberate strategy. It would have to be seen, rather, as the result of powerful psychological and political forces it has been, itself, unable to comprehend. Let me, then, finally draw together the threads of the argument.

This feminist deconstructive thinking can be seen to be, first of all, like psychotic thinking in so far as it provides the means for a simultaneous recognition and avoidance of a fundamental issue. I have been insisting that it is to the credit of this kind of thinking that it grasps – or rather alludes to – something which is recognised very rarely, namely that the simple assumption that we can be 'more' or 'less' human is at the core of human oppression. (Clinically psychotic thinking also often has a disturbing ability to latch onto mostly unperceived essentials.) Although this is grasped only by way of its 'binary' form, that it is indeed a recognition of the centrality of this idea is suggested not just by the fact that it is its form which is identified, but more significantly by the fact that the human dynamics which develop around this idea are also described. These are likewise grasped in a pale and abstracted fashion only through their form which is then seen as the form of a conflict- ual relationship between signifiers. Nevertheless, the fact that what we have here is some kind of indirect understanding both of the hidden assumption of the 'more' and 'less' human and of its role is confirmed by the moral credibility which this kind of thinking has managed to accrue. This, I have been suggesting, is due to the presence of moral intuitions expressed more commonly as essential Christian morality than in the political terms of liber- ation theory, which would also (tacitly) identify the same assumptions of human inferiority and superiority as central to the way we wrong each other.

The crucial point, though, is that the apprehension of this crucial assump- tion only through its form also means that the consequences of this under- standing can be avoided. By ignoring the content of the oppressive notion, this sort of feminist deconstruction does not have to face up to what liber- ation theory clearly understands to be the morally demanding, although con- ceptually simple, implication that we should develop a way of life which refuses to compare the worth of human beings as such. It is therefore possible for its advocates to step back from risking whatever their place in the world may be (their social status that is) – the risk which liberation theory showed is the only way through to such a moral position. This partial recognition of a fundamental problem accompanied by its partial avoidance is analogous, I have been suggesting, to the way in which psychotics can accurately identify the oppressive and inhuman behaviour of their own parents or of other really existing human beings, but find it safer to attribute this behaviour to God Himself or someone almost as remote, such as Hitler. The need to recognise the problem is balanced by the fear of facing it and so there is developed a means of doing both at once.

However, as I have intimated before, this now very prevalent thought form is unlike psychosis in that, instead of simply moving to a concept like God which has a different reference from that of the 'real life' one whose use might create intolerable conflicts, it moves to the *form* of the ideas it identifies. It is this difference which confers certain 'worldly' advantages which do not accrue to those who participate in classically psychotic thinking. First of all, since it is common for those working in educational or intellectual environments to take up issues concerning logical and theoretical form, it is not immediately obvious when discussions of these constitute bizarre projections of real life conflicts as opposed to genuine reflection on the logical and conceptual issues. I am not sure that it is in fact that much less crazy to think of political conflicts as taking place between categories of 'sameness' and 'difference' or between 'bourgeois formal logic' and 'proletarian dialectical thought' than it is, say, to believe that one is being pursued by Hitler around one's local neighbourhood. But it does look a lot less crazy. Second, there is the advantage that the obsession with theoretical form provides, in the right circumstances, access to power, in so far as it allows for a quick and easy way to denounce ideas one probably does not understand and to promote others which may have very little coherent meaning. And while it might be thought that this has something in common with the compensation for their degraded social condition that psychotics can find in believing their conflicts to be with the famous or powerful, there is nevertheless the important difference that the former approach too often yields real power which the latter almost never does. It is the projection onto theoretical form which largely makes this difference.[4] This concludes my attempt to understand the prevalence of some of the cruder kinds of contemporary feminist academic thought.

Now only some of this analysis applies to 'serious' deconstruction. There are two main differences. First, while the more serious version of deconstruction, like the surrational version I have just analysed, focuses on the form rather than the content of ideas, it has an argument for doing so. It cannot be seen so simply, therefore, as an unconscious response to a psychological/political need to both recognise and avoid a situation. Nor does it take up the second of the above advantages, that of using a facile, seductive, but intellectually unsound means to denounce intellectual opponents. (As I have said before, the serious deconstructionist will expend some intellectual effort in demonstrating that a certain binary opposition informs a particular text.) For this reason, it cannot be said to embody directly opposing aspirations nor to have the actual investment in conceptual confusion that we found in ideological deconstruction. Nevertheless, we do find a projection of the 'real life' conflicts described as such by liberation theory onto conflicts between theoretical forms and between signifiers. We find this projection, however, in the much more intellectually reputable and completely traditional form of classical idealism. What is at issue, I shall show, is just what was at issue between Marx and Hegel, namely the question whether human 'alienation' or oppression is the necessary form of human existence or whether it is a very pervasive fact about it which can be transformed within it. On the answer to this question hangs the choice whether to search for authentic existence beyond social life in the mystical or its equivalent, or whether perhaps to look for the mystical and authentic within the processes of human and social life.

Part III

Feminism, deconstruction and the divided self

... love is the true *ontological* demonstration of the existence of objects apart from our head: There is no other proof of being except love or feeling in general. Only that whose *being brings you joy* and whose *non-being, pain*, has existence. The difference between subject and object, being and non-being is as *happy* a difference as it is *painful*.

(Ludwig Feuerbach)

... the recognition of the 'subject–object' relation, or relation between knower and known, implies that each of these is an independent thing, or thing with an existence and characters of its own, and that it cannot be properly described in terms of the other thing or of the relations between them.

(John Anderson)

6 Deconstruction

> The only thing that is certain is that whatever you may say of this procedure, someone will accuse you of misunderstanding it.
>
> (William James on Hegel)

In Chapter 3 I distinguished between what I have described as the 'surrational' and the 'serious' versions of deconstruction in terms of the fact that the latter asks questions at the point where the former provides answers. While both theoretical approaches maintain that binary oppositions have a fundamental role in both Western thought and in Western oppression and while they both insist, therefore, on the political importance of deconstruction, 'serious' deconstruction has an account of why this theoretical form is supposed to be so central. Since my analysis of the more popular, surrational, preoccupation with binary oppositions centred on the absence of argument on this point it is clear that it does not straightforwardly extend to the more serious kinds of deconstruction. If, then, I want to persist in advocating a return to the general approach of liberation theory – in which dualisms are not thought to be constitutive of either Western thought or of oppression but are said, rather, to be established as a misuse of concepts in situations of domination – these more respectable arguments for deconstruction will have to be met. And if I wish to go further, as I do, and maintain that even this more intellectually credible deconstruction has elements which function as a projection – a simultaneous reference to and avoidance – of the basic ideas of liberation theory then I must show, not only that the arguments fail, but also that they are the result of political and psychological forces their advocates have failed to comprehend.

In pursuing the latter theme the kind of projection involved in the better versions of deconstruction must be distinguished from that in its poorer counterpart. Not only is the character of the thinking quite different but so, too, are the practical/political stakes. In both cases, it is true, these practical stakes involve an inability to confront issues concerning power where it counts at the same time as there is an identification with being 'truly' radical. However, the more popular kind of deconstruction, I have tried to show, evolved as a means of a *new* strata taking power in universities. (This is E.P.

Thompson's 'lumpen intelligentsia' – see the epigraph to Chapter 5.) It is this strata's grasping for the power previously denied to it, together with the political necessity of presenting itself as radical, which has meant that its theoretical productions are unable to meet the requirements of reason. The relatively intellectually respectable deconstruction is, by way of contrast, the work of a more traditional intellectual elite for whom this kind of 'take over' of public institutions is not necessary. The more limited contradiction it involves, between appearing to be very radical at the same time as doing very little, is not such as to generate anything like the same amount of intellectual confusion.[1] On the contrary, it is a contradiction which can be made intellectually coherent by means of a very conservative understanding of what the possibilities are with respect to undermining power. Nevertheless, even this intellectually more legitimate deconstruction can be shown to indirectly refer to, and at the same time divert attention away from, the more basic ideas of liberation theory.[2] The difference remains, though, that whereas one projection is such as to depend on intellectual confusion and a closing off of important questions, the other has its own internal coherence and a measure of argument to support it.

I claim no particular originality for the argument which follows, not because it has been derived from anyone else's work, although others have arrived at similar conclusions by different routes,[3] but because the issues can be shown to be fundamentally those which were at stake between Hegel and Marx and the general ground, therefore, has been well covered.[4] Both the effective criticism of deconstruction as well as its analysis, I shall argue, is at bottom a matter of repeating the sorts of moves by which Marx replaced Hegel's 'conservative' understanding of alienation with his own 'radical' conception. (It could be noted here that in the various discussions of the relationship between Derrida, Marx and Hegel, this argument, the import of which is to distinguish social/ political problems from basic philosophical ones, is scarcely mentioned.[5]) So in somewhat the same way that Marx argued against Hegel that it is inappropriate to conceive as problematic the very distinction between subject and object but not so the form of the relationship between them, the argument can be made against deconstruction and allied thought that repression, etc. is mislocated in the allegedly fundamental binary oppositions between ourselves and the world but that it can be identified in the manner in which we conceive ourselves when making this distinction. Moving from criticism to analysis we can still broadly follow Marx. In the way that he showed that Hegel's conception of alienation was the basis of the latter's reconciliation of revolutionary hopes with conservative politics it can be argued that the deconstructionist conception of the necessary repression of 'différance' is central to its simultaneous projection of a radical image and the adoption of an extremely limited critical stance and cautious politics, a politics which, it is repeatedly insisted, can only proceed from the 'inside' of power. This conception is the intellectual means, in other words, by which deconstruction is able to avoid political and moral questions which are both intellectually and practically soluble.

Taken as a whole, my argument amounts to the insistence that there are both intellectual and political reasons for distinguishing practical and worldly problems from what are, or are very close to, philosophical and/or religious questions of the ultimate relationship between consciousness and reality.[6] For the price of conflating such issues clearly has to be conservative – political problems are identified with the 'ultimate' questions, the solution to which, if there is one, is profoundly difficult. Deconstructionist thinking, it emerges, is at bottom that of absolute idealism. Marx's argument against Hegel provides the form of both a philosophical argument against its philosophical content and a political case against its likely political consequences. What is shown to have occurred is an abstraction from practical 'real life' issues such that they are transformed into eternal philosophical questions or, in other words, a projection of such concrete issues onto an abstract philosophical plane.

DECONSTRUCTION RECONSTRUCTED

The difference between the more and less intellectually serious versions of deconstruction consists in the fact, first, that the latter, unlike the former, has an argument both for the prevalence of binary oppositions in Western thinking and for their necessarily hierarchical character and second, in the fact that on this basis it also has a more or less intelligible account of the mysteries of the second phase of deconstruction. There is a problem, however, in attempting to reconstruct this argument. Deconstructionists like to describe themselves as making 'gestures' rather than as advancing claims with arguments, and they are, I think, quite right about themselves. There is a resistance to clear argumentation – 'clarity fetishism'[7] – which is sometimes justified in terms of the aim of revealing a hitherto unrecognised multiplicity of meanings. As well as this, the exponents almost always fail to identify the problem points which those who are not convinced might wish to explore.[8] They therefore tend to repeat the very formulations which require explication, giving rise to the suspicion that they may not themselves fully understand the positions they advance. In spite of these difficulties, if one persists in searching for a coherent line of reasoning an argument can be reconstructed. The following account aims to be general enough to capture a number of related positions. (It should be noted – and this will be important for the argument in the next chapter - that it is not only the ideas of deconstruction which are described below. If one is not too strict about the notion of 'différance', allowing in its place similar notions of that which, being the basis of meaning, cannot be represented within meaning, then the argument here captures the more general assumptions and moves of a good many instances of what is classed as poststructuralist thought.)

In summary the argument is this: there is a basic premise to the effect that there is a 'movement' or 'force' which produces meaning and which cannot itself be meaningfully represented.[9] This movement is that which Derrida, for example, calls 'différance', meaning, amongst other things (and for reasons we shall see), that which produces differences in space and deferrals or delays in time. For reasons which shall also emerge, but to do with the difficulty of referring to what allegedly cannot be referred to, the movement 'referred to' by 'différance' is 'referred to' by a series of other terms – 'the gram', 'trace', 'becoming-woman', etc. (Derrida 1972: 39–44). And this same movement is also very close to that which Kristeva, for example, calls the 'semiotic' and Lyotard calls the 'unrepresentable'.

If this is the basic premise, the central thesis is that the structure of our language and, therefore, of our thinking is such that this movement is positively repressed. This repression of 'différance', it should be emphasised, is therefore something over and above its unrepresentability. Given the widely accepted further premise that the subject is structured through language, the repression of 'différance' will be said to be the key to the problematic aspects of the human condition, manifesting in the violence of Western imperialism, patriarchy, ethnocentrism, etc.[10] Now this repression – again for reasons I shall try to reconstruct – is also said to be a function of the distinction between subject and object and it is from that point that the argument proceeds to explain why our thinking is dominated by dualisms, why these are necessarily hierarchical and then to an account of the efficacy of deconstruction in undoing some of the repression inherent in language and thought. But let's begin by trying to understand the central thesis. So first, what is the repression of 'différance'?

It occurs, it is said, when (either in our spontaneous experience or in philosophical thought) meaningful terms are conceived of as deriving their meaning from their reference, from something, that is, which is thought of as originally existing 'in-itself' (according to 'the metaphysics of presence') rather than from this prior and more fundamental movement of 'différance'.[11] It is the reference understanding of meaning which, it is claimed, is not just mistaken but is actively repressive. To understand why we have to explore the reasons why 'différance' was posited in the first case.

It all began, it would appear, with Saussure's insistence that meaning derives from relations between signs. From this deconstructionists draw two conclusions, both of which are shaky, but the latter of which marks the thinking as essentially that of absolute idealism. First, it is inferred that reference plays no role at all in meaning – the apparent dichotomous assumption being that either the meaning of a linguistic sign consists entirely in its reference or it is not relevant at all. (The thinking here has been criticised often and effectively, for example, in Callinicos (1989: 79–80) and in Ellis (1989: Chapter 2.) Second, because it is now exclusively the relations or differences between signs which are of significance in language – the specific signs themselves having been shown to be arbitrary – it is thought that there is a problem which must be addressed of explaining where these come from.[12] This is a very peculiar step which requires some examination. Normally differences are understood simply to be relationships between real terms and so where they come from (in the sense of what produces them) is not something which is thought to require explanation. They simply are, as it were. The generation of things themselves and their properties might be appropriate subjects for explanation but not the logical relations, such as difference, which hold between them. One reason why deconstruction appears to hold that the specific differences which are regarded as responsible for meaning must themselves be explained is because Saussure's now famous statement, 'in language there are only differences *without positive terms*', is construed as a rejection of the normal understanding.[13] Differences, it now seems to be assumed, cannot simply be understood as logical relations between positive terms, because positive terms have either disappeared or been deemed irrelevant. Some other explanation is required. The rationale of the notion of 'différance' as the condition of meaning is to resolve the absurdity of the position so generated in what seems to be a patently faulty way.[14] (The fault lies in the step which moves from the idea that specific terms and their properties are irrelevant to the system of language, to the idea that therefore the relations of difference are ungrounded, that they are not between any positive terms and that they therefore require other explanation.) What we get, then, is an important, fundamental 'différance' which generates all the little and specific differences responsible for meaning. But what this amounts to, although as yet only in the domain of language, is a transformation of a realist and/or common sense ontology into an ontology which is at bottom that of absolute idealism.[15] This transformation occurred when things and their properties dropped out of the picture and only relations of difference were left with any ontological 'bite'. In the classic manner of absolute idealism these relations were then thought to be entirely constitutive (in this case of meaning). This, though, was only the first step for, still in the classic manner of absolute idealism, the ontology so constructed was thought to require another deeper level which generates it. In the case of deconstruction this more fundamental ontological level consists of the elusive 'différance', although it is important to note that the move here is precisely analogous to the Hegelian one which would insist that this deeper ontological level is that of the 'Absolute'.[16] All that is essentially at issue is that relations are now seen to be, first of all, entirely internal or constitutive of what we allegedly mistakenly perceive as things and properties and second, that these relations, themselves, are therefore thought to require explanation. But we shall meet again the effects of the absolute idealist manner of thought so I shall proceed now with the attempt to reconstruct the deconstructionist theory of meaning.

All that we have so far is the accusation that reference theories of meaning are mistaken, that they locate meaning in reference rather than in 'différance'. The further point concerning their repressive role would appear to rest on the idea that the relations of difference in 'the chain of signifiers' are infinite in number, each term being related to the infinity of all the others. The movement – the 'play' – of 'différance' extends into the whole chain and so 'exceeds' any manifestation in a single – or even a finite number – of signifiers. The 'reference' understanding of meaning, then, does not only deny 'différance' by locating meaning elsewhere but it represses its 'infinite play' by fixing meaning in a single or finite number of signifiers. The referential 'metaphysics of presence', spontaneous experience of meaning, forces the 'excess' underground. Or, if you prefer, madness, the openness to the infinite play of meaning, is repressed, so constituting reason (Braidotti 1989a: 57). So, at this point in the argument, the important claim of the repression of 'différance' depends on a basic (badly argued) claim about 'différance' as the producer and condition of meaning, the associated rejection of the idea that reference is anything but an illusory source of meaning and the claim that the failure to recognise the infinite play of 'différance' is the repression of this infinite play. If we now move from the 'How?' to the 'Why?' and ask the reason for this repression of 'différance', we see that deconstruction has to locate the major problems of human existence in the distinction between subject and object or in associated dualisms.

So why is the movement of 'différance' repressed? What emerges is that it is not only repressed but that it is necessarily repressed. The reason (in so far as it can be found) appears to be in terms of the necessary formation of the subject as divided and the illusions which attach to this. The deconstructionists conceive 'the division of the subject' (the arguments will be discussed in the section 'Against Deconstruction' below) in this way:[17] In a manner reminiscent of Fichte's philosophy of consciousness, what we 'really' are, it is suggested, is both terms of that distinction between the 'I' and the 'Not-I' by means of which we are constituted, although we necessarily identify ourselves with only one term, usually the first.[18] In the deconstructionist version, this Fichtean distinction between the 'I' and the 'Not-I' can be made in any number of ways. With respect to the formation of the subject, it is equally the distinction (or dualism, because its exclusive and exhaustive nature is in-built) between mind and body, between subject and object, between spirit and matter, between nature and culture, the inside and the outside, etc. (Here we get a glimpse of where the dualisms of Western thought are supposed to come from.) The location of ourselves in only one term of the division, that is, as a 'unified' rather than 'divided' subject, is a kind of necessary illusion. It is an illusion because what we 'really' are is both terms: we are mind and body, for example. And it is necessary, because on this account we are division and were we to grasp that we were the whole division then we should not be divided. (Here the similarities with Hegel's notion of the Absolute as Spirit necessarily divided against itself in matter begin to emerge.) So how does this divided nature of the subject result in the illusions of the 'metaphysics of presence'?

The next point to grasp, before we can relate this conception back to problems of meaning and the alleged illusions of reference, is that this formation/division of the subject is, on the deconstructionist account, itself a manifestation of the 'metaphysics of presence' and the repression of 'différance'. For in the necessary identification of itself with only one of its terms, the subject sees itself (mostly) as a consciousness (necessarily self-reflective or 'present to itself', Cartesian-style) opposed to things or objects given and present to it. What the subject ignores/represses is not only that it consists of two terms rather than one, but, more importantly, its own formation as a division neither of whose terms is self-present because each essentially refers to the other, and which is generated from a movement whose nature is to make divisions or differentiate. Now this movement, on Derrida's account, just so happens to be also that of 'différance' – the movement which we have just seen is responsible for the differences between linguistic signs which generate meaning. 'Différance' produces the subject in such a way that it differs from itself in space and differs from itself in time.[19] So it is in the very nature of the human subject as divided to repress the movement of 'différance' which produces it and so to remain oblivious to its own nature as division. (More simply, the divided subject necessarily obscures the relations which constitute each of its terms, conceiving them instead as independent, self-contained existences. Once again, it should be noted, there is the absolute idealist insistence, this time in the context of a view of the subject, that only relations are real and that things and their properties are essentially illusory.)

At this point we might ask why this repression of 'différance' in the formation of the subject relates to the repression of 'différance' in language, 'the movement of the signifier', and so to the task of deconstruction. Essentially because, following Lacan, the two movements, that of the formation of the subject and that of language, are thought to coincide and to be conditions for each other. This means, first, that the repressions required for the formation of the divided subject will necessarily manifest themselves in repressions at the level of meaning. Now we have just seen that a divided subject relates to itself in terms of a 'metaphysics of presence'. This metaphysics will carry over into the subject's understanding of the sign, which will naturally be in terms of a mediating role between oneself as self-present consciousness and the given things which are also present to us. This in turn means that the meaning of the sign will be thought to lie in its reference, in the object it denotes for us. Hence the manifold relations of the sign with other signs will be ignored/repressed and so we have the repression of 'différance' in language, thought, or 'the text'. It would now appear that the more fundamental ideas of deconstruction concern the repressions necessary for the formation/division of the human subject.

However, this is to fail to take into account that for deconstruction the inessential role we supposedly attribute spontaneously to the sign is at the core of the problem. There is, then, a further thesis concerning the formation of the subject and the constitutive role of the sign, which is necessary for the idea that our problems are fundamentally at the level of the signifier. The stronger Lacanian notion on which the thinking here is based is that the subject is produced in its divisions only by way of language itself. The subject distinguishes itself from the world and from others in talking/writing about the world to others. And the point here, of which I shall shortly make much, is not that we require language, thought and meaning in order to recognise the distinction between ourselves and the world but that it is required in order to make this distinction. The subject in its necessary division is produced by 'the movement of the signifier', although it is then deluded into the opposite belief that it produces the signifier.

We have reached the point where the familiar theses of deconstruction begin to fall into place and so this basic account can be completed. To begin with, we can now see why it is insisted that our thinking is necessarily structured by dualisms. For if one of the necessary tasks of language is to produce and then maintain the subject in terms of the subject/object dualism, and this can be formulated in an endless number of ways, then it might seem plausible that such dualisms will at least pervade, if not dominate, our language and hence our thought. Moreover, it is the way in which the illusion of the subject/object dualism is said to be maintained which accounts for its allegedly necessary hierarchical character, and therefore for the hierarchical character of all the associated dualisms. To seal off the possibility of perceiving or releasing the movement of 'différance' behind our own constitution, and to confirm the experience of the distinction as 'real', what happens, it is suggested, is that one term of the subject/object dualism or its variants will be understood to be grounded in the other term. In this way, the 'reality' of both terms of the distinction is assured and any productive movement is thought to be not of the distinction itself but only of one of its real, given, self-contained terms by the other, real given, self-contained term. This 'false' grounding is at once the act of repression of 'différance' and the institution of the 'violent hierarchy' of binary oppositions. For the hierarchy simply is this grounding, the 'superior' term being that which is thought of as ground of the other. And it can, of course, be easily reversed. (The concealed dependence of the two terms, the exposure of which is essential to deconstruction, lies, it is suggested, in the production of the distinction between them by 'différance'. This dependence, not manifest in the text, becomes apparent when the prioritising which is supposed to conceal this dependence is shown to be so easily reversed. For this suggests that what is at stake is not 'given' properties of objects but rather a presupposed dependence, the terms of which can be made to slide either way.)

And finally we arrive at an account of the role of deconstruction itself and the mysteries of its second phase (that succeeding the moment of reversal of a hierarchical opposition).[20] There are two reasons which can be derived from deconstruction's own account of itself as to why its second phase can be described only with difficulty and obscurity. The first is that deconstruction understands itself as an attempt to in some sense release the repression inherent in the way we think and use language, at the same time that what it is which is repressed cannot be meaningfully spoken (or written) about. What is required is the demonstration of the supposed illusions involved in grounding meaning in a relationship to things and the concomitant grounding of subjects in objects or vice versa. What is sought is some kind of revelation that the basis both of meaning and of the subject is not in differentiated, self-contained things but is rather this 'différance' which manifests itself in the 'endless play of differences' (or which, manifesting only relationally, refers 'present' objects to 'absent' objects, nothing being therefore entirely present or absent but constituted rather in the endless play of absences and presences). The obscurity stems from the fact that this movement as the basis of meaning, prior both to language and the subject, cannot itself be meaningfully described. It can allegedly be shown but not stated. And it is for this reason we get the endless and obscurantist play on the fact that 'différance' is neither a word nor a concept. It is also why it is insisted that new terms are constantly required to mark the place of 'différance' in order to prevent its appropriation (which 'happens very fast' (Derrida 1972: 58)) as an ordinary concept, which on this understanding would imply reference to some ordinary but illusory self-contained presence. Deconstruction's second movement insertion of the 'undecidable' is then supposed to mark but not to conceptualise the place of 'différance'.

The second reason for the difficulty in describing the latter phase of deconstruction brings us to its conservative understanding of power. What I mean by this is just what Marx meant by the description of Hegel's account of alienation as conservative, that the problem is conceptualised in such a way as to imply that its practical overcoming is impossible. (This of course provides no argument against either deconstruction or Hegel. But if there are other reasons for rejecting the ideas in question, the implied conservatism may then be seen to have provided some of their rationale.) Now the conception of power in deconstructionist thought is substantially that of the conception of repression just outlined. In a chain of reasoning (rarely made explicit) which involves the idea that the divided self-present subject must posit the 'Other' in the place of the 'not-self' with all the attendant projections and repressions required to maintain the illusion of this 'Other's' separateness, the acts of violence of Western racism/imperialism/sexism, etc. are traced back to the repression of 'différance'.[21] The conservativeness of the view consists, then, in the idea that the repressions and divisions of the subject are both necessary and illusory/repressive. For, since the division of the subject is necessary, there is no question of simply transcending it, of moving into a place where the repressions inherent in 'the metaphysics of presence' no longer occur – for this, I take it, would be madness where meanings and associations proliferate endlessly. The second phase of deconstruction, then, aims only to 'unsettle' or 'destabilise' the self-certainty of the subject as to its self-present nature and not to destroy it. There is a delicate balancing act required where somehow, at the same time as the fixity and repressions of meaning are maintained, it is indicated (without of course being stated) that meanings are not so fixed as they might appear and that both the subject and meaning are the result of the movement of 'différance' which cannot be named. In other words, what we can achieve in relation to power and repression is necessarily very limited.

Similarly, Marx was able to describe Hegel's conception of alienation as conservative, because it was based on the idea that the subject/object division is both necessary and a manifestation of alienation, with the implication that what could be done about it was also necessarily limited. But deconstruction's strategy is inherently obscure in a way that Hegel's is not and this difference deconstructionists regard as important. (Although it is not important to the overall argument I am making here.) The difference is this: on Hegel's view, alienation cannot be transcended, but we can be reconciled to it by under-standing. The subject, at the same time as it is divided from the object, can move (through epochs of world history) from the conviction that the distinc-tion is complete and just as it appears, to grasping the underlying unity behind it. This underlying unity consists in the fact that both its terms are a manifestation of the Absolute and that the division is necessary. In this way the contradiction is reconciled by means of the famous 'Aufhebung' that deconstructionists strive to avoid. The reason that they do so is because the movement of 'différance', unlike that of the Absolute, is thought precisely not to resolve distinctions and dualisms within the conception of a 'higher unity' – it just differentiates, or produces differences and that's the end to it. The positing of the 'Absolute' as the ultimate self-present Being is then thought to be the final logic, not of the process of undoing the repressions of the subject but, on the contrary, of 'the metaphysics of presence' itself – that which has to contain differences in presences and consequently 'différance' itself in Absolute Presence.[22] So while Hegel is able to come to a clear (at least in principle) conception of alienation, what deconstruction does has to remain obscure, not only because 'différance' is unnameable, but because the conservative concept of repression requires that the strategy be neither to open the subject to the infinite play of meanings nor to allow it to remain closed to this play. What it does do has to be (depending on one's sympathies) very subtle or very murky indeed. There is now an extra dimension to the conservativeness of deconstruction which emerges in the implication that only the extremely astute and clever are able also to be very good and remain uncorrupted by power. At this point, to those who are unimpressed by the imputations of subtlety and cleverness, the account of deconstruction looks more like its *reductio ad absurdum* than the solution to Western imperialism/ ethnocentrism etc.

AGAINST DECONSTRUCTION

What deconstruction has achieved, it would appear, is a synthesis of the most basic questions of ontology, religion, meaning, psychology and power. It is not surprising, perhaps, that an initial impression might be that it therefore constitutes something of a revolution in all these areas and this might partially explain the enormous excitement it has generated within tertiary institutions from those who can have at best only a surface acquaintance with the ideas. There is clearly something very seductive about the notion that one's immediate political stance – say opposition to sexism, racism, etc. – is such that it will at the same time change the way we think and behave about everything else. At the same time, perhaps, it is understandable that, given the intellectual nature of their occupation, academics with more than a surface acquaintance with these deconstructive ideas would also tend to be drawn to ways of understanding political questions which identify these with ultimate philosophical questions. The question is whether this synthesis is the radical breakthrough as which it presents itself or an illegitimate conflation of issues which therefore acts as an obstacle to any of them being adequately addressed. I want to now argue the latter.

It cannot be maintained that ontological questions are not related to political questions. Rather, the former necessarily inform the latter. Indeed, the argument I want to make that political questions are different questions from those concerning the distinction between subject and object, consciousness and matter, etc., is best made by way of the insistence on the ontological status of each term or in other words on the reality or truth of these distinctions. It therefore presupposes a definite ontological stance. And so, clearly, does the opposing argument of deconstruction whose near identification of political with ontological questions relies on the fact that full ontological status is conferred only upon the movement of 'différance', the subject/object distinction meanwhile being given a sort of quasi-ontological status which constitutes it as both necessary and illusory – both unchangeable and supposedly modifiable in some way. Generally, the way in which one conceives the relationship between politics and ontology is not independent of the particular ontology one adheres to. So, following the lines of the young Marx's thinking about Hegel I shall assert, first, an ontological disagreement with deconstruction, second I shall identify a limited political agreement and third, from these two premises I shall deduce the extent and nature of the implied political disagreement. (In this way Marx argued that while Hegel is right that there is a problem of alienation, ontological considerations required that this problem not be located in the subject/object distinction itself but rather in the form of the activity of labour by which the subject and object are connected.)

First, the ontological disagreement: we have seen that the core of deconstruction's argument is that the subject/object distinction is the key to the metaphysics of presence and hence to the repression basic to the West in so far as it posits given and self-contained things over and against, but present to, a given consciousness. Now to have such mistaken/repressive results clearly there must be something wrong with the distinction itself. What is wrong with it, according to the argument of deconstruction, is that the subject/object distinction is not a 'true' one – not one which we learn about because there really is such a distinction – but it is a distinction which is made for other reasons, namely that a viable psychological subject requires the illusion of separateness and distinctness from the world. It is a distinction which is mistakenly taken to be real.

Suppose that against this it is simply asserted that there really are material things and that there really are minds or consciousnesses and that no matter how closely connected these might be and no matter whether or not we want to ultimately insist that they are of the same or of different kinds of substance there are nevertheless real distinctions between them. Suppose, in other words, we assert that the distinction between subjects and objects refers to a real distinction and that it is not, therefore, entirely relational although there are, of course, still relations between subjects and objects. What will follow is that *no* political/ human problem can be located in the subject/object distinction itself and that at most such problems could lie only in a more specific way in which either the distinction or its respective terms might be (mistakenly) understood. I shall begin, therefore, with the assertion of an ontology which contains material and mental existences as opposed to an ontology of 'différance'.

But second, my argument in Part I implies a large area of agreement with deconstruction concerning the broad determinants of political/psychological problems – specifically, that many of these result from a divided human psyche with illusions both about its own unity and the extent of its independence. In order to maintain the 'liberation theory' version of such problems it will have to be shown that what is agreed to does not require an ontology of 'différance'. So in more detail the agreement is this: on the basis of the account outlined in Chapters 1 and 2, it can be maintained with deconstruction that operations of power are closely connected to mistakes people make about their own psychological constitution. Moreover, and still with deconstruction, it can be said that these mistakes fundamentally involve an illusion of autonomy which consists in a failure to recognise our essential dependence on (relatedness to) others. More precisely, the illusion consists in mistaking what are in fact internal or constitutive relations for external or non-constitutive relations. The failure to recognise internal or constitutive relations as such occurs when we fail to recognise that the attributes we recognise as ours as well as the value we put upon them can be the effect of power relations with others – that is, that relations with others are to this extent constitutive, determining us to some degree. The illusion that these relations are external or non-constitutive consists in the assumption which we have when psychologically immersed in power in this way to the effect that our place in the world is a consequence only of our attributes and their intrinsic merits or defects (in other words that our relations with others are a result of what we are and do and not vice versa). The point of agreement is then that while we are in fact intrinsically related to others we are persistently deluded, for reasons closely bound up with power, into believing that we are only extrinsically related. It can be further agreed – and indeed this is probably the most important point – that all of this amounts to a division within the human psyche, for what we have is a dependent, relational constitution which is in conflict with our own convictions of autonomy. It is agreed, then, that power conflicts are mapped onto conflicts within the psyche itself. So in the way that Marx agreed with Hegel that there is a problem of alienation, we can agree with deconstruction that there is a problem of the illusion of autonomy of the human subject and that this problem is also that of division within the human psyche. The area of disagreement, we shall now see, concerns how these agreed claims are more specifically construed.

I wish then to reject the ontology of deconstruction but accept that there is a deep problem concerning our divided psychological nature and the resulting illusions we have about ourselves. This will require understanding the problem as a much more specific one than deconstruction would have it, as one which arises from concrete circumstances rather than from the necessary ontology of human subjectivity. Such an understanding is contained in the 'liberation' account which is specific in two ways that deconstruction's version is not. First of all, on the 'liberation' account the illusion of autonomy is not thought to be endemic to human subjectivity as such but rather to be a response to definite social relations which it also sustains – namely, relations of power. The divided subject arises in the same way as a result of the same relations, the division being between, on the one hand, our own self-evaluation with the attendant recognition of dependence and, on the other, the 'taking in' of the values of others, with the attendant illusion of autonomy. Deconstruction, by way of contrast and despite its own anti-essentialist rhetoric, posits that it is the essential nature of the subject to be divided and that the illusion of autonomy is based in this essential division. For this division, in its nature as division, necessarily demands that the subject is 'caught up' in one or other of its terms, repressing any perception of the relations which constitute it as division. Second, the content of the autonomy illusion on the 'liberation' account is specific in so far as it is alleged that only certain and specific perceptions of apparently 'given' attributes are illusions which deny the operation of very specific relations with others. In specific instances, the argument is, we wrongly perceive ourselves as having 'given' attributes rather than as being constituted by specific relations with others. But it is not claimed that any perception of a non-relational attribute is an illusion which conceals a constitutive relationship with others because there is no claim that the human subject is entirely relationally constituted. We saw earlier that what is denied is, first of all, our intrinsic dependence on others for recognition and respect and as a result of this the relations of power which this denial sustains. And we do this, it is argued, by falsely attributing to ourselves certain properties. Deconstruction's analysis, on the other hand, is that the illusions of the subject are the illusions of 'the metaphysics of presence' and are therefore such that recognition of any and all constitutive relationships (of the subject, the object, or the signifier) are necessarily repressed in favour of a perception of the 'present and self-contained' and, conversely, that any perception of an apparently non-relational attribute is an illusion concealing a constitutive relationship. It is a general philosophical argument based on an absolute idealist ontology in which the subject – and indeed the rest of the universe – is constituted entirely out of its relations.

We are faced with a choice between being realist about consciousness, material reality and the differences between them and consequently locating psychological/political problems in the specific way that the subject understands itself in specific circumstances or regarding the subject/object distinction itself as the core of the problem and locating the problem in ontological necessities. The choice is between understanding the divided personality as a specific and contingent formation and understanding it as a necessary formation. It is once again the choice between relating to alienation in world-historic ontological terms and relating to it as a practical concrete problem.

At this point, what has happened is that the argument has been pursued to its most fundamental level, to a point where arguments can no longer decide.[23] From the realist point of view what can be claimed is that the manoeuvres of deconstruction – at bottom those of absolute idealism – which split reality into illusory properties and constitutive relations, with the result that these relations, now left hanging, have to be based in some deeper more absolute movement, are both unnecessary and unproductive. Particularly they are unproductive when it comes to rendering practically soluble problems mysterious and almost insoluble. These are the sorts of reasons offered by Marx and Feuerbach for rejecting absolute idealism, for locating problems of alienation in practical 'real life' considerations and they are the sorts of reasons which I think are still sufficient.[24]

DECONSTRUCTION AND LIBERATION THEORY

I have been arguing the case for the idea that the poverty of a common mode of contemporary radical and feminist thought stems from the fact that it is a projection of 'real life' political conflicts onto theoretical categories with the result that some genuine oppositional aspirations are expressed while the costs of pursuing the real conflict are avoided. This thesis holds most clearly in the case of surrational deconstructionist thinking where the focus on theoretical form functions to hold in place contradictory identifications both with, and in opposition to, power. But we have now seen this more intellectually sound version of deconstruction also locates political conflicts in the domain of theory by treating them as a function of relations between signifiers. It does so, though, in a different way. First, as I have said repeatedly, it has an argument to justify its focus on theoretical form, that is, upon binary oppositions. So whereas in the surrational version the lack of argument on this fundamental orientation is an indication that the point of the exercise is something else, namely to identify politically sound and unsound theoretical forms, this is not so here. Second, the character of the supposed political conflict is different. It now consists in the 'hierarchy of signifiers' which is to be 'unsettled' or 'displaced' and so the results of deconstruction itself are not held up as an alternative theoretical form to that of 'logocentrism' as in the cruder version.[25] The conflict is not between logocentrism and deconstruction after the manner of 'bourgeois' versus 'proletarian' thought but is rather between the supposedly dominant and dominated signifiers. I have argued that this serious version of deconstruction is an inadequate view mainly on the grounds that political conflicts are better conceived as 'real life' conflicts rather than as conflicts between signifiers but the question now is whether it can also be considered to be a projection of a 'real life' understanding of political conflicts onto the domain of signifiers.

That it is worthwhile to pursue the possibility of this sort of projection is suggested by a contradiction whose existence has been mentioned several times but which has now emerged clearly. It is this: on the one hand, deconstruction is a classically conservative view. It insists that the possibilities for radical political change are extremely limited and, moreover, that these can be pursued only from a point within the network of power relations themselves. Power is thought to be the necessary form of human psychological and social life. This conservatism means that the kind of confrontation with power which is the aspiration of liberation theory is ruled out from the beginning since this is thought to be positioned in a point outside the determining influence of power. This external point – no 'God's eye' view even if some interpret it as 'God's ways' – is just the real conviction (real enough to manifest in dispositions) that respect is due to the human beings as such. The conservatism of deconstruction consists in its insistence that it is impossible to confront power as such and that one must always partly uphold, to some extent, some kind of power. On the other hand, despite the awe of power so expressed, deconstruction presents itself as an extremely radical view and its appeal is clearly due to this self-presentation. If its surrational counterpart effects the synthesis of an oppositional stance with a bid for power, it seems as though 'serious' deconstruction manages to synthesise a deeply conservative stance with a radical image. It is this which suggests that in practice it may function partly as the projection, that is as a partial expression and a simultaneous avoidance of, a genuinely radical view. If so, and if the 'real life' understanding in question were to be substantially that provided by liberation theory, then the case for a return to this approach is considerably strengthened.

Aside from the above differences, all the considerations I adduced for regarding surrational deconstruction as 'really' about the concerns of liberation theory apply to deconstruction. We have two competing theories about the same sort of thing (domination and its overcoming) with the same general structure (insisting on the necessity but limitations of a 'moment of reversal') and where one avoids the morally difficult consequences of the other. We have also the fact that the popularity of one approach succeeded that of the other in time. However, the decisive factor which allowed us to say that surrational deconstruction was a projection of another view was its intellectual incoherence and this is missing. Instead of this, however, the bizarre character of the serious version's intellectual approach can be pointed to as reason for thinking it is 'really' a displacement of the other view. What I mean is this: I have tried to show that the choice between liberation theory and deconstruction partly comes down to a disagreement over what philosophical questions are considered legitimate. Deconstruction is committed to the idea that, contrary to everyday perceptions, it is the existence of relations as such which requires explanation. It was argued above that the basis for this conviction is the absolute idealist view that everything is constituted by relations – in other words, by the idea that things and their properties are illusions, that they cannot therefore ground relations and that these therefore require a different explanation. (It is the consequence of this view that the subject/object relation must be explained in a non-realist way.) The question so posed is a general philosophical one. This is a coherent, but also a very strange idea of what needs to be explained. By way of contrast the philosophical assumptions of liberation theory (although these have not been articulated) amount to the realist and/or common sense view that there are both things and their properties and that relations hold between them and require no other explanation than this. That this is the implicit philosophical position is brought out by the fact that when some of the properties we attribute to ourselves and others turn out to be both illusions and the result of concealed relations between ourselves and others, this is not thought to be due to their nature as properties as such but rather to specific and contingent circumstances. Things and properties as such are not held to be illusions and so it is not relations *qua* relations which require explanation but the specific relations which generate these specific illusions. But the nature and causes of these special circumstances do not themselves constitute a philosophical question for the explanation sought will be concrete and specific. This is not at all a strange approach.

The strangeness of deconstruction is in posing abstract philosophical questions where more specific questions can be put, so transforming concrete practical questions into mystical and insoluble ones and philosophical questions into directly political ones. If we see it as a projection of these problems and their concrete apprehension, in the manner of liberation theory for example, then this strangeness can be explained as an avoidance of the morally demanding implications of facing them more directly. In the same way that Marx argued that the Hegelian theory of the alienation of Mind was a projection and a filtering of the perception of the reality of alienated labour which avoided the core of alienation it can be insisted that deconstruction projects and filters out the more disturbing aspects and implications of power. Why the difficulties should be avoided in this specific way is not hard to understand, for it is both a natural and an easy move for those who regard themselves as intellectuals to make. It is natural, first of all, for intellectuals to understand real problems in terms of their theoretical reflection and it is easy in this case because what is at stake in the existence of power relations is something which is both specific and contingent and very close to universal. The slide to seeing it as a metaphysically based necessity is, perhaps, almost imperceptible. That it is a significant slide with disastrous effects becomes apparent only when a while later we find ourselves talking about signifiers dominating each other, resisting each other, etc. and human beings seem to have disappeared.

This chapter has been an argument against replacing the more alarming modes of feminist and radical thought described in Part II with their intellectually superior counterpart. However, for the most part, even feminists who are very influenced by this superior version do not uncritically accept it. Many of them also see it as embedded in, rather than as confrontational of, significant networks of power. What I shall argue next is that their attack is, itself, based upon the deeper assumptions of deconstruction and it is for this reason that it has resulted in another feminist version – more argued than those discussed in Chapter 3 – of the 'two sciences' thesis. It has also led to a focus on what I would maintain is the 'wrong' division in the divided subject, a division which cannot be overcome by the processes of living but which requires fundamental world-historic transformations in every area of life. The 'right' division of the subject, of course, is essentially that which was posited by liberation theory.

7 A different divided subject[1]

What are the politics of the female split-subject?

(Rosi Braidotti)

Unless ye be born again, ye shall not enter the kingdom of heaven.

(John 3: 3)

Julia Kristeva once remarked, in passing, that there are two ways in which the increasingly popular notion of the divided subject could be understood.[2] One way, her own, and also that of postmodern/poststructuralist thought derives from Lacan's account of Freud and refers first of all to the idea that human beings are divided between their conscious and their unconscious aspects. Since, further, the conscious is identified with the use of language (more generally the symbolic) and the unconscious with what is a precondition for this use, something which is allegedly necessary for language but which cannot in principle be represented within it, then the division is also effectively understood as being between that which represents and that (aspect of the subject) which cannot be represented.[3]

This division is an interesting division for psychoanalysis (rather than, say, for philosophy) when it is understood to bear upon, not only the essential nature of consciousness and representation, but also upon the constitution of the subject as such. The further (presumably contingent) thesis then becomes that the subject is actually formed, both chronologically and structurally, by way of this division. There is said to be a dynamic relation between the two poles of the division consisting, first of all, in the fact that the conscious, representing pole is formed not only by way of distinguishing itself from, but also by way of repressing, the unrepresentable, unconscious pole; and, second, in the fact that the latter pole does, nevertheless, appear – 'it speaks' – although it cannot be spoken about. The former notion implies a subject necessarily deluded as to its own nature – aware of only one side of the division through which it is constituted since the other side is repressed. (This is a different division, it should be noted, than that which is thought by poststructuralists to be subsequently posited by this conscious representing subject between self and other, mind and body, etc. This posited division, the basis of the subject's alleged dualistic thought, is the mode of repression of the fundamental division between its conscious and unconscious aspects.) The latter idea implies that, nevertheless, there are clues to our self-delusion which, although necessary, is not therefore absolute. If, then, we replace the notion of 'différance' with that of 'the unconscious' as here described, this understanding of the divided subject can be seen to be broadly along the lines of deconstruction as reconstructed in the last chapter. (The differences will be discussed shortly.) It is a division which is understood to be constitutive of the subject and therefore necessary to it. When the further division just noted, that said to be posited by the conscious aspect of the psyche between subject and object etc., is also assumed, as it is by those who adopt this conception of the divided self, then the conception which results is even more closely along the lines of deconstruction and these two articulated divisions are, for reasons given in the last chapter, regarded as the source of problems of power.

The alternative understanding of the divided subject, which Kristeva mentions and then by-passes, does not regard the division as essential to subjectivity as such. Rather, it is conceived as a contingent division which, although widespread, is constitutive only of disturbed psychological formations and is, in principle at least, the kind of division which can be overcome. This is the division of R.D. Laing's 'divided self', the conception of which is broadly derived from Winnicot and which can also be found in Freud's early case studies – those undertaken when he was in the process of formulating the notion of the unconscious.[4] It is understood as a division between two whole personality fragments which are at odds with each other - sometimes so much so that that the one is unknown to the other.[5] Of these two personalities the least dominant could be said to be unconscious or repressed. While it is true that only the dominant personality fragment has an obvious voice, this is not because the other fragment is by nature unable to speak or to be spoken about but purely because of the specific character of the dominance as dissociation. If one were to think in terms of this sort of notion of the divided subject, power would not be identified as a relation between the speakable and the unspeakable, embedded in the nature of subjectivity as such, but would be seen rather as a function of particular and contingent forms of subjectivity. (The splitting of personality fragments and the dominance of one fragment over the other – itself a kind of power – could be explained as the result of the person being subjected to traumatic forms of power.) And even if it were subsequently thought that the effects of this power had in fact, in some people, disturbed the very process of formation of their subjectivity (or sense of identity), what would be posited would be an instance of a contingent intertwining of this kind of power with the fundamental process of subjective formation.[6]

Kristeva, however, having given a rare acknowledgement that the notion of the divided subject is not the exclusive property of structuralists and post-structuralists, proceeded with her own preferred conception. Despite the passing nature of her comment I understood her to be suggesting that subjects can be thought of as divided in both of the above ways and that both approaches are therefore legitimate in so far as they have a different focus. To a point, such a view must be right. There are issues concerning the formation of the subject as such and there are issues concerning the particular disturbed formation of some subjects – even if the latter turn out to be almost all subjects. These two sets of issues may well interconnect but they are nevertheless distinct. But to the extent that it might be implied that there are correspondingly, therefore, two appropriate ways of looking at the operations of power in the psyche, I would be opposed to such tolerance.

Building on the argument in the last chapter I shall argue that questions of power are badly posed if they are conflated with questions of the nature of the subject as such. In the last chapter the general arguments for this kind of identification were addressed and it was shown that they relied upon a very conservative view of the possibilities of undermining power. Here I shall focus on the problems created specifically in the context of feminist psychoanalytic theory by this implied but unacknowledged conservatism. The conclusion to be drawn is that the second of the above conceptions of the divided subject is more fruitful for those interested, as most feminists are, in psycho/ political change. (Here I am not even taking up the many considerations which would appear to conflict with the thesis of the construction of the self through language.[7]) This conclusion will relate to my overall argument in so far as this second conception of the divided self can be shown to provide the elements of a psychological framework within which the insights of liberation theory could be further pursued. And so it will be on this note of showing how the unique and powerful combination of moral, political and psychological understanding opened up by liberation theory might be deepened that I shall conclude.

KRISTEVA AND IRIGARAY

The tension between the radical stance which deconstruction suggests about itself and its actual inherent conservatism comes dramatically to a head when this kind of theoretical framework is adopted by feminists. For feminism, especially feminism of 'the second wave', is fundamentally about personal or psychological change. It is this tension which is the basis of the dispute between feminists of a poststucturalist/psychoanalytic orientation over the relative merit of the works of Julia Kristeva and Luce Irigaray, the best known representatives (outside France at least) of what is widely referred to as French feminism. Both theorists take as their very general point of departure the broad framework of deconstruction which incorporates the first of the above conceptions of the divided subject. And although they both use this framework only in a more developed psychoanalytic version, this development, it will emerge, is not such as to affect its general conservative character, which stems from the location of issues of dominance in the very distinction between subject and object.

The main point at issue between Kristeva and Irigaray as it tends to be seen in the feminist discussion is over the former's relatively conservative stance and the apparently 'over the top' character of the latter's radicalism.[8] For reasons which will soon become clear, this conflict condenses over the issue of 'the specificity of sexual difference'. This is the issue of whether there is a specifically feminine desire and, therefore, (presupposing the particular psychoanalytic framework where desire is thought to be constituted only in language/discourse) a specifically feminine language/discourse which is different in principle and not just as a result of circumstance from masculine language/discourse (and desire). Ultimately the question becomes posed in terms of an ontology of sexual difference. It is here, then, that we find the 'serious' discussion of the idea of 'sexed' discourse and hence of specifically feminist theory, meaning by this a radically different kind of theory.

What I would show, however, is that the more fundamental issue is that of the choice of the basic framework of deconstruction itself. For the ideas of both Kristeva and Irigaray can be seen to be more or less consistent developments, although in opposite directions, of this shared, implicitly conservative framework. The price of an inherently conservative framework is that the possibilities for change are seen to be either very limited or if they are not, then they must be supposed to shatter what is posited by the theory as quasi-necessary structures. That is to say, on conservative assumptions, one cannot be radical and think about more than minimal change without being extremely radical and advocating change in the allegedly most fundamental structures of human existence. Irigaray pays this price of adopting a radical stance whereas Kristeva remains within the constraints of the framework. But if the underlying shared assumptions were abandoned and a differently divided subject was made the focus of feminist theory, a radical position with respect to power could be articulated which did not require the positing of apparently wild and obscure notions such as that of a female language and female discourse.

KRISTEVA

The very general account of the human subject outlined in the last chapter becomes a psychoanalytic account with specific relevance to feminism in Jacques Lacan's version.[9] In this, the construction of the divided subject through language is identified historically with the process which Freud described as the resolution of the Oedipus complex, the process in which the child, through fear of the father, represses its early bond with the mother. (That which is repressed, the unconscious, is thought to consist largely in this bond, rather than in 'différance' as deconstructionists might maintain.) Language (the symbolic order) is therefore regarded as a specifically masculine order, first of all in that the child allegedly acquires it ('enters' it) by and large by way of the specific intervention of actual fathers. But second, because of this, it is structurally identified with the 'place of the father' or the paternal function (also referred to as 'the Name-of the-Father'), so constituting it as a masculine order independently of the role of the actual fathers. When this structural place is further identified as that of society itself, then the location of power in the subject/object distinction, which I complained about in the last chapter, here becomes, first, the location of psychological subjection in the process of the child's separation from its mother (for this is induced by the authority of the father, through fear) and second, the location of social authority ('the Law') in the symbolic order, the order of representation.[10]

These ideas imply conservative conclusions in two ways. First, there is clearly a general conservatism because it follows that the price of overcoming both psychological and social subjection of the kind advocated by the early 'liberationist' feminists can only be psychosis. This is because any fundamental challenge to either or both kinds of authority is simultaneously a challenge to the very processes of signification. Both civilisation and sanity, it is thought, depend on the repression effected by the Law. There is also a more specific conservatism, regarding the supposedly necessary patriarchal form of this authority which is imposed by actual fathers and relies upon an allegedly masculine symbolic order. (These conservative conclusions, it can readily be seen, are no more than the psychoanalytic version of the conservative conclusions which follow from the insistence that the subject/object distinction is both necessary and the illusion responsible for power. This is because we are here discussing the psychoanalytic version of the latter idea.)

Despite the fact that she accepts both kinds of conservative implications Kristeva has substantial feminist credentials.[11] These depend on the fact that while she broadly accepts the Lacanian picture, she emphasises what it neglects, namely the psychological relation to the mother and the associated structural 'place of the mother', as far more than the site of both an original and sustaining repression. Her theory of the 'semiotic' (the pre-oedipal, that is pre-symbolic, and therefore in principle unrepresentable manifestations of drives associated with the mother's body)[12] is essentially an account of the manner of 'return' of this repressed material (in the form of the material embodiment of the symbolic, that is, the sounds, marks, etc. which are its means) which would show that it is an essential aspect of signification – as essential as the symbolic itself. It follows that the subject must be considered as a unity of the symbolic (structurally the place of the father) and the semiotic (structurally the place of the mother). In this way Kristeva criticised Lacan's focus on the exclusively symbolic aspects of language as reproducing the original rejection and repression of the relationship with the mother's body, a rejection which Lacan himself maintained is necessary for subjecthood and entry into the symbolic. (These are also the general lines of her criticisms of Derrida.) She insists on the importance of 'the place of the mother' as constitutive of subjecthood and signification and explains women's subordinate position in terms of its repression. So in the first instance Kristeva's feminist credentials depend on the fact that she clearly brought out the issues in Lacanian psychoanalysis which are of significance for feminism by insisting that its devaluation of the 'feminine' semiotic was a mistake, not just of evaluation but also of theory. For the most part these credentials are accepted even by those feminists who otherwise find her position antithetical to feminism (for example, Braidotti 1989a: 229).

But there is more that might have been thought, at least at first glance, to further enhance Kristeva's standing amongst feminists. First, she insists that revolutionary change, limited as it may be to conserving the symbolic order, comes about only through a kind of 'shaking up' of the symbolic by 'irruptions' or 'transgressions' of the semiotic, the 'feminine' aspect of signification. Because of her acceptance of the constraints of the framework, what is politically at issue in such change cannot be thought to be the nature and function of the symbolic itself. The politically significant factor is then identified as the extent of the rigidity of the repression of the semiotic. A too rigid repression, Kristeva maintains, can be loosened by the transgression of the symbolic by the semiotic. The 'feminine' semiotic, the place of the mother, is then the source of revolutionary change. Second, among the several groups which Kristeva argues are in a specially advantageous position to effect such transgression, she includes women – along with poets, dissident intellectuals and psychoanalysts.[13] (For women, being mothers, have a special interest in the kind of relations we have with the mother's body.) The feminine is the source of liberating change and women are specially placed to be its agents – an attractive position, one might think, to those of a feminist persuasion.

These last two points, however, cut no ice at all with Kristeva's feminist critics who on the contrary see these positions as a retreat from feminism. This is because, they say, they amount to a denial of the importance of sexual difference.[14] Indeed, they see her more general conservatism, consisting in an acceptance of the bifurcation of both society and the psyche into the powerful place of the father as against the unspoken and, she supposes, literally unspeakable place of the mother, as intrinsically connected to these later, only apparently feminist positions. To understand this very different feminist response to Lacanian psychoanalysis, a response which nevertheless is broadly derived from it, we can begin by asking why these 'difference' feminists locate the essence of Kristeva's conservatism in what look like radical and feminist positions.

IRIGARAY

In what follows I shall refer rather more to the writings of those feminists who see themselves as broadly propagating Irigaray's ideas than to her own works, which are generally found to be too obscure to interpret with confidence.[15] It is, in any case, the kind of theoretical moves being made in feminist theory which are my concern more than the accuracy with which these may be attributed to certain theorists. Generally, the proponents of Irigaray's ideas are quite clear that they believe that the weakness of Kristeva's approach (both as feminism and as theory) is due to her refusal to recognise fundamentally different kinds of subjectivity in men and women. Because of the close link which is assumed on both sides of the debate to exist between subjectivity and the symbolic, this amounts to her refusal to recognise that discourse is also sexed. As Rosi Braidotti puts it: 'On the level of discursive production, then, sexual difference counts for nothing' (Braidotti 1989a: 231). It is on these grounds that the last two, at least superficially feminist, positions of Kristeva's referred to above are regarded as both conservative and anti-feminist by these stronger advocates of sexual difference, for they both presuppose that the subjectivity of both sexes will be constituted in the same way. Kristeva's insistence that revolutionary change requires the movement of the semiotic is predicated upon the assumption that the subjectivity of both sexes is constituted by the unity of the semiotic and the symbolic and that therefore both sexes will be affected by such changes in the same kind of way.[16] Nor does the attribution of a special interest to women in such revolutionary change do anything to undercut the underlying idea that subjectivity, both as such and therefore also at the level of discourse where it manifests, is not sexed, if this interest is due only to the circumstances of their positions as mothers, and is in principle no different from the interest of dissident intellectuals, psychoanalysts or whoever. Rather than an affirmation of the revolutionary importance of women this latter thesis is therefore seen as amounting to a denial of the revolutionary potential of female subjects *qua* female subjects (Braidotti 1989a : 233). (Kristeva does, of course, follow Freud in positing an important difference between male and female subjectivity – due to the different effects of the castration experience. But this difference consists only in the fact of different psychological histories resulting from different circumstances and so is not a difference which is intrinsic to the sexes as such.) If the actualisation of different-sexed subjectivities is thought to be the crucial issue then both of the above positions must be seen as backward and conservative.

The question which now needs to be answered to make sense of this argument concerns its basic assumption. Why does feminism depend upon the assertion of a 'strong' sexual difference, a difference so fundamental that it determines both subjectivity and discourse? More specifically, why is it assumed that an insistence on fundamental sexual difference would be able to overcome the inherent conservatism of a Lacanian conception of the subject? To put the same question differently: feminists of strong difference correctly perceive, I think, that Kristeva is conservative about the possibility of fundamental change in the Lacanian/Derridean kind of symbolic, which operates on allegedly violent dualisms and which is masculine in the sense described above. Why do they think, though, that an insistence on 'strong' sexual difference will enable them to maintain this broad conception of the subject and assert radical feminist possibilities at the same time? Unfortunately, this question is not often explicitly addressed, for the equation between feminism and the insistence on difference has become so automatic that the two are now assumed to presuppose each other. Nevertheless an answer can be reconstructed.

Suppose that we are radical feminists who accept, for whatever reasons, the broad Lacanian or deconstructionist conception of the subject but who do not wish to accept the conservative and patriarchal consequences. The standard radical move in the face of an argument to conservative conclusions is to insist that what appears to be necessary and universal is in fact only a contingent and historical result, that is, it is to argue with reference to history that what appears to be unchangeable is in fact changeable. But this move is not open to us here, for the particular framework we have adopted is explicit that the subjective formation it posits and which is here in question is prior to society and history.[17] (This is a consequence of locating the problematic aspects of the subject in the subject/object distinction itself.) But there might be another way of relativising the absolutist assumptions other than through history. This would be to insist that the subjective formation they describe belongs to only one kind of subject – the male subject.[18] What appears to be universal would then only be male. Female subjectivity, the subjective formation of women, would at least potentially not coincide with insertion into the masculine symbolic order. There may be a distinctively female symbolic.[19] The idea would be that subjectivity is necessarily sexed, that it is either male or female and that poststructuralist theory has recognised only its male form. (This does not mean, as the resulting debate on essentialism has made clear, either that the sexed character of subjectivity is fixed or unavailable to the other sex, but only that it comes in forms specifically appropriate to men or to women. As Rosi Braidotti argues, the thesis could be interpreted as the idea that awareness of oneself as female (or, I assume, male) is an essential constituent of subjectivity (Braidotti 1989b).) If such a move were to work then it may provide a way, after all, of beginning with Lacan and concluding with radical feminism. Let us then follow through its implications.

What follows, more or less intelligibly and more or less consistently, are most of the major 'Irigarian' theses which almost all except the enthusiasts have found so bewildering. My conjecture is that the above move is central to the 'logic' of how these theses are generated, although this is rarely if ever made apparent.[20] My further point, though, is that what we shall find after these theses have been generated is that the position as a whole has landed in an insoluble contradiction. Clearly, I am anticipating here a reinforcement of my argument in the last chapter that if one is interested in radical conclusions then a framework which locates political issues in the formation of the subject as such will not do. In other words, I want to show that poststructuralist feminism has been led into strange ideas about ultimate differences between men and women by assumptions which are themselves highly questionable.

Now if we make the move of claiming that the Lacanian or Derridean subject is the specifically male subject (leaving aside the question of the grounds for such an assertion) then we no longer maintain with Kristeva that women, like men, are necessarily inserted into a masculine symbolic order, but we insist, more strongly, that in so far as women attempt to adopt that form of subjectivity – which may well be the only one available to them – they mimic men. Lacanian subjectivity is no longer masculine, in other words, but rather it is male. And if our culture, by disguising it as human subjectivity, makes a place for male subjectivity alone, then women have no place – they are in exile.[21] They have no symbolic and no language and have the subjectivity, therefore, of a hysteric whose anguish cannot be expressed in language but only in physical symptoms. And these are just the sorts of things that 'strong difference' feminists do say, often in the name of Irigaray. It seems that some sense can be made of these apparently strange theses when it is seen that they follow directly from the attempt to relativise Lacan for radical feminist purposes in the only way possible, namely by insisting that he and other poststructuralists describe only a male subject. But these theses are only the consequences of such a relativising move. The question which must arise, assuming that only male subjectivity is recognised, is what has become of female subjectivity and what hopes are there for it?

The answer to the first question emerges when we look more closely at the alleged nature of the male subject. It involves another obvious move, which also reinforces the original position that the poststructuralist subject is the male subject, by offering something like an argument for it. It consists in returning to the thesis of the dualisms allegedly posited by the fully formed subject in a way which would show that these are more appropriate to male than female subjects. To repeat: the general idea here is that the subject constitutes itself by positing a division between 'self' and 'other' in order to maintain the necessary repression of 'différance', the semiotic, the unconscious or whatever. This 'self/other' division is then supposedly maintained and reproduced by the dualisms which consequently constrain the subject's thinking. What can now be fruitfully maintained from the point of view of the current project is the idea that the first and most basic of these dualisms, both in terms of psychological chronology and therefore perhaps also in some tenuous logical sense, is that in which the subject distinguishes himself from his mother by positing her as an object. It can be further suggested that it must be a specifically male subject who does this because it would be distinguishing itself as subject and as male from its mother as object and as female.

Such a move would be going beyond the basic picture in two ways: first, it would be being maintained that the dualisms by which the subject constitutes itself necessarily oppose subject to object, where the basic picture insists only that it is a self/other distinction without the implication that this must at the same time be a distinction between subject and object (although, of course, it may be). Second, it is asserted that the most basic of these differentiations is also sexed, in such a way that maleness emerges as essentially 'of a subject' as opposed to femaleness which is essentially 'of an object'. It follows from this that the Fichtean/Derridean/poststructuralist subject (now properly a male subject) has no capacity to recognise other subjects as such since it is essentially a subject/object formation. These ideas, I am sure, will be familiar to those at all acquainted with poststructuralist feminist discussion, even if their rationale has not been clear. (Margaret Whitford, widely regarded as the author of the authoritative account of Irigaray in English, interprets her as making these last two moves, although not for the reasons I am suggesting here (Whitford 1991: 45).) The persuasiveness of these moves to those with a feminist consciousness, I imagine, is that it brings in to the discussion the 'real life' experience that men do very often seem to be backward in recognising women as subjects. What is assumed, however, and it is an assumption which we shall shortly see creates insoluble difficulties, is that this incapacity, if not quite thought of as innate, nevertheless is thought to stem from the very construction of the male subject *qua* subject. It is assumed, in other words, that these concrete 'real life' problems can be dealt with by a framework which locates them in the formation of the subject as such. To see where all this leads we must first get back to the question of what 'strong difference' feminism thinks has happened to female subjectivity.

If now we were to focus on the basic objectification of the mother as the key to this specifically male subject, we might want to proceed to say that what is repressed in its constitution is something more than the relationship with the mother's body which precedes the differentiation of self from the world and which would have to be repressed in any form of subjectivity, male or female – in something more than Kristeva's semiotic, in other words. For the division which constitutes the consciousness of the subject as well as the division between his conscious and unconscious aspects now becomes pertinent. If this former division is based on the objectification of the mother, which on the above assumptions is also the objectification of women, then what could also be said to be repressed is the subjectivity of women – women as subjects. The answer to the question of what has happened to female subjectivity is that it has been repressed by way of a fundamental objectification of the mother and of women and that this objectification is constitutive of male subjectivity. Male subjects, this means, cannot recognise women as subjects and because male subjectivity is the only culturally recognised form then women have no alternative but to adopt it also, so denying to themselves a form of subjectivity appropriate to them as women. It is not only a feminine semiotic, common to the subjectivity of both sexes, which is now thought to be repressed, but any form of subjectivity which is specifically appropriate to women.

There would be, then, two aspects of repression to the dominant male subjectivity, one a quasi-necessary sex-neutral aspect and the other both contingent and sexed. The former refers to the repression of the unconscious, the relation to the mother's body etc., the latter to any recognition of female subjectivity. The positing of these two aspects allows for a retention of the broad poststructuralist, deconstructive conception of the subject (due to the first) and an insistence on the possibility of change (due to the second). Before we see whether we do indeed have a solution to the problem of how to be at the same time a radical feminist and a poststructuralist of the Derrida/ Lacan mould, let's briefly consider how these changes might come about and what they would mean. Once again familiar propositions from 'strong difference' feminism provide the answer.

The possibility for change now lies in the emergence of a distinctively female subjectivity, that is, in women becoming subjects *as women* rather than, as hitherto, as men.[22] Given, still, poststructuralist assumptions about the coincidence of language and subjectivity, this means women speaking, writing, communicating, etc. as women. Which idea in turn naturally leads to that of a female language and a female symbolic. The point here is that if the patriarchal structure depends on women being silenced as women, then their speaking as women will unhinge it.[23] And so we should advocate the emergence of women's discourse, women's theory, even women's science (although this time there is some kind of theoretical rationale behind this last position). Another essential and much discussed aspect of the emergence of women *female* subjects is the corresponding transformation of the mother/ daughter relation. For if the idea is that the male subject (including the women *male* subject produced by the current order) is constituted by way of defining himself as subject against the mother as object, then it follows that women being of the same sex as their mother would have to constitute themselves as female subjects in a subject–subject relation with their mothers.[24] The female subject would necessarily be constituted as capable of recognising other subjects as such, unlike the male subject which recognises only objects. There would seem to be some hope for the future generally in the emergence of women subjects.

The difference between women writing or speaking and their doing so as women is an important one in Irigaray's theorising and it is much discussed in 'strong difference' feminism. Some sense can be made of it, in the way I just have, by showing where the idea comes from. It is notoriously much harder to make sense of it in terms of understanding what it might amount to, what it might look like, as it were. In this connection we are given descriptions of the morphology of the female body and suggestions to the effect that female communication would be fluid as opposed to linear, with multiple rather than single meanings etc. – the sorts of suggestions that more 'straight' feminists find disturbing because they appear to amount to an abandonment of the requirements of rationality. I don't want to enter the debate at that level, although my sympathies are with those who think that no useful or clear conception of women writing as women can be formulated. This is because I think it can be easily shown that, leaving this question aside, the line of argument does not have to be pursued very far before it leads into a basic contradiction and so becomes untenable.

CONTRADICTIONS IN DIFFERENCE

The contradiction becomes apparent when we ask the question: what happens to male subjectivity in the process of emergence of female subjectivity? If it is predicated upon the silence of women as women, that is upon the repression of women as subjects, then either it must remain completely out of touch with the new reality, when women are no longer silent and become specifically female subjects, or it must change. If the former, and male subjectivity continues to be formed by an original objectification of the mother and by implication of female subjectivity, then in the new circumstances where women themselves do not collude with this denial, it will be a semi-autistic kind of subjectivity. In the old circumstances where, according to the theory, it was able to impose itself as the only form and women were in fact silenced as women, there was a degree of reality to the positing of women as objects. But that degree of reality would now disappear and men, at least if they adopted specifically male subjectivity rather than the new form of female subjectivity, would be cut adrift from women. This is what must happen if the 'maleness' of male subjectivity is thought to consist even partly in the original objectification of women.

Although the question I am asking here is not addressed very explicitly by the advocates of 'strong' difference – and, I think, for good reason – I do not think that this is what they envisage. I believe that they assume that the second possibility, namely that male subjectivity will also change, is both what is likely and what is desirable. But the difficulty with this is that it is no longer clear where the 'maleness' of male subjectivity lies. For if male subjectivity is no longer based on the objectification of the mother then, like female subjectivity, it would also be formed by way of the recognition of her as a subject. It, too, would be a subject–subject form of subjectivity. And that of course would be 'a good thing' – except for the fact that the theoretical strategy which leads us to this conclusion now seems to come unstuck. The problem now is of where to locate the difference between the two forms of subjectivity. Both forms are subject to subject, neither form is able to or wanting to impose itself as the only form. And both forms, we are to assume, are available to both sexes.

This *is* a problem because the starting position which, in conjunction with 'mainstream' poststructuralism, generated all the controversial 'strong difference' theses, was that subjectivity must be sexed and so there are, at least potentially, two different forms. This difference is quite explicitly not a contingent one, due to social or historical circumstances, but is fundamental in some way. (That it is intended to be fundamental is shown by the debate on essentialism which it has generated.) Moreover, it must be fundamental, in the constitution of subjectivity as such, prior to social and historical influences, or else the whole point of the retention of the poststructuralist conception of the subject is lost. From the beginning this was a conception which was thought to be necessary because it depended upon issues far deeper than those of society or history, for it depended upon our very ability to conceptualise and identify ourselves as separate beings. If different kinds of subjectivity are being posited then the difference must also be at this fundamental level. But if this fundamental difference must now be thought to disappear due to the effects of a social movement then the whole position becomes untenable.

One possible way of retaining the notion of a fundamental difference in the subjectivity of the sexes together with the assumption of a radical transformation in both forms, and a way which is in fact taken by leading advocates of 'strong' difference, is to locate the required difference in the recognition of oneself as male or female. This 'ontological' understanding of sexual difference asserts that awareness of oneself as sexed is an essential aspect of subjectivity.[25] I do not want to take issue with the contention itself, for the prior point is that, whether true or false, it cannot do the job it would be supposed to do. For what was thought to be repressed in the construction of male subjectivity was not just the mere recognition that we are women, no matter how fundamental this recognition may be thought to be, but a whole way of being a subject. The simple awareness of oneself as male or female does not on its own imply a different way of being a subject.

The problem, I think, results from a basic confusion built into the strategy from the outset over whether the alleged male poststructuralist subject has the subjectivity of the powerful and the dominant or whether it has the subjectivity specifically of men. The former position implies that it is a subjectivity which can be changed through social and historical influences, the latter implies that it is not. It is, then, only the latter position which can be held in the spirit of poststructuralism itself. And it is the latter position which I hope I have shown in fact generates the strange and controversial theses of this form of feminist thought. But when, through the latter position, the whole enterprise falls apart, the tendency, I think, is to fall back on the former historical account and insinuate that it is only the subjectivity of dominance which is disappearing, overlooking the fact that the alleged fundamental maleness of this subjectivity has also disappeared.

It is by means of this kind of poststructuralism of difference that feminist theory seems to have come into its own in the sense of there now being an argued position for the notion of specifically feminist theory. For this is now understood to be the discourse of women constituting themselves as women, with a distinctively female subjectivity. It must therefore be a different kind of theory from previous theory, which on this sort of account has now to emerge as specifically male theory. Many feminist poststructuralists believe that engagement in women's writing, discourse, theory or whatever, is the specific contribution they have to make both to feminism and to poststructuralism. With respect to the latter, however, they complain that 'mainstream' poststructuralists tend to overlook their contribution.[26] I think they are right, that they do develop poststructuralist assumptions in a distinctive way and that other poststructuralists are uneasy about it. I suspect, though, that the reason for this unease is that the bizarre and extreme conclusions which feminists have developed (with some consistency, after all) in attempting to use this framework, which purports to be radical for genuinely radical ends, reveals how difficult this is to do. Tacitly, therefore, this kind of feminist poststructuralism of 'strong difference' points to the inherent conservativeness of the framework which I tried to establish in the last chapter.

A DIFFERENT DIVIDED SUBJECT

The instincts of Irigaray and those inspired by her, that women have been silenced and that repression involves more, therefore, than a pre-conceptual semiotic, for it extends further to something quite specific which demands articulation, can be retained and developed within the alternative conception of the divided subject described above. Such a direction would enable questions of the formation of the subject as such to be distinguished from questions of personal and psychological change. Kristeva would then be seen to be answering the former while Irigaray's political instincts would be pursued in relation to the latter. The choice between the conservative conclusions forced by taking Kristeva's approach and the barely intelligible and ultimately inconsistent ones which result from following Irigaray would no longer be required. One could retain both Irigaray's radicalism and Kristeva's important understanding of the semiotic.

The second conception of the divided subject as outlined above is not necessarily incompatible with a theory of the subject as formed, although, since Juliet Mitchell's *Psychoanalysis and Feminism* (1974), it has widely been taken to be so.[27] Nor, therefore, is it incompatible with a theory which might want to suggest that the formation of the subject necessarily involves aspects of subjectivity being rendered unconscious. As a theory of the sorts of things that can happen either to fully formed subjects who then become damaged or about damage which can occur during the process of subject formation, it is simply about different sorts of things. In line with the considerations I was putting forward in the last chapter, it could be said to be about some forms of subjectivity rather than about what constitutes it. (Although obviously the two sorts of theories may well interrelate.) If feminists were, then, to approach the questions of psychological change which concern them primarily by way of this alternative conception of the divided subject, they would no longer be conflating questions of the necessary constitution of the human subject with more specific, political issues.

Although this approach to divisions in the subject appears in the psychoanalytic literature as a theory of the splitting of a personality which can occur as the result of trauma, it is an analysis which can be readily cast in terms of power and, moreover, the kind of power which silences. For the splitting whereby one aspect of the personality, that which rarely if ever directly expresses itself, is unknown to the rest of the personality which does speak freely, can clearly be characterised as the dominance of one personality fragment over the other.[28] Moreover, this exercise of power within the psyche as it were, being regarded as a contingent phenomenon, can itself be seen to be both due to and to contribute to external relations of power, also now viewed as contingent.

Such a framework would appear to be tailor-made to articulate the insight that there is much about women's experience which has been silenced, and that this silencing is internally as well as externally imposed – the insight that the 'strong difference' feminists find absent from Kristeva's account. This 'divided self' approach has the immediate advantage over the 'strong difference' position that it can posit the kind of psychological change necessary not to collude with power as something which is non-mysterious and perfectly attainable, even though it might be difficult. For such change would now be conceived as a conflict between the two separated aspects of the psyche, a conflict which would take place if the dominated side became stronger for some reason, of if the whole split became untenable. A psychological conflict it may be, but not one which necessarily leads to a complete unravelling of one's very subjecthood (although in some cases it may do). It has all the advantages over Irigaray, it would seem, which in the last chapter I argued that Marx has over Hegel when it comes to understanding political change.

However, since it is a general theory, when it comes to the question of what it is which is repressed in this divided psyche, the answer does not come out immediately in sexed terms as we have just seen that it does in the 'strong difference' account. It would not be a distinctively female subjectivity, nor a distinctively female discourse which is silenced. What then would the silencing of women amount to on this framework? And why and how should feminists use this mainly psychological account in a directly political and feminist way?

LIBERATION THEORY AND THE DIVIDED SELF

It should already be clear that what would be thought to be repressed on the 'divided self' framework would not be, as in the poststructuralist approach, the preconditions of subjecthood but rather one of its aspects. In line with the more usual psychoanalytic understanding, the objects of repression would be thoughts, desires, and feelings, the kinds of things which belong to already-formed subjects, which in principle can be articulated and which sometimes need to be. The 'silencing' or repression of women would then be regarded as an instance of this more general kind of repression. And precisely because it would be seen in this way, this psychological framework would provide a straightforward way of articulating Irigaray's instinct that in order for the position of women to shift, something which has not been spoken must be spoken and that this, therefore, cannot be in principle unsayable. But now, because what is repressed is thought to be an aspect of subjects and not their conditions of existence, this 'speaking' would not necessarily be supposed to lead to a revolution in language, categories of thought and the most fundamental ways of being a subject. The 'speaking' of what has been repressed in women would change their psychology, but not immediately and in the same move, logic, science, metaphysics and whatever else.

The question is now raised: even if such a framework does accommodate this fundamental feminist thesis why, even so, would we use it? Why not revert immediately to liberation theory which, as we saw, also operates on the idea of a division with the psyche (where the search for conditional love works by way of repressing the need for unconditional love) and which also develops the idea that women (and other oppressed groups) have been silenced? Why bother with any psychoanalytic account of the divided self at all? The answer is that although the two respective approaches to divisions within the self are different – for they posit different divisions within the psyche – they have sufficient in common to mutually enhance each other. The different divisions within the psyche can be shown to connect with each other and the resulting understanding can be shown to have the capacity to address fundamental problems which raise themselves, only to be left hanging when the two approaches remain separate. To really bring these two conceptions together would, of course, be a major work, but I can conclude this minor work by sketching briefly how it could be done and where the benefits might lie.

To begin with, if we consider some elementary Freud in the light of these two theories (liberation theory and the non-Lacanian theory of the divided self) we can see how they could be brought into line with each other to constitute, perhaps, a unified theoretical approach. First, the account of the divided self we are now considering is such that no universal explanation would be offered for the dividing of subjects – a variety of traumas or psycho-logically untenable situations, it would be assumed, might be dealt with by a splitting of the self into fragments, that is by a failure of personal integration. Nevertheless, the basic picture contained in Freud's theory of the resolution of the Oedipus complex could readily be accommodated within such a theory as one very common example of a 'dividing' process. For, as is well known, Freud maintains that repression can be induced either by a need to identify with a father, in the male case, or alternatively, in the female case, by a conviction of one's own castration resulting in the need to seek approval first from one's father and then from other males.[29] These two formations could then be seen as dividing processes resulting in a repressing father-oriented sub-personality being pitted against a repressed childish sub-personality. They could be broadly regarded as the result of trauma, since one formation is thought, following Freud, to be brought about by fear of the father and the other by a sense of oneself as deficient (castrated), manifesting in overwhelm-ing need for his approval. Now if this resolution of the Oedipus complex is further seen, as Freud would have seen it, as the process of separation from the mother, then the repressed sub-personality would be that of the child still dependent on its mother – the child before it has attained any significant ability to regulate its own behaviour.[30] And if, following Freud, this sort of case is regarded as so common as to be typical, then such a development of the theory of the divided self would posit as both a typical and a fundamental

division that between repressed mother-dependent aspects of the personality
and a repressing father-identified part or superego.

We can begin to bring this 'divided self' version of Freud into line with
liberation theory when we recognise that what is crucial in this splitting is the
fact that the father (and hence maleness) comes to be seen by the child as
superior to the mother (and hence femaleness). For this means that the
repressing part of the personality must be understood to operate essentially
on the 'higher/lower' form of evaluation of human beings discussed in Part I.
At the same time, there would be no reason to posit that the differential
evaluation of human beings is present in the repressed parts of the child's
personality and every reason to assume, therefore, that it is not. It looks as
though some contact with this repressed part of the psyche might be necessary to overcome the differential evaluation of people which is central to the
psychology of power.

But before we now, as feminists, join the rush to find the 'lost child within',
it is important to recognise that while liberation theory and this kind of
'divided self' psychology might both posit the same or at least a similar
repressing aspect of the psyche, they are nevertheless concerned with different (although almost certainly related) intra-psychic conflicts. For the conflict
between an aspect of a child's psyche and a repressing superego which meas-
ures people as more or less 'important' is a different conflict than that
between this same repressing force and a highly conscious ethic that 'respect
is due to the human being as such and is not a matter of degree'. A child's
psyche is marked, I should think, more by an absence of a developed ethic of
how to relate to others than the active presence of that broadly Christian one
of liberation theory. When the typical repression of Freud's resolution of the
Oedipus complex sets in, it would be between aspects of a child which have
not yet learned to relate to others and an authoritarian superego which
induces that 'higher/lower' way of relating shown by liberation theory to be at
the heart of what is called oppression. But the conflict which concerns liberation theory is between this already-instituted superego and an alternative,
non-oppressive way of relating.

Nevertheless the two theories can be brought into connection with each
other in ways that could be of benefit to both. In the case of liberation
theory, first of all, it was almost certainly the absence of anything but a
surface psychological understanding which was one of the factors responsible for its practical failure. What was not grasped when women were
attempting to apply liberation theory to their lives was that in opposing the
part of the psyche which measured the value of people differentially, the
hold of something akin to a Freudian superego was being challenged and
loosened, with the inevitable result that all kinds of hitherto repressed psy-
chic material was being tapped. The high incidence of women bound up with
Women's Liberation who subsequently had psychotic episodes or other
kinds of severe mental disturbances testifies to the fact that this challenge
was not just words and that little was understood of the psychological pro-

cesses involved. (The rapid transformation of the notion of 'the personal is political' into a set of abstract and repressive rules also testifies to a lack of understanding of the nature of the repressive part of the psyche.) If, however, liberation theory were to incorporate an account of the repressions which can occur in early childhood, it would be in a position to understand the depth of the psychological processes it may be unleashing in striving to evolve a consciousness incompatible with power. And clearly, the sort of 'divided self' version of Freud I have just sketched would be tailor-made for this purpose.

It is perhaps less clear what the psychological theory of the divided self might have to gain from liberation theory. The prevailing understanding of psychotherapy is that psychological understanding is sought for its own sake and that no morals can or should be imposed on those undergoing it. The sort of ethic, then, which is the guiding inspiration of feminism and liberation theory would appear to be out of place in this context. If people want to discover their 'lost child', it is usually said that it is up to them where they go from there and that it is not the concern of psychotherapy. The 'child' itself can lead them.

This, though, is without the argument I made in Part I to the effect that personal autonomy does not mean a complete freedom to choose one's moral position, for the reason that it can only be attained by way of an actual incorporation of the morality of respect being due to the person as such – an actual refusal to make human respect a matter of degree. If this argument were to be accepted, it would follow that any 'divided self' psychology which aimed to be more than explanatory and which genuinely valued autonomy would have to incorporate aspects of liberation theory. It would have to be recognised that the recovery of the 'lost child within' could only be integrated into an autonomous personality as the old repressive 'higher/lower' part of the psyche gave way to one centred upon this human and humane ethic. Otherwise, with a straight punch-up between the 'lost child' and the Freudian superego, all that could be really expected is that the repressive superego would simply reassert itself, very possibly by way of using the aspirations of 'the child' as a means of repression. And indeed, given what appears to be the increasing hysteria associated with people discovering what they see as their own lost and abused child, the freedom with which others are accused of abuse, the abandonment of normal rules of evidence in establishing victim status, this seems to be very much what has happened with this sort of psychotherapy. The powerful and liberating insights of R.D. Laing have been transformed into an irrational and self-righteous aggression. The point would be then that, while a challenge to that part of oneself which is caught up in status and which does not understand that respect is due to the human being as such must lead to renewed contact with the repressed child within, such contact on its own, without a different ethic to guide it, leads nowhere. In truth, one is no longer a child and one can – and must – develop from within oneself a new relationship with what is now only one's 'inner' child. The emphasis is on the 'again' in the injunction that unless you are born again you shall not enter the kingdom of heaven.

This kind of integration of psychoanalysis with liberation theory would extend the scope of the latter beyond wisdom, where this is understood as that self-understanding of the soul which is at the same time the understanding of the good (in the Socratic sense that self-understanding is understanding of what the soul perceives as good and not just that self-understanding is itself a good). It would bring together this sort of wisdom (the particular form of which I described in Part I) with a purportedly more objective or scientific account of psychological development.[31] The synthesis is needed, I am suggesting, because on the one hand, without the moral understanding of liberation theory psychoanalysis is unable to adequately grasp the nature of personal autonomy and it is inhibited, therefore, in its ability to assist in its attainment. On the other hand, it is largely because of its relative lack of psychological knowledge that liberation theory was doomed to function as an abstract moral position, divorced from life and unable to become that kind of knowledge of the whole person, of mind, feeling and behavioural disposition which is wisdom.

The aspiration for freedom all too easily becomes realised in the form of increasing repression, however much the latter uses the language of freedom itself. To understand why this is so, we have to understand ourselves. And to understand ourselves we have to, with Socrates, continue the search for the good. The Christian morality that we are all equal before God may not be our ticket to heaven but it is one of the elements of this self-knowledge and so of what it is to be human.

Conclusion

A man who really fights for justice must lead a private, not a public life, if he is to survive for even a short time.

(Plato)

I have been trying to show that there was something very special about the Women's Liberation movement, something which made it different in kind from most social and political movements. This specialness consisted in the fact that it was a *social* movement, engaged in the search for a personal and individual ethic of a Socratic nature, that is for an ethic which recognises that the search for the good is the primary focus of human life, which is essentially tied to a behavioural disposition to seek that good and which is sought more against than with any prevailing social norms since, typically, an element of the latter is that easy assumption of certainty which is incompatible with any search for the good.

I made it clear in the preface that I am not specifically advocating that feminism return to this Women's Liberation ethic, summed up in the thesis 'the personal is political'. For the circumstances which brought about this strange synthesis of the intense moral searching of individuals with a social movement are, I suspect, long passed. Were this general moral position, discovered (or rather rediscovered) by Women's Liberation, to be once again taken seriously by large numbers of people in the context of some kind of movement – and this is unlikely – I think that it would, perhaps, find its point of application less in opposition to the assumed superiority of men over women than in the rejection of the increasing emphasis placed on 'appearances', both on physical appearance and on the appearance of achievement and efficiency. The evil activity of measuring the worth of human beings as such now flourishes rather more in the latter terms than in the former. Moreover, the appropriate focus of a women's movement is now, I should think, of a more practical political nature. In recovering the forgotten moral position of Women's Liberation, part of my aim has been simply to preserve this valuable legacy by insisting that along with the many social and political achievements of second wave feminism there is also this other contribution to human life, one made on a more universal and enduring plane.

But there is something else, also of enduring importance. The very existence of Women's Liberation, no matter how short-lived, leaves us with a question which I for one don't know how to answer but which strikes me as worthwhile, if not necessary, to pursue. This question is also a part of the legacy of Women's Liberation and arises from its special nature, in which the sort of moral quest usually regarded as antithetical to the political life is combined with a political movement itself. Let me explain.

The substance of my argument has concerned the failure of Women's Liberation in its own terms as a social movement based on a deeply moral position. For the political success of the women's movement has been possible, it would seem, only by way of the repression and distortion of its morality. This failure, I suggested, reproduced the sort of fate one might generally expect of the kind of morality at issue, a fate symbolised by the deaths of Socrates and Jesus, the stories of which show how the search for the good is likely to be destroyed by those who are compelled to present themselves as, as it were, already good. Since political movements tend, for good reason, to be populated by the latter, it would appear that the failure of Women's Liberation is just the result of the fact that it was aiming at the impossible in attempting to base a political life on something fundamentally opposed to it. If we come to that conclusion we should end, perhaps, by endorsing Socrates' rejection of the political life on the grounds that it cannot be reconciled with the search for the good. But it is not as simple at that.

What is at stake, I think, are two opposing traditions about the nature of wisdom, the necessity for a reconciliation between which is demanded by the experience of Women's Liberation, despite the fact that it was unable to bring it about. One of these traditions stresses the necessity of withdrawal from the world as a precondition for wisdom and is usually presented in elitist terms, the other emphasises non-separation from the world and is fundamentally anti-elitist. The reconciliation of these traditions would be effected by the development of a political and/or social life which both makes possible and depends upon individual moral searching. It is in this way that Women's Liberation was an argument for something it was, itself, unable to effect. This, briefly, is how.

The tradition which focuses on wisdom as withdrawal from the world becomes elitist when it interprets this withdrawal as a rejection of 'the masses' and maintains that only in isolation from 'the herd' can one attain wisdom. Some in this tradition go further and speak of the necessary 'veiling' of wisdom such that 'the masses' interpret it in one way and the enlightened, penetrating the veil, in another. Repellent as I find these ideas, they are not without their strong basis in the Women's Liberation position I have expounded here, in which the transition from a life lived 'in the opinions of others' (and so veiled) to a life led on the basis of self-knowledge is the central focus. That this transition is thought of as a passage through a 'dark night of the soul' provides further support for the idea that wisdom is found only in isolation. Given the value placed on wisdom, it seems, perhaps, not too hard to proceed from the recognition of the necessity of a kind of isolation from one's fellows to the assumption that by way of this isolation one has become superior to them and so to a perspective where they now appear as 'herd-like'. I think that it is at this point that the association between the search for wisdom and elitism often gets a hold. The immediate point, though, is that although the elitism itself is absent from the Women's Liberation conception, the basis of this elitist tradition is very present in the recognition that for a time at least one must set one's face against one's fellows.

The reason elitism does not get a hold in the Women's Liberation conception is because it combines the insights of this first tradition with those of the second, opposed tradition in which wisdom is thought to be possible only as an act of non-separation from others. Here it is thought to imply the kind of self-knowledge where nothing human is regarded as alien to oneself, where one does not search for the mote in one's brother's eye because one is too aware of the mote in one's own eye and where one does not, therefore, cast stones, for one is not, oneself, without sin. I have tried to show that this opposed conception, according to which wisdom, self-love and love of others all mutually presuppose each other, is part of the Women's Liberation conception by placing the latter in the Christian tradition. And it is the fact that it belongs to this more democratic tradition which enabled, if not required, this morality to manifest in a social movement. For this kind of wisdom is not only about discovering the 'humanness' in one's own nature but, since it moves from there to both an awareness of the need for love and to the ability to love, it must be expressed in a 'solidarity' of the kind I have described. It must, that is, be expressed, *with* others in some way.

The point is that 'liberation theory' coherently combines the basis of both these traditions concerning the nature of wisdom by maintaining that what it is which is understood in one's necessarily isolated search is just the essentially social character of one's nature (by which I mean one's need to be recognised as a member of the species whose value therefore is not measurable). This forces clarity on the fact that the rejection of social and political life necessary in the search for the good is not a rejection of one's fellows as such but only of the attachment to 'honour' or 'status' necessary to successfully live the orthodox conception of the political life. It is a rejection, only, of an immersion in the prevailing social norms, where this immersion is based on the compulsion to have a social place. The apparent incompatibility between the elitist and non-elitist conceptions of wisdom falls away, as does the antithesis between withdrawal from the world and a social existence. It may be thought, therefore, that the legacy of Women's Liberation is not so much a question about what to do about these different traditions as it is a possible answer to such a question.

This rendering of rival traditions as compatible and mutually enhancing, however, takes place only at the level of 'pure' theory. That there is here no 'real life' solution to the opposition between the political life and the autonomous individual search for wisdom is shown by the very failure of

Women's Liberation. The practical synthesis only lasted a moment before the movement transformed into an orthodox political movement strongly attached to and motivated by considerations of social status. Given that, as I have stressed, the wisdom being sought, at least implicitly, was of the kind to manifest in action and so bridge any gap between theory and practice, this failure of Women's Liberation was a very real one. The question we are left with is how Women's Liberation wisdom might manifest itself socially and not just privately, given that we are persuaded of the necessity of this. It is this question of how to pursue our essentially human search for the good, both in solidarity with others so that we do become more fully human, and autonomously so that we stop reinforcing the workings of power, which is the most valuable legacy of Women's Liberation.

Notes

INDRODUCTION: THE LOSING OF WISDOM

1 The classical notion of 'critical theory' which I use here is that which is derived from Marx, propagated mainly by Habermas, and refers to theory in which explanation is thought to be secondary to the aim of social change. For a detailed account of this conception of critical theory, see Guess (1981). In recent years the notion of 'critical theory' has been broadened to include just about any theory which contains social criticism.

2 Since Foucault has been widely embraced as *the* theorist of power, the notion of taking a stance in opposition to power per se, rather than resisting its specific localised manifestations in a form of resistance doomed, itself, to develop into a form of power, has been regarded as naive, or worse, as 'totalising'. In this context, it could be pointed out that this attitude is based on confusing what are in fact distinct issues. One issue concerns the moral basis of one's opposition – whether it is to power as such or to the fact that someone else holds it – and the other concerns projections of likely social developments. The two are logically indifferent.

3 In this reference to Socrates I am assuming the interpretation advanced by, amongst others, Gregory Vlastos, according to which the distinction between the 'real' historical Socrates and the one who is 'Plato's mouthpiece' consists in the intention of the former to seek answers to the 'what is virtue?' question in terms of 'this worldly' considerations rather than in either transcendent or metaphysical terms (Vlastos 1991: 45–80). It is only to the question posed by this 'real' Socrates that the analysis of liberation theory can be construed as a reply. The metaphysics of forms is an answer to a different question, incorporating different assumptions. (See the discussion in Part III for a different argument about the importance of not conflating ethical and metaphysical questions.) It should be noted, however, that if liberation theory can be construed as a response to the question of the 'real' historical Socrates, it cannot be construed as a result of Socratic dialogue. Rather, as the following chapters show, it comes from an attempt to struggle with 'real life' experiences.

4 Gregory Vlastos suggests that the 'strangeness' of Socrates' philosophy is one of its essential aspects (Vlastos 1991: 1–19). I have, I am sure, taken from Vlastos the general idea that the strangeness of a philosophy might be an indication of its profundity.

5 In Plato's *Apology* Socrates discusses why he did not enter politics.

6 This identification is most clearly articulated in Plato's *Meno*.

7 Sara Evans (Evans 1979: 29–35) documents the Christian background of many of the early feminists who became feminists as a result of their experiences in the civil rights movement.

8 Liberation theory is quite closely related to liberation theology. For an introduction to the latter see Boff and Boff (1987)

9 By 'Women's Liberation' I mean the radical women's movement which emerged in the late 1960s, lasted until the early 1970s and adopted that name. It was the first form of that 'second wave' of feminism which is still flourishing.

10 This claim must be qualified in several ways. First, the fact that Women's Liberation involved an intense exploration of the personal and the private in terms of power considerations is definitely remembered by some, at least. See, for example, Rowbotham (1989), especially Part One and the interviews in Evans (1979). What does not seem to be remembered, however, is that there was a theory accompanying this. It is more difficult to reference the absence of an idea than its presence but see the discussion at the beginning of Chapter 1 for a description of (and references to) some of the relevant material.

Second, 'feminist standpoint theory' (for a 'seminal' account see Harstock (1983)), which is regarded as a major position in feminist epistemology, contains some elements in common with what I am calling 'liberation theory'. The former, however, is an epistemological theory and refers in very general terms to the role of 'women's experiences' in the development of theory. Women's Liberation theory, by way of contrast, elaborates upon the specific character of these experiences which is necessary for its role in their transformation. This central notion of the transformation of experience is absent from 'feminist standpoint theory', which is a highly abstract version of the ideas of Women's Liberation. Perhaps the strongest surviving remnants of Women's Liberation theory are to be found in the psychotherapy developed by Susie Orbach and others (see, for example, Eichenbaum and Orbach 1982), although it should be noted that the political emphasis of the former has here been watered down by the latter into a therapeutic concern.

Third, however, neither of the above qualifications – failure to remember that there was a theory or the treatment of it in abstracted terms – applies to the influential work of Catharine Mackinnon, which explicitly relies on the ideas of feminist 'consciousness raising' and so to some extent is a genuine counter-example to the generalisation I am about to make that there has been a 'forgetting' of the ideas of Women's Liberation. (See for example Mackinnon 1991: 83–105). However, I disagree with Mackinnon over just what ideas did emerge from consciousness raising. See note 8 to Chapter 1.

11 See, for example, Barrett and Phillips (1992). This collection is largely devoted to bringing into some kind of dialogue what is seen as the theories of the 1970s and those of the 1990s. Seventies theory is identified as 'grand' theory. It should be noted, however, that many of the contributors work in Britain where 'liberation theory' did not have the impact it did in Western countries more directly affected by the Vietnam War.

12 This is my deduction from Weil's argument. The text itself here refers to the difficulty of facing another's affliction, a condition which Weil defines as corrosive of the soul. The point, though, is the difficulty of seeing that one's apparent advantages are not one's own personal qualities.

13

> A condition of complete simplicity
> (Costing not less than everything)
>
> (T.S. Eliot, 'Little Gidding' in Four Quartets)

14 'For the intellectual of goodwill, Communism is a struggle of conscience. To understand this explains many things.' (Spender *et al.* 1950: 241).

15 This claim, essentially of the corruption of second wave feminism, is a major background assumption of my argument. It has been argued by others in different

ways, including Garner (1995), Hughes (1993), Paglia (1990), Roiphe (1993), Tapper (1993) and most strongly by Hoff Sommers (1994). My concern is to analyse its effects on theory rather than to establish its existence. I am aware, however, that it is not a claim which will be readily accepted by many feminists.

16 It was extremely common in the 'official' philosophy textbooks of the old Communist movement to find proletarian 'dialectical' thinking opposed to bourgeois formal or mechanistic thinking. For one example, see the entries on 'Dialectics' and 'Formalism' in Frolov (1984). See also the prelude to my Part II, 'Flashback'.

17 The idea that psychotic thinking can be understood as a metaphorical expression of genuine conflict is probably most often associated with R.D. Laing (as, for example, in Laing (1965)). But it is also the assumption of most psychoanalytic understanding of psychosis. For one example see Stierlin (1987).

1 THE PSYCHOLOGY OF POWER

1 The connections here have not been well documented for the reasons I am advancing. As well, a lot of the literature of the time was ephemeral, consisting of roneoed discussion sheets etc. However, the main available sources do make possible an objective reconstruction of the route of the ideas of liberation theory. (My own initial source was my own memory.) The movement of the ideas from Fanon to Black Power can be clearly traced; see the following note. As for the connection between ideas of Women's Liberation and of Black Power, I would point, first of all, to the fact that the content of the early Women's Liberation writings (Firestone 1979, Morgan 1970, Tanner 1970) is extremely close to the ideas of Black Power (particularly as exemplified in the writings of James Baldwin) and, second, to the fact that Women's Liberation emerged after the Black Liberation movements but also overlapped with them. More significantly, Sara Evans (Evans 1979) supplies a lot of historical evidence for the connection between the early ideas of Women's Liberation and Black Power. Working largely on the basis of interviews, she documents in detail the relationship between the anti-racist movements of the 1950s and 1960s and the emergence of Women's Liberation. She also takes the view that 'the sweeping critique of sexual roles that characterised the more radical women's liberation movement of the late sixties first developed from within the ranks, and revolt of young southern blacks' (Evans 1979: 25). Although she does not identify what I am calling 'liberation theory' as the specific set of ideas at stake, her description of the emergence of personal politics is in accord with my thesis. See also Wandersee (1988: 4) for the suggestion that the insistence on the autonomy of women's movement was introduced by way of a comparison with Black Power. Rowbotham (1989: 6) also mentions the link between Black Power and the organisational form of 'consciousness raising'. That these connections are not generally known even by the most committed feminists is indicated, I think, by Sandra Harding's apparent surprise when, in 1986, she discovered a strong parallel between the ideas of African American movements and her own 'feminist standpoint' theory, which bears similarities with what I am calling liberation theory (S. Harding 1986a).

2 A crucial event in transmitting ideas between the movements was 'The Dialectics of Liberation Congress' held in London in 1967 (see Cooper 1968). See also Gendzier (1973: Chapter 3) and Caute (1970: Chapter 2) for different accounts of the development of the relevant ideas.

3 Both Caute and Gendzier in the works just cited maintain that in fact the reception of Fanon's work was greater in the West than in the 'Third World' nations to which it was directly addressed.

4 The 'anti-psychiatry' of R.D. Laing and David Cooper and others was also influential at this time and also went under the name 'the politics of experience'. See for example Cooper (1968).
5 See Freire (1972: 48) and Freire (1970: 34n).
6 The significance of this deserves further comment. In orthodox Marxist terms, the possibility of peasants attaining to a revolutionary consciousness or performing any kind of progressive role without the intervention of a communist party is heresy. To different degrees the heroes of the time – Guevara, Debray, Fanon, Freire – participated in the heresy, which consisted less in the fact of a more positive assessment of the peasants than it did in the undermining of the theoretical justification of the leading role of the Communist Party.
7 More lately Sandra Lee Bartky (1990) has developed an approach which is strikingly close to this early feminist understanding, although she appears unaware of this precedent – a fact which confirms my thesis of the repression of this period of feminist intellectual history.
8 Mackinnon, like myself, found something very special in the activity of consciousness raising, so special in fact that she claims that this activity is the epistemological practice of feminism. And, as in the account of liberation theory which follows, one of the things she maintains is so special about it is that it 'denaturalises' phenomena which had hitherto been regarded as natural. That is, it enables one to see as social products what had previously been assumed to be somehow 'in nature'. From there her account of consciousness and that contained in liberation theory depart from each other. The key difference is with respect to what it is which is 'denaturalised'. Mackinnon maintains that it is our perception of sexuality and that what the consciousness-raised feminist has discovered is the objective fact that 'Sexuality is socially organised as to require sex inequality for excitement and satisfaction' (Mackinnon 1991: 243). Liberation theory, as the following exposition reveals, maintains that what changes is a subjective perception of oneself as inferior.

The difference here is not, first of all, one of fact. It is not about what ideas actually did and do come out of consciousness raising, for conceivably both could do so. Nor does it immediately concern whether or not Mackinnon's theory of sexuality is a good one. The difference concerns the kind of theory that could have consciousness raising as its epistemology. There were two related aspects of consciousness raising with epistemological import. First, it involved the sharing of women's experiences and second, at least ideally, there was a 'solidarity' (see the account in Chapter 2) or 'sisterhood' amongst those present. Now while these things could clearly assist with the realisation that the conception of one's own inferiority derived, not from an inferior nature, but from external ideas one had 'taken in', it is difficult to see how they could provide much evidence for an objective theory of sexuality (although they may, of course, suggest one). The sharing of experience occurred on far too small a scale to provide anything like adequate evidence for such a social theory, even if (which I deny) the experiences shared mostly provide it with confirming instances. Consciousness raising can constitute some of the epistemology of subjective change but social theories which purport to be objective must conform to more orthodox epistemological criteria.

But Mackinnon wants to do even more than this with the epistemology of consciousness raising. Not only does she put forward a theory of the social organisation of sexuality but she also wants to claim – and it is this which constitutes her as a 'grand theorist' – that this social organisation is the fundamental basis of women's subordination:

A theory of sexuality becomes feminist . . . to the extent it treats sexuality as a social construct of male power: defined by men, forced on women, and constitutive of the meaning of gender. Such an approach centres feminism on the perspective of the subordination of women to men as it identifies sex – that is, the sexuality of dominance and submission – as crucial, as fundamental, as at some level definitive, in that process.

(Mackinnon 1991: 128)

But if consciousness raising does very little epistemologically for the claim concerning the social organisation of sexuality, it does nothing more than this to base this stronger claim that this social organisation is fundamental. Mackinnon's account of consciousness raising is not, I submit, an adequate one.

9 This is a much more important point than I realised until I read Judith Grant's *Fundamental Feminism* (1993). This was one of several works I came across too late to discuss in the body of the text so I will briefly discuss it here. To explain the importance of the point that liberation theory, properly understood, did not purport to explain the social basis of power, but only the psychology involved, let me first briefly describe Grant's thesis. Grant maintains that there are three 'core concepts' of feminism, namely those of 'Woman', 'experience' and 'personal politics', all of which, in various ways, are presupposed by the major varieties of apparently different feminisms we now find. These core notions were established as such, she claims, by the theoretical discussions of Women's Liberation movement, although the very fact that this is a thesis which Grant feels she must argue at length indicates that the feminists who use these concepts do not recognise that they are doing so. The crunch of the argument, though, consists in the demonstration that the first two of these concepts are embedded in futile theoretical programmes, the insoluble difficulties in which have been unwittingly inherited by most contemporary feminisms.

   Now it may seem that if Grant is tracing the theoretical faults in contemporary feminism back to the ideas of Women's Liberation, when I claim that it is the forgetting of these ideas which are the problem, then she and I must be at odds over something. What we are at odds over, though, is not the history of feminist theory she reconstructs, which I think is very perceptive, nor the criticisms she gives of its muddled conceptual foundations with which I would also concur, but rather it is over just what was going on in Women's Liberation. For the confused core concepts which Grant attributes (and this also correctly) to Women's Liberation, I would maintain were already a transformation of the ideas of liberation theory which occurred under the pressure of using these ideas in the context of a political movement. And this transformation was probably the first move in the ultimate forgetting of liberation ideas (which I did not realise until I read Grant's book). Let me explain.

   The core concept of 'Woman' in feminist theory, Grant argues, stems from an early feminist programme which needed both to assert and to explain why 'all women were oppressed'. (This need, Grant, thinks, was due to the fact that Women's Liberation operated in the broad environment of the left, where social explanations of exploitation and oppression were an important part of the general currency.) It could not be a part of liberation theory, understood as a theory of psychological transformation, to prove or to explain why all women were oppressed. Its theoretical scope was limited to explaining what happens, given that they are. (See, also, note 8 to this chapter.) The social basis of male power was a distinct question, and my memory tells me that it was also understood to be a distinct question in Women's Liberation, at least for a time. But this explanatory project became a distorted version of liberation theory when it was welded with Grant's second core concept of 'experience'. In this distorted version of liberation theory, now feminist experientialism, the claim was to be able to explain the basis of power rather than its psychological effects. For what happened, Grant shows, was that the project of finding a transhistorical basis for female oppressions failed to find any appropriate social categories and so the notion of 'women's experience' was brought in from the theory of consciousness raising to do the job. The proof that women were oppressed was that our experience told us so. Moreover, the basis of this oppression was the 'essential womanness' which was the object of this experience, if not the experience itself. (And from then on it naturally became a necessity to insist on irreducible differences between women's and men's experience, men's and women's knowledge, etc.)

Grant, however, is unaware (understandably, because she is younger than the Women's Liberationists) that the feminist concept of 'experience' she has, I think, correctly and very insightfully located as the common source of current projects and confusions is a distortion of a very different notion of 'experience' in another set of ideas of Women's Liberation, namely liberation theory. She is unaware of this because she is unaware that consciousness raising in fact had a theory and so was more than just a bland emphasis on experience. The differences in the two concepts of experience are these: first, the use of the former concept means that one cannot differentiate between the experiences of different women, nor even within one woman, without putting the political project in jeopardy, whereas the latter is part of a theory whose point is to distinguish between different sorts of experiences. Second, the former notion of 'experience' is used epistemologically, as a justification for a theory, whereas the latter is the immediate object of the theory. (More on this point in note 12 to this chapter, and see also note 8.) Third, the former concept leads to the positing of radically different kinds of experience between men and women, while the latter is predicated upon the possibility of human beings understanding the apparently different experiences of others. (It was only because of liberation theory, for example, that early Women's Liberationists saw Gay Liberation men as their brothers, for they thought they had some understanding of their situation, and similarly, it was only for this reason, too, that we immediately and more readily than the rest of the white left wing, supported a black movement which insisted on black leadership.) In short, the problems with the former notion of experience stem from the fact that it was taken illegitimately from an analysis of the psychology of power and made the basis of a theory of the social basis of power.

Finally, I was sad to see Grant partially endorse a postmodern solution to the problems of the core concepts, despite her recognition that feminist postmodernism, too, assumed the overwhelming importance of these concepts in its very rejection of them. I should like to be able to persuade her that there is another alternative, namely the one I present here as liberation theory, for which these problems do not arise.

10 See Brennan (1992: 9–17) for a convincing argument that Freud's notion of femininity is not restricted to women and also for an outline of Freud's specification of the phenomenon as the turning of aggression against oneself.

11 See pages 9–25 of Whitford (1991) on the utopian aspects of Irigaray's thinking and page 44 for an account of her definition of the problem of others.

12 Jardine (1985: 145–55) (reprinted in Docherty (1993)) gives a standard formulation of the first point. (The fact of its reprinting in what is a reader indicates that it is regarded as a classic statement.) Here it is maintained that 'experience' is a 'universal' and 'pure' (extra-linguistic) category which would allegedly 'found' a 'True' theory. This kind of epistemology being rejected, so too is the category of 'experience'. I shall leave aside the question of whether the concept of experience can and has been used this way (I think the characterisation could be applied to various versions of positivism) and whether it is therefore automatically to be abandoned (for most epistemologists now argue against this sort of epistemology) and simply point out that the description does not apply to the account of experi-

ence in liberation theory. The main reason is that experience, in the first instance, constitutes the object of liberation theory, not its epistemology. The theory is about why certain experiences of oneself are unstable and why, in certain conditions, they have tendencies to develop in certain directions. Nevertheless, 'experience' of some sort is clearly relevant to the epistemology of liberation theory. But does this make it an epistemology of guarantees? The theory has a strong phenomenological component which means that a condition of accepting it is that it successfully produce an 'understanding' (in the sense of Weber's 'verstehen'). That is, it must, by providing an appropriate description, enable one to grasp the experiences of others as though they could have been one's own. Such experiences are clearly not 'pure' or 'extra-linguistic', since they can only be apprehended through an adequate description. They may, at a stretch, be said to be 'universal' if by that is meant that the theory works on the assumption that it is worthwhile for people to enlarge their understanding of the experiences of others. While it is not always clear what is at issue when postmodernists sneer at the idea that theories can be 'founded', if their point is to have any substance at all it cannot be a point against the idea that theories should have some grounds for acceptance. It can, I submit, only be a point against the view that theories should be reducible to simple (non-theoretical) elements which are self-validating. It must be a rejection of the view that there is ultimately only one kind of reason for accepting a theory, namely its reducibility to these basic elements. Clearly, then, in not purporting to be reducible to non-theoretical experience and in relying on 'experience' as only one ground amongst others for its acceptance, liberation theory does not come within the scope of the possible criticism. (The other kinds of ground for accepting liberation theory would also be broadly as spelled out by Weber – internal coherence, fit with empirical data of the non-phenomenological kind, etc.)

The second postmodern concern that might be thought to relate to liberation theory concerns the rejection of what is described as the 'politics of identity'. What is at stake here is the fear that a common experience of oppression might be thought to ground the unity 'women' (their quotation marks) as a political group. This is regarded as undesirable because, it is claimed, such a unity would be conceived as having a quasi-natural basis and would therefore result in oppressive dynamics between self and other, in 'exclusion through naming'. (See, for example, Haraway 1991: 196–203.) Similar objections to the political use of women's experience of oppression are expressed by Chandra Mohanty (1992: 77): 'Being female is thus seen as *naturally* related to being feminist, where the experience of being female transforms us into feminists by osmosis'. There are two reasons why liberation theory is not an appropriate target for these fears. The first is that its account of 'the experience of oppression' is not an account of a single experience of the kind which could 'ground' anything. It is rather an account of the kinds of movements and developments experiences could undergo under certain conditions. The second reason is even more powerful. The 'solidarity of the oppressed', which could be seen as the practical aim of liberation theory, is not conceived as the unity of a political group but as an attitude of opposition to the psychological demands of power. This attitude amounts to the refusal to evaluate people (all people) on the basis of their qualities, natural or otherwise. In other words it is the very attitude which renders the oppressive dynamics of self and other impossible. All of this is shown in the following chapter.

13 This theme in Socrates emerges very clearly in Plato's *Meno*, where the slave boy's ability to learn is contrasted with that of the powerful and power-hungry Meno.

14 The reference is to Plato's *Euthyphro*, where Socrates persuades Euthyphro that the gods love the holy because it is holy and that it is not holy because the gods love it, as had been proposed by Euthyphro.

15 There is a difference about where the problematic aspects of binary oppositions

are thought to lie in my account and the prevailing postmodern one. I shall explore this fully in Chapter 2 where it is more relevant to the argument, but briefly here. A binary opposition consists of two predicates which are exhaustive and exclusive of a field, such that for any element of the field one or other predicate must apply, but not both. For example, all things are either red or not-red but not both, so the predicates 'red/not-red' constitute a binary opposition. So with the evaluative predicates 'fully human/lesser' in the field of human beings. These are logical points and so any problems must lie in the usage of the binary opposition. The problem which liberation theory pinpoints here is not so much in the pair of predicates 'fully human/lesser' itself (although the idea of the 'less than fully human' is of course problematic) but in the fixing of the application of the predicates on different elements. It is the polarisation of the terms to which they apply rather than the polarisation of the predicates which apply to them that is at issue. In Chapter 2 I shall argue that the postmodern preoccupation with binary oppositions abstracts and inverts the problem by focusing on the polarisation of the predicates, not that of the terms.

16 For example, Irigaray (1993: 12): 'The demand to be equal presupposes a point of comparison'.

17 John Locke, *The Second Treatise of Government*, Chapter 54.

18 Karl Marx, 'On the Jewish question' in Marx (1975).

19 See Fanon's outrage at Mannoni's positing of this dependency complex as a psychological given (Fanon 1967a: 83–108).

20 Fay Weldon (1972) *Down Among the Women*, London: Penguin. The title phrase caught on.

21 There is a popular myth amongst the tertiary educated that it was Foucault who 'discovered' that power is always accompanied by resistance. In Foucault's works, however, I can discern no explanation of why this should be so.

2 THE GETTING OF WISDOM

1 For example, John Locke, *The Second Treatise of Government*, sections 55–7.

2 This idea is found most clearly in the writings of the young Marx. It is particularly unambiguous in his very early article 'On the Jewish question', although it is also central to 'The economic and philosophic manuscripts of 1844' and other early writings. See Marx (1975).

3 *Meno*:   Is this true about you Socrates, that you don't even know what virtue is? Is this the report we are to take home about you?

   Socrates: Not only that, to the best of my belief, I have never yet met anyone who did know.

   (Plato, *Meno* (71 c) trans. W.K.C. Guthrie, in Allen 1985)

   As to the kind of answer given by liberation theory, it will emerge to be more a theory of a particular virtue than a general definition of the kind sought by Socrates.

4 George Orwell in 'The shooting of the elephant' (Orwell 1950) discusses the experience of 'superiority' of an Englishman in India, but although he clearly recognises the illusions it embodies, it is also clear from his account that this alone does not result in the desire to abandon this superiority. Freire, however (1972: Chapter One), discusses how 'oppressors' may join the movement of the oppressed, on condition they abandon motives of charity which presuppose their continuing superiority and adopt the standpoint of the oppressed.

5 The hierarchy of terms upon which deconstruction focuses allows for only one kind of reversal, because it is a hierarchy of terms and there are only two terms. So

note that the reason *why* there are two sorts of reversal here is because the key assumption concerns a binary mode of *evaluation*, where both the standard of evaluation and the attributes of the terms subject to evaluation can be reversed. Note also that the two sorts of reversal posited by liberation theory both actually occur in political life.

6 See Tapper (1993) for an account of some of the ways in which this is now occurring.

7 The argument in Plato's *Euthyphro*, which establishes that something is holy not because the gods love it but rather that they love it because it is holy, is to this general effect.

8 Richard Robinson (Robinson 1953: 17–19) maintains that this lack of interest is due to the fact that Socrates was concerned that the recognition of ignorance led to the search for wisdom and not for the causes of ignorance. It may be, however, – as the argument from liberation theory would imply – that the two are intrinsically connected.

9 Plato's *Gorgias* contains an important argument between Socrates and sophists, including Gorgias over whether effectiveness or power is the main good.

10 There is, perhaps, a small missing link in the argument here. What about the unlikely possibility that she comes to the conclusion that she, specifically, is due unquantifiable respect but does not extend this right to others, failing to even raise the question of their evaluation? This is impossible for the simple reason that those from whom she needs the respect in question must themselves be judged as fully human in order to make the respect itself worthwhile.

11 I am glossing over the complexities of MacIntyre's argument, which are not relevant to my own. One of these is that MacIntyre's focus is on the concept of a virtue more than it is on morally recommended behaviour. Another is that his conception of virtue is itself multi-layered, the notion of a telos having its place only in the second layer, which refers to the unity of a single life and which therefore functions to integrate the virtues as these are defined at the first level in terms of the notion of 'practice'. A practice is understood as a human activity which seeks goods defined internally to the practice itself and which therefore requires whatever qualities of excellence are necessary to contribute to those goods. It is put forward as a historicised version of the Heroic tradition which regarded 'the good' as relative to one's functioning in a social role. Chess, philosophy and some sporting activities would count as practices. The third layer of the definition refers to the fact that both the cultivation of the virtues and their integration into a unified human life take place in the context of a tradition – an ongoing argument about the good for human beings – in a way that functions to ensure the continuity of that tradition.

12 As a preliminary, because of the current intellectual climate, it should be pointed out that in arguing for a notion of what it is to be human there is no commitment to positing the existence of a 'human essence' in the sense of some fixed set of attributes which determine behaviour. All that is necessary is that the conception of 'the human' has some content and that this content includes a telos, a project of some kind. There are certain things which will be thought to be distinctively human because they are regarded as both necessary for us to behave specifically as humans and are unique to this behaviour. But the notion of a 'human essence' is no more necessary for a concept of what it is to be human than, say, the notion of a 'musician's essence' is necessary for a concept of what it is to be a musician.

13 I have not confronted the question of from just how many people one might need this recognition. Ideally, it would be everyone one comes across and our heroine would, like Fanon in the opening quotation, make it clear in one way or another that this is what she expected. But as far as the actual removal of the agony and intensity arising from an unsatisfied need, I suspect that not many people at all

would be required for one to begin internalising a conception of oneself as properly human.

14 It might have been more straightforward, perhaps, to translate the whole problem into the language of virtues. Then it could have been argued (provided the reciprocity inherent in the demand for recognition as human is stressed) that the disposition to accord others an irreducible respect as human is a virtue and conversely that the disposition to treat some as more important than others is a vice. The reason I didn't approach it this way was that I wanted to stress the inherently interdependent nature of this telos in different individuals.

15 Karl Marx, 'On the Jewish question' in Marx (1975).

16 See Kymlicka (1989).

17 This is the core of Bernard Williams' argument in Williams (1991).

18 In defence of this conception I would point out, first of all, that it has a very strong basis in common sense. We do tend to think that the more we live the more we understand about ourselves and others, that the living itself is the condition of this and, I think, the more we live, the more we think so. This counts as a defence, because what is going on is that the understanding of 'human nature' is here being put in a very special category, as the kind of knowledge to which everyone, independently of training or ability, has in principle the same kind of access, because everyone has the life experience which is its source. If so, one would expect some kind of confirmation to be found in that more general, non-privileged understanding, namely common sense.

19

> *Socrates*: Isn't it clear then that this class, who don't recognise evils for what they are, don't desire evil but what they think is good, though in fact it is evil; those who through ignorance mistake bad things for good obviously desire the good.
>
> (Plato, *Meno* (77c), trans. W.K.C. Guthrie, in Allen 1985)

20 Most famously in Plato's *Apology*.

21 The idea that 'radical' needs make us 'rich' belongs to the young Marx and has been explored in Heller (1974).

22 See Strauss (1953).

23 'It [communism] . . . is the solution of the riddle of history and knows itself to be the solution.' In Marx (1975: 348).

24 The idea that the women are typically constructed psychologically to experience themselves in terms of relationships with others, while men are typically constructed as autonomous, in the sense of being relatively oblivious to such relationships, is almost a commonplace of feminist theory. The classic sources are Chodorow (1979) and Gilligan (1982).

25 See Whitford (1991).

26 It may be ironic that what is produced here is the kind of idea of love found in Aristotle and not in Plato. (See Vlastos 1981: 3–6.) What liberation theory shows, I think, is how this Aristotelian answer can be given to the Socratic question once it is shown that the good of one's own soul is dependent on relating to others as ends rather than means.

27 This interpretation of the notion of 'solidarity of the oppressed' clearly does not (although I suspect it may be thought to) come within the scope of, say, Chandra Mohanty's criticisms of the use of the category of 'experience' by some feminists in such a way that 'Being female is thus seen as *naturally* related to being feminist, where the experience of being female transforms us into feminists by osmosis' (Barrett and Phillips 1992: 77). On the origin, and continuing presence in feminist theory, of the use of 'experience' in the way criticised by Mohanty see Grant (1993). See also my notes 9 and 12 to Chapter 1.

28 Analogously, it has been often claimed that a similar Christian prophecy can be discerned in the theories of Karl Marx.

POSTSCRIPT TO PART I

1 See Hoff Sommers (1994) on the extraordinarily rapid expansion of Women's studies courses in the US and the authoritarian character of the Women's Studies movement. See also Tapper (1993) on feminism in Australian universities.

2 This sort of account is so widespread that one could not begin to comprehensively reference its appearances. Hester Eisenstein and Alice Jardine in the 'Introduction' and 'Prelude' to *The Future of Difference* (Eisenstein and Jardine 1980) were amongst the first to articulate this perception of the development of recent feminist thought. More recently, the theme has been developed in text book form in Gatens (1991b). It should be noticed also that it is only relatively recently that feminist theorists are beginning to recognise that the fusion of the idea of 'sameness' with that of 'equality' is to misread the liberal tradition to which it purports to refer. See, for example, Ann Phillips (1992).

As mentioned in Chapter 1, there is another, often related, perception of the history of recent feminism which misses the existence of liberation theory. It is that which sees earlier forms of feminist thought as instances of 'grand theory' as opposed to later emphases on heterogeneity, multiple causes, specificities, etc. (e.g. Barrett and Phillips 1992, Nicholson 1990: 1–15). This is a more respectable historical perception because such 'grand theory' was very much around and is often mixed in with liberationist ideas. Firestone (1979) is one important example of this mix.

3 One example of many: Gisela Bock and Susan James (eds) (1992) *Beyond Equality and Difference: Citizenship, Feminist Politics and Female Subjectivity*.

FLASHBACK: THE INFAMOUS HISTORY OF THE 'TWO SCIENCES' THESIS

1 For accounts of the 'Lysenko Affair' see Joravsky (1970), Lecourt (1977) and Medvedev (1969). On the 'crank' nature of the theories see note 5 to 'Flashback'.

2 The strong support of the new Soviet state for science was not the only factor in this dramatic success. Another was the accident of the extraordinary cheapness of the main research material, the fruit fly *Drosophila*, for it was this which made genetics research, specifically, economically viable. Depew and Weber (1995) explain the importance in the history of genetics of the 1922 visit to Russia by the geneticist H.J. Muller. Muller gave his fruit flies to the Moscow Institute of Experimental Biology, with the result that very soon after there were three institutes devoted to genetics research in Russia (Depew and Weber 1995: 287). The extent of the early Soviet achievements in genetics helps to explain the enthusiasm of the famous British geneticist J.B.S. Haldane for positive effects of socialism on science (Clark 1984: 90 and Haldane 1932).

3 Michurin (1855–1935) was a Russian horticulturalist who had experimented with grafting and hybridisation and to whom Lysenko attributed the founding of the 'school' of biological thought which he saw himself as developing. See Joravsky (1970: 40–53) and Langdon-Davies (1949: 18–19) for rather sceptical accounts of Michurin's abilities.

4 Langdon-Davies (1949: 74–6) gives an accessible summary of the crucial decisions (closing laboratories, dismissal of leading biologists, rewriting of texts, etc.) from the 1948 Congress which banned genetics. For a full account of these decisions see

The Situation in Biological Sciences: Proceedings of the Lenin Academy of Agricultural Sciences of the USSR Session: July 31st–August 7th 1948, Verbatim Report (Moscow: Foreign Languages Publishing House). The most complete account of the repression of biologists is in Joravsky (1970) of which the Appendix A (pp. 320–8) is a list of repressed specialists. The list is long but almost certainly incomplete since it was prepared without access to the Soviet archives.

5 Some of these are Hudson and Richens (1946), Joravsky (1970: 39–62), Langdon-Davies (1949).

6 The notion of 'sexual difference' is not always formulated in purely social/political terms like the Marxist concept of class, but this fact does not undermine the analogy which stresses that both arguments move from the recognition of some important difference between two groups of people to the conclusion that this difference fundamentally affects the nature of their thinking. With respect to the concept of sexual difference, many feminists maintain that a purely social analysis of the idea ignores the importance of 'the body' in the manner of patriarchal reasoning. This, however, is not to be construed as the thesis that 'pure' biological differences are involved. For such a thesis would allegedly buy into a binary opposition between the bodily and the social. The argument seems to be that in order to avoid the effects of this binary opposition, the concept of sexual difference must have reference both to the nature of the body (where an understanding of this cannot be taken from biology) and to its social situation. For the logic of the supposition that the presence of a binary opposition automatically invalidates a theoretical position, see Chapter 3. For a short account of the position just described see Gatens (1991a). For a long account see Grosz (1994).

7 See Beyerchen (1977) and Walker (1995).

8 It should be remembered, in all fairness, that Lysenkoism emerged roughly during the period of the 'new synthesis' of Darwinism with Mendelian genetics (that is when the synthesis *was* new) and so some time before the identification of the gene with DNA. Equally, though, it should be noted that Lysenkoism was not a part of the long and respected rival tradition in biology of Lamarckism and so it cannot be said to share in any lingering credibility the latter may have had at that time. This is both because any link with Lamarck was explicitly denied and because Lysenko's central propositions were in fact rather different from those of Lamarck. The Lamarckian hypothesis was that those acquired characteristics which became inheritable would then survive (as inheritable) in different environments. Lysenko maintained that the environment must always affect the hereditary substance of the organism (Lecourt 1977: 97).

9 Alan Morton, a British communist supporter of Lysenko, put it this way:

> to these material particles are ascribed a series of properties which no material particles can possess. They are integral parts of biological systems, yet they do not develop, and on the other hand they are assumed to control development. . . . Thus the 'material' gene is seen on analysis to be an idealist concept.
>
> (Morton 1951: 55)

I should add that the exposition of Lysenkoism found in Morton is amongst the clearest, the most informed, and the best argued. I am tackling the argument in its strongest version. Joravsky (1970) contains many examples of much worse arguments advanced during the Lysenko period.

10 The geneticists of the time admitted the exceptions of some treatments of the organism by X-rays, by colchecine or by formaldehyde, treatments which were thought to alter the structure of the gene itself. See Langdon-Davies (1949: 91–3).

11 Evelyn Fox Keller (Fox Keller 1995) argues that this sort of mistake – that of attributing too much agency to the gene by way of overlooking the mechanisms within which it necessarily operated – did in fact arise from the kind of language

and metaphors used by Morgan and his student, Muller (the same Muller as in note 2 to Flashback), to describe their programme. However her case is not that this mistake arose from the very concept of the gene, but rather from too much excitement about it and the associated separation of the study of embryology from that of genetics. For while embryology studied the development of the organism and could scarcely avoid trying to identify the actual mechanisms involved, this was not true for genetics, which focused on the transmission of characters. Her argument would imply, I think, that there was, after all, some kind of point in the Lysenkoists' attribution of idealism to genetics, but that it was a point which was illegitimately used to reject a whole programme rather than to rectify an unwarranted emphasis within it.

12 Jacques Monod's reaction is worth noting:

> What for me was the most revealing aspect of these astonishing documents (of the Lysenko affair) was the fact that the real debate did not concern experimental biology itself, but almost exclusively ideology or rather dogmatics. The essential argument (ultimately the only one) tirelessly repeated by Lysenko and his supporters against classical genetics was *its incompatibility with historical materialism.* This was the real debate, the heart of the problem.
>
> (quoted in Lecourt 1977 : 100).

3 FEMINIST THEORY AS 'POWER/KNOWLEDGE': THE 'TWO SCIENCES' THESIS REVISITED

1 The popularity of the criticism of binary oppositions is due largely, although not exclusively, to the fact that it is regarded as central to deconstruction. An indication of how central it is thought to be is that Diane Elam, an advocate of deconstruction, complains that many deconstructionists – including leading feminists – reduce deconstruction to a too easy attempt to dismantle binary oppositions (Elam 1994: 6, 20).

2 Diane Elam (1994: 20) quotes Joan Scott (1988: 41):

> If we employ Jacques Derrida's definition of deconstruction, this criticism means analyzing in context the way any binary opposition operates, reversing and displacing its hierarchical construction, rather than accepting it as real or self-evident or in the nature of things.

3 My presentation of the argument here is influenced by the wonderfully demystifying account of deconstruction in Ellis (1989).

4 There are some structural analogies between the 'women's studies' movement, where we have for the first time in the West an explicit integration of a political movement with public education, and the merging of a political movement with the social bureaucracy, including education, in what was until recently 'existing' state socialism and which occurred also in Nazi Germany. Christina Hoff Sommers (Hoff Sommers 1994) documents the shocking extent of the former merging in the US. There is very little documentation of the phenomenon in Australia. But Susan Magarey (1989), for example, makes it perfectly clear that the women's studies movement sees itself both as directly political and as having enormous rights within public education. Marion Tapper (Tapper 1993) describes and criticises the merging of academic feminism and university management.

5 An indication of how extremely prevalent this idea is is the fact that this last quote is taken from an article in *New Scientist*, a magazine which is for the most part devoted to serious reporting of science. It is particularly worthy of note in this context that the author makes no attempt whatever to establish her assertion.

6 There are more cautiously worded versions of the idea, the caution consisting in a specification of the domain under discussion and perhaps an acknowledgement that some substantiation is required. For example: 'The objective/subjective dichotomy is but one of several dichotomies that have structured mainstream Anglo-American epistemology and have become a central focus of feminist analysis' (Code 1991: 28). Further down on the same page it is acknowledged that some demonstration is required: 'Feminist theorists have argued, persuasively, that dichotomous thinking is peculiarly characteristic of malestream thought.' However, the latter claim is unreferenced and the persuasive arguments are not given, unless it is intended to be Code's own argument which follows. But this is an argument for the 'maleness' of dichotomies (consisting in the fact that they 'run parallel to a taken-for-granted male/female dichotomy, not just descriptively but evaluatively'). The persuasive argument that dichotomies characterise 'malestream thought' is not recounted.

7 One of the more shocking anecdotes in Christina Hoff Sommers' *Who Stole Feminism?* concerns the practice in some US universities of excluding from appointments committees academics who are not well versed in postmodern/ feminist theory (1994: 129–30).

8 The opposition between 'Aryan' and 'Jewish' physics made within the German physics movement of the 1930s also focused, not on the content of ideas, but on their form or manner of derivation. Excessive abstraction was said to characterise the Jewish mind, and therefore 'Jewish' physics, whereas a respect for nature and an emphasis on the experimental method allegedly characterised 'Aryan' or 'German' physics (Walker 1995: 30). The other point to note here is just how flexible was the label of Jewish mind or 'Jewish' physics, being applied to those who were politically undesirable, irrespective of whether or not they were Jewish (Walker 1995: 24, 27).

9 See, for example, Threadgold (1990: 1):

> Phallocentrism, located in all our dominant malestream Western ways of thinking and talking about and making our world, is a discursive and representational construction of that world in binary terms such that one term is always regarded as the norm and highly valorised, while the other is defined only ever in relation to it and devalorised. Thus: masculine/feminine, rational/irrational, active/ passive and so on.

While, in the succeeding pages, Threadgold seems to want to explain the dominance of binary opposition in terms of the production of 'truth' effects which she sees as the repression of the recognition that meanings are 'made', she offers no account at all of why there should be this connection. (Nor does she offer any account at all of why a recognition of the production of meaning is incompatible with the notion of a reality which cannot be collapsed into meaning so produced. But then, nor does anyone else of her general orientation.)

10 The most famous example of this is Hélène Cixous' discussion (Cixous 1981) which was a point of departure for many feminist theorists. See, for example, Toril Moi (1989: 193).

11 Louis Althusser distinguishes between 'closed' ideologies, in which the answers are logically prior to and therefore determine the questions asked, and the 'openness' of science, where the questions are logically prior to, and in no sense contain, the answers. See, for just one instance, Althusser and Balibar (1968: 55).

12 The move is very common. Cixous (1981) is again, I think, the main original source. Some examples taken more or less at random are Code (1991: 28), Kirby (1994: 126), Spanier (1995: 17).

13 I do not include here the famous article by Nancy Jay (Jay 1981). Jay is quite clear that the dualisms she would explain are those which embody logical mistakes and

therefore do require external explanation. Moreover, she produces an argument for the thesis that the male/female dualism is their psychological and not their logical basis.

14 Val Plumwood has recently called for a distinction between dualisms and dichotomies (Plumwood 1993: 446–7). The former she regards as having a cultural component which allows for the systematic attribution of inferiority to one term, while the latter she sees as simply the drawing of a distinction. Her concern is that the (legitimate) feminist attack on dualisms may lead to an attack on the making of distinctions as such. The analysis she gives of what constitutes a dualism makes it, I think, very close to what liberation theory identifies as the logical relationship between the alleged attributes of oppressors and oppressed, a relationship which holds in the context of oppression. However, unlike my reconstruction of that theory, she does not recognise an evaluative dualism of more or lesser human worth as being pivotal. Her argument could, though, be reconstructed as a more complex version of my point here, that a distinction must be drawn between the way a dichotomy may be systematically used because of social factors and the dichotomy itself.

15 Some feminist philosophers, though, do begin to perceive the difficulties they are getting into. Moira Gatens, for example, in her textbook on feminist theory, articulates an ambiguous position (Gatens 1991b: 93–9). On the one hand she begins by explicitly distancing herself from the position I am criticising here: 'The claim here is not that dichotomous thinking is bad or oppressive per se' (ibid.: 92). But she very soon goes on to identify phallocentric thought as that which 'operates by way of dichotomous thought, where one central term defines all others only in terms relative to itself', a definition which, given the feminist identification of the author, would seem to imply that there is a problem in dichotomies themselves as opposed to their use or misuse. Gatens' actual arguments, however, tend to attack the misuses of dichotomies in much the way advocated here and it seems to me that she gets caught up more in the rhetoric of dichotomies 'dominating' Western philosophy than she does in the implications of the thesis itself (ibid.: 4, 91).

16 As well, there is a general theory to explain why such hierarchisation systematically occurs. I expound and criticise this theory in Chapter 6. Moreover, the existence of this general theory is not thought to undercut the fact that one of the theoretical tasks is always to demonstrate the presence of the hierarchy in each new text under consideration.

17 It is not Haraway's stated disagreement with the feminist critique of binary oppositions in her 'cyborg manifesto' (Haraway 1991: 149–81) which renders her position the more intellectually sound, for in this she only assumes the general force of this critique. Her disagreement consists in the insistence that the time of binary oppositions as a form of oppression has now passed, because we live in a postmodern age where the 'dichotomies between mind and body, animal and human, organism and machine, public and private, nature and culture, men and women, primitive and civilised are all in question ideologically' (ibid.: 163). The agreement which is here assumed with the feminist critique of binary oppositions extends beyond the fact that its validity is recognised for an earlier historical period, to an implicit endorsement of the manner of argument. Haraway's advocacy of the political fiction of the cyborg is heavily based on the idea that cyborg imagery transcends the above oppositions, so offering us 'a way out of the maze of dualisms in which we have explained our bodies and our tools to ourselves' (ibid.: 181). In other words, what is good about the fiction of the cyborg is just that it transcends dualisms. In the absence of any discussion about the alleged deficiencies of any specific dualism, it is once again the binary form as such which is being regarded as offensive.

What does place Haraway's discussion a little on the more serious side of the spectrum is that she does gesture towards a theory of personal identity which would purport to explain why the binary form has held its allegedly dominant position until recently and why it has been a concomitant of oppression (ibid.: 155–60, 177). This theory is so briefly described that it would be difficult to assess it on the basis of Haraway's account alone but it does at least indicate an awareness of the need for explanation of this crucial thesis. (In Chapter 6 I discuss a more developed version of an argument of this kind, namely one which would show why the binary form is oppressive, not in terms of considerations of logic but in terms of a theory of personal identity.) It should also be noted that, despite using rhetoric which suggests the opposite, Haraway is actually very careful not to allow for a position in which the objective or scientific component of science (which she maintains is indissolubly linked with fiction, myth, culture, etc.) would be thought to be subject to criteria of being non-binary or feminist. Unlike the feminists described below, her use of the idea that the better ideas are the non-binary ones is limited to the arena of political fiction and personal identity.

18 The paper 'What is feminist theory?', which is one of several by Grosz in which substantially the argument which follows is articulated, has been reprinted at least twice. The original is in Gross and Pateman (1986) but it appears also in Gunew (1990) and in Himmelwait and Crowley (1992). The only criticism of her argument of which I am aware is Olding (1992/3).

19 See Gross and Levitt (1994) for an account of the extent of the ignorance about science on the part of some of those who would now dismiss it on political/ philosophical grounds of this kind.

20 I am not quite sure what to make of the fact that those who operate in the way I am here describing are those who are quick to insist that all knowledge is power (power in the political sense). The position clearly is a projection of their own specific way of conducting intellectual life onto intellectual life as such (it is a universalisation of their specific perspective), but why such a projection should manifest itself so obviously escapes me. The further (tragic) point is that the more control theorists of this kind gain in universities the more their claim does truly describe existing intellectual activity.

21 When we consider the arguments of the more intellectually serious forms of deconstruction we find that what is at stake between those feminists who confine themselves to the activity of deconstructing oppositions and those who would look to an alternative form of thought (one which is not dominated by the binary form) is a dispute over whether the binary form is necessary to all subjectivity or just to the male subject. Those who take the former position maintain that binary oppositions cannot be transcended and that all that can be done, therefore, is their perpetual deconstruction. This itself, then comes to be seen as distinctively feminist theorising. Those who take the latter position, often influenced by the writings of Luce Irigaray, maintain that feminine/feminist theory is outside this alleged binary domination.

22 For some examples of the extraordinary respect accorded to this position by feminists academics who do not themselves adhere to it, see Holland (1990: 8–16 and 85–9) and Antony and Witt (1993: xv). Val Plumwood takes on what she shows is the implicit authoritarianism in Andrea Nye's attempt to dismiss logic as male but nevertheless insists that feminist understanding 'has been immeasurably advanced by scholars such as . . . Nye' (Plumwood 1993: 438–9). Just as disturbing is an exchange of letters in the *New York Review of Books* (Vol. XLII, No. 6, April 6, 1995) where, after an incisive criticism of the position that feminism requires a different conception of reason, including the possibility of abandoning *modus ponens*, philosopher Martha Nussbaum moves on to express her 'unequivocal admiration' for those just criticised ('the pioneers in this new discipline') 'for their vision and for the courage with which they risked their careers'. For an

alternative view of the extent to which one must risk one's career to do feminist philosophy of this kind, see Hoff Sommers (1994).

23 Huxley (1949: Chapter Two).

24 These sorts of claims are made frequently. See, for example, Grosz (1990: 166–70), Harding (1991: 9–15) and a more argued version in Code 1993.

25 The main source of these commonly found ideas is, again, Cixous (1981). Another randomly chosen example not referenced earlier is Hewitson (1994). Even Donna Haraway whom, in note 17 to this chapter, I credited with being comparatively careful not to fall into this sort of position with respect to the scientific component of science, makes statements like 'Feminist accountability requires a knowledge tuned to resonance, not dichotomy' (Haraway 1991: 194–5).

26 The notable exception to this is Plumwood (1993) who attempts to argue the case that the A/not A form is intrinsically connected to situations of oppression.

27 There are quite a lot of feminist theorists who, in different ways, do present a case that theories with allegedly feminist characteristics are better as theories. This is broadly what feminist standpoint theorists attempt, for example, in arguing that women's experience of oppression gives them a scientific advantage. Some of these arguments nevertheless collapse into the position I am criticising, see notes 31 and 32 to this chapter. But these theorists are not my immediate concern, for they are aware of some of the difficulties and are attempting to avoid a full-on 'truth is political' conclusion.

28 The point is evident in the popular dismissal of the position described as 'feminist empiricism', which asserts that while ideas do in fact gain acceptance on (usually unacknowledged) political grounds, they ought not do so. See for example Code (1991: 316–17) and Grosz and de Lepervanche (1988), discussed in detail below.

29 Elizabeth Grosz, whom I have credited with being unusually straightforward, explicitly asserts the political character of theory choice. After arguing that there are no shared theoretical criteria of choice between theories, she advocates that feminists 'insist on retaining the right to judge other positions, to criticise them and also to supersede them' (Grosz 1990: 167; also Grosz 1993: 194). This, she claims, distinguishes feminist epistemology from relativism.

30 Most of the adherents of Lysenko wanted to argue that 'proletarian science' was also objective. See Morton (1951: 9–20) for examples of the kind of argument advanced.

31 Helen Longino's working out of a feminist epistemology (which is a genuine intellectual endeavour and by no means 'surrational') is illustrative of this point (Longino 1990). The case is both interesting and important because it is clear that Longino wishes to avoid the 'wilder' kind of feminist epistemology, to which end she argues strenuously against the kind of essentialism which would maintain that men and women naturally tend to produce different sorts of theory (ibid.: 187–8). A more sensible position which nevertheless maintains a strong connection with feminism, she argues, is one which sees theory choice as necessarily political: 'we can choose between being accountable to the traditional establishment or to our political comrades' (ibid.: 193–94). Now Longino is clear that she does not advocate political criteria as the only basis for theory choice: 'The feminist scientist is responsive to the ideas of a political community as well as to some subset of the standards endorsed in her or his scientific community' (ibid.: 192).

   However, as James Harris has argued (Harris 1992: 182–7), since she insists that the standards of the community are themselves influenced by its political commitments – 'scientific methods generated by constitutive values cannot guarantee independence from contextual values' (Longino 1990: 191) – then any notion of a commitment to scientific standards must dissolve. For if the political can be sorted out from the scientific, then we are back with the 'value free' conception of science which Longino opposes (ibid.: 191). But if not, then the position reduces to the idea that theory choice is political. Harris does not believe that Longino understands the full implications of her position (Harris 1992: 184).

Harris's argument reveals, I think, that the basic problem with Longino's argument consists in her rejection of the notion of 'objectivity' and its replacement with the notion of the 'constitutive values of science'. The recognition that 'objective' or 'constitutive' values of science (however understood) are affected by political 'contextual' values and may not be completely separable from these is, I think, both correct and important. (The political/contextual may well be necessary both as conditions for 'constitutive' values and to provide the means for their articulation.) Given this lack of separability, the only way to conceive the 'scientific' or 'constitutive' aspect of science in such a way that it does not reduce to the political or the contextual is in terms of its being geared to 'objectivity', where this in turn is understood as 'of the object' and not as a 'God's eye view' (see the discussion in this section of the text). In other words, it must be understood that what Longino calls the 'constitutive' values of science are constitutive only because they strive 'for the object'. In that case the lack of separability between the contextual or political and the constitutive does not amount to the latter sliding into the former because the latter has its own independent determination. But when the 'constitutive' values are understood 'subjectively' entirely in terms of values, then it is difficult if not impossible to see how their lack of separability from other values would not imply their collapse into these.

A similar case could be mounted against Donna Haraway's feminist epistemology (Haraway 1991). Like Longino, Haraway appears not to want to fall into a complete 'knowledge is power' position (ibid.: 183–201). And although she does use the term 'objectivity' (with quotes to separate herself from any naive usage) the idea is discussed only very subjectively, in terms of the possibilities of a 'fractured' identity (ibid.: 155–61). Mostly, however, she refers to the 'technical' language of science (ibid.: 204). In any case, her notion of 'objectivity' is like Longino's 'subjective' rather than 'of the object'. Finally, Haraway is also wary of attempts to separate out the 'pure' or technical scientific language from other parts of the language of science, such as the mythical, fictional, political, ideological, etc. (ibid.: 85, 205, 215). It can be argued, then, that she, too, is left with no way of defending scientific values against their eventual reduction to political values. If so, despite my acknowledgement in note 17 to this chapter that this is not what Haraway appears to intend, her 'cyborg manifesto' becomes just another prescription for the direct interference of politics in science. For if political considerations are rightly dominant with respect to the political components of science, and the technical or scientific components are inseparable from and ultimately reducible to these, then it would seem to follow that political considerations should influence the technical scientific component. It would follow that the 'oppositional' cyborg imagery which Haraway advocates for the fictional component of science (as a basis for objectivity) must directly influence the content of the objective component itself. Once again we are in the position of politics deciding scientific questions. (In fact, Haraway's criticism of Sarah Blaffer Hrdy's feminist sociobiology would confirm that her thinking leads very much in this broadly Lysenkoist direction (ibid.: 98–101). The only theoretical point brought against Hrdy, made after an extraordinary attack on her acknowledgements for revealing an association with the likes of Edward O. Wilson, is that her use of the sociobiological notion of reproductive investment strategies involves 'an appeal to profit calculations under conditions of the market (species biology and habitat)' (ibid.: 101). Sociobiology is criticised here only on the grounds of its political resonances and not in any substantive terms.)

32   It is resisted on the grounds that feminists do choose between competing theories –

on feminist criteria – see for example note 29 to this chapter. By relativism I mean the denial of any shared criteria of validity between two competing theories. Most feminist epistemologies are relativist in this sense although many recognise that this is problematic and attempt to deal with it in different ways (for example, Code 1993; Longino 1990). The argument of 'feminist standpoint' epistemology is an argument that there is 'male' and 'female' theory in the sense of theories which are based respectively on 'male' and 'female' experience. This epistemology claims not to be relativist and to be concerned with the production of 'objective' knowledge, which is said to be possible by starting from the experiences of the oppressed. It is, however, relativist in the sense in which I am using the term, in so far as it is implied that there are no rational criteria of theory choice relevant to the 'context of justification' (S. Harding 1991: 143–4). It would also, therefore, fall within the scope of my general argument, for theory choice is now made on the basis of criteria drawn from the 'context of discovery', namely upon the degree of 'oppressedness' of the theorist (S. Harding 1991: Chapter 6; S. Harding 1993: 49–81). Harding claims that there are arguments for the thesis that the situation of oppressed people is an epistemologically superior one and that 'those arguments must be defeated if the charge of relativism is to gain plausibility' (S. Harding 1993: 61). But this is not the point here. What is the point is that what is in Marx, for example, a thesis that, say, the working class situation is epistemologically advantageous, has here been transformed into a criterion of objectivity. If this is denied, one would want to know what a criterion of objectivity does look like according to feminist standpoint theory.

33 Harding is here purportedly describing, but not endorsing this position. However she does maintain that it is widespread and this is my present point. But see note 32 above.

34 The claim is often made that the absence of shared theoretical criteria does not amount to the absence of any criteria, grounds for discussion, etc. For example, see Code (1991: 2–3). But the point which is at issue here is that of the existence of theoretical criteria of validity.

35 Because of the influence of French structuralism and poststructuralism on recent feminism I am assuming that the 'standard' argument is that in Gaston Bachelard's *The Philosophy of No* (Bachelard 1968). It was this argument which was taken up by Althusser and others, including Foucault. But Feyerabend's famous version of the argument in *Against Method* (Feyerabend 1975) is more akin to the argument I am criticising here.

36 Huxley (1949: 47–61) and see note 15 to the previous section, 'Flashback'.

37 This unfortunately applies also to those academic feminists who, on my criterion, would have to be classed as of the more intellectually 'serious' variety. For example, in both Lovibond (1993) and Fraser and Nicholson (1993) there is an awareness of (and some argument against) the misuse of the postmodern opposition to 'meta narratives' (which in the domain of theory amounts to the rejection of 'external' criteria of adequacy of truth) to imply an opposition to 'global concepts' (concepts which are posited by the theory itself). Despite this recognition that the whole postmodern package cannot be generated from the idea of the 'internality' of criteria of adequacy, there is no recognition of the more fundamental point that the insistence on this internality is more consonant with a rationalist outlook than otherwise.

38 Claims of this kind are so widespread, that exhaustive referencing is impossible. But, for example, all the articles by academic feminists referenced in this section use some of these expressions.

39 Lorraine Code at times explicitly advances this 'strong' version. While claiming to propose a view of knowledge which is 'both subjective and objective' she states:

> My claim . . . that the sex of the knower is epistemologically significant intro-
> duces a *subjective* factor – a factor that pertains to the specific, subjective
> 'nature' and circumstances of knowers – into the conditions that bear on the
> nature, possibility, *and/or justification* of knowledge.
>
> (Code 1991: 27, my italics)

It is the idea that the sex of the knower can bear on the justification of knowledge
which effectively renders this the strong version of the argument (see below) and
which is also incompatible with notions of objectivity according to which the
procedures of justification aim to ensure conformity with the object and not the
subject. Code more often explicitly advances what amounts to the 'weak' version,
about to be described: 'it is unlikely that information about the sex of the knower
would count among criteria of evidence or means of justifying knowledge claims'
(ibid.: 7). It might be tempting to think that the first formulation was a slip of the
pen and not intended to imply that the sex of the knower bears upon the justification of knowledge. This temptation is thwarted, though, for when discussing Sheila Ruth who very clearly insists, according to Code, that 'the sex of the knower *is*
fundamentally significant at a fundamental level, with all-pervasive implications'
(ibid.: 19), the only disagreement she finds is with the fact that Ruth assumes that
there is a single male and female stance where Code argues these will be many and
varied. The fact that she does not comment on Ruth's assumption that the sex of
the knower is relevant to truth claims indicates that she does not clearly distinguish this from her own position. Moreover, her criticism of the so-called feminist empiricists who aim to eliminate from the context of justification those differences which necessarily inform the context of discovery, indicates that she believes
that such a programme necessarily relies on the 'knowers are the same' assumption. This is clearly a 'strong' version of the thesis. Finally, she uses the formulation that epistemologies 'bear the marks of their makers' (ibid.: 48 and 1993: 24),
which I argue below contains an equivocation between the strong and weak versions of the 'knowers are different' thesis.

40 See note 39 above.
41 Harding, however, goes on to confuse them. Her thesis is that such universalist
claims are hypocritical because science in fact discriminates between different
groups. But the discrimination which exists in the practice of science is relevant to
the second of these claims and does not establish the first.
42 Notes 32 and 39 to this chapter establish this with respect to Harding (1991) and
Code (1991) respectively. See also note 31 on the implications of the feminist
epistemologies of Helen Longino and Donna Haraway.
43 Compare the following:

> Within the sciences, she [Irigaray] argues, the 'common force of production'
> (1985: 74) has always been man. But if man, men, produce science, where is it
> possible to locate this force of production in the product (science, knowledge)
> this produced? Irigaray suggests that man effaces his masculinity.
>
> (Grosz and de Lepervanche 1988: 25)

and

> This development [of science] always has a social content: as such it is always
> relative to the state of the productive forces, always linked to class struggles
> (often by remote links), always expressive of the interests and consciousness of a
> class. . . . This explains how the content of science can be objective and yet
> express the viewpoint of the rising or ruling class.
>
> (J.T. Desanti, 'Science, a historically relative ideology', in *Science
> bourgeoisie et science proletarian*, quoted in Lecourt (1977: 24–5))

The thesis that the forces of production affect the character of the theoretical product depends in both cases, I am suggesting, on equivocating over whether the former is a necessary and/or sufficient condition for the latter.

44 It has become very common to advocate the reconstruction of biology as a theoretical discipline (that is as theory) according to desirable political principles. For example, Vandana Shiva begins her paper 'Democratizing biology' (Shiva 1995) like this: 'The dominant paradigm of biology is in urgent need of reinvention and democratization because it is inherently undemocratic' (Shiva 1995: 50). Admittedly, when she goes on to say why the paradigm of biology is undemocratic, she refers to considerations normally regarded as external to the theory itself, namely to the fact that biology is the basis of many food production systems, to the idea that social behaviour is biologically determined and to the idea that humans should be dominant over other species. But this lack of clarity about what the paradigm of biology is doesn't improve the situation. The collection in which this paper appears is called *Reinventing Biology* and it is published by Indiana University Press. The editors (Linda Birke and Ruth Hubbard) introduce it by telling us that it is devoted to answering the question 'what would science look like if it respected the living organisms it studied as individuals with their own histories and integrities? What would it look like if scientists thought of other organisms as rational and capable of intelligent thought?' (Birke and Hubbard 1995: ix). Now to answer this question it is not necessary that one rewrite biology according to these very admirable ethical principles alone, ignoring the internal requirements of the science. But the project would easily lend itself to such an attempt unless scientific limits on such 'reinvention' were insisted upon. They are not.

45 As is suggested by some of the references which follow, my views on this paper were developed in discussion with Alan Olding. We came across it together and were equally shocked by its contents. It should be said, in possible defence of the authors, that the paper is not one of their major publications. It is more an instance of that run-of-the-mill academic feminism which forms the substance of the large number of anthologies, collections, etc. which are now in circulation. But it is precisely these sorts of feminist publications, most of which, like this one, are used as teaching materials for undergraduates, which are my concern in this chapter.

46 This is also stated explicitly by de Lepervanche in her Introduction to the collection in which the paper appears (Grosz and de Lepervanche 1988: 4).

47 The following is a footnote from Olding (1991: 34) referring to this paper:

> The scholarship is enthusiastically appalling and cannot be excused on the grounds that their article is only an 'overview'. Here is one example, purporting to give, with quotation from *The Double Helix*, James Watson's view of the crystallographer Rosalind Franklin: 'Reduced to a bundle of whims, neuroses and symptoms, Watson even speculates that she was "the product of an unsatisfied mother who unduly stressed the desirability of professional careers that could save bright girls from marriages to dull men" ' (Grosz and de Lepervanche 1988: 15). Scholarly hackles should stir at the information that Watson's sentence begins with the words 'So it was quite easy to imagine her . . . ' (this follows a passage describing her lack of dress-sense, etc.); and they should be as erect as an offended porcupine's quills when the immediately succeeding sentences from Watson are supplied: 'But this was not the case. Her dedicated, austere life could not be thus explained – she was the daughter of a solidly comfortable, erudite banking family' (Watson 1968: 17). In fact, further research has revealed that the offensively misleading, out of context quotation has been directly (lack of context and all) lifted from Jacobus (1982: 129). Students of the art of impressively learned quotation might note that two other bits quoted from Watson have come

via the same route (see Grosz and de Lepervanche (1988: 14–15) and Jacobus (1982: 128–9).

4 RADICAL PRETENSIONS

1 See Krupnick (1987: Introduction) for the history of this description.
2 Strictly speaking, Derrida here is referring to the fact that the phase of reversal is interminable because 'metaphysical appropriation happens very fast' (Derrida 1972: 42) But this clearly implies that the third phase must also be interminable.
3 Compare Ellis (1989: 139) who is also unable to make much of this so called second phase and maintains that effectively much of the practice of deconstruction stops at the moment of reversal.
4 This qualification explains nothing and takes us on to the ground of equivocation. The force of 'axiologically', I take it, is to refer to the way the terms are valued, which refers us once again to the use of terms and to the conceptual relations which may be established when people try to dominate each other. The force of 'logically' can only be that logical relations can be described as political relations.

5 THE MYSTERY OF SPECULATIVE FEMINIST DECONSTRUCTION

1 For example, Alice Jardine says this about the reasons for rejecting liberal humanism: 'The major reason has been cautiously and painstakingly laid out in texts written over the last twenty-five years: our ways of understanding in the West have been and continue to be complicitous with our ways of oppressing' (Jardine 1985: 24). The cautious and painstaking texts are, unfortunately, unreferenced.
2 One difference between the reasoning here and what I am describing as the more 'serious' version of 'deconstruction' (as found, for example, in Derrida's own writings) is that these things are explained on the basis of an account of the nature of the subject and language. The general (essentially Fichtean) idea seems to be that the subject can only be posited as a distinguishing between self and not-self. Since, however (unlike Fichte), it is maintained that this positing takes place in language or discourse, the impact of this formative binary opposition is such that language, 'our thought', 'Western metaphysics' or whatever will be permeated by a resulting whole series of binary oppositions.
3 See note 2 above.
4 Another difference which implies that the deconstructionist is much closer to reality than the clinical psychotic is the widespread use of equivocation, some of which I have discussed. When an absurd position is pushed, the approach allows for a falling back onto a saner view (which is usually something quite straightforward and without the glamour of the absurd view). But the fact that this can be done indicates an awareness of absurdities which the strong commitment of the clinical psychotic to their own view does not. This difference, though, is to the moral credit of the clinical psychotic.

6 DECONSTRUCTION

1 There are a few 'serious' poststructuralist feminists, of whom I would single out Rosi Braidotti, who are clearly genuinely concerned by the distance between poststructuralist theory and women's political struggles. Braidotti, however, accepts the general importance of poststructuralist theory and would locate the source of the difficulty in a combination of the failure to think through the ontological

implications of sexual difference and the personal sexist biases of male poststructuralist theorists (Braidotti 1989a: 91). By way of contrast, I locate the problem in
the character of the theory itself, the whole thrust of which is to present a conservative and idealist conception of power by means of identifying it with ultimate
ontological issues.

2 I have insisted that an idea can only be described as a projection of another idea
with reference to the way it is used. My perception of *your* jealousy, for example, is
only a projection of *my* jealousy if I can use the perception to reassure myself that
all the jealousy around is in you and not in me. Since the ideas of deconstruction
could be used in a number of ways, my argument can be at most that it is suited to
act as a projection and that it often does so.

3 For example, Dews (1987).

4 Derrida himself acknowledges at least a surface similarity of the issues but denies,
of course, that the critique can be made straightforwardly in the way I think it can.
He is usually very cautious in his rare discussions of Marx and Marxism, insisting
that more work needs to be done. The main reason I can reconstruct from what
has been said against what I am about to do is that Marx's critique of Hegel has
not yet been sufficiently understood (Derrida 1972: 63). In this connection, note
Derrida's caution in replying to Goldmann's early suggestion that the obscure
notion of 'différance' can be best understood as 'practice' in the Marxist sense
('Interview with Derrida' in Wood and Bernasconi 1988: 88–92). See, further, the
exchange with Jean-Louis Houdebine in Derrida (1972: 77–96). (Very recently,
Derrida has returned to the subject of Marx to explain that his previous 'prudent
and sparing' references were due to the fact that the Marxist ontology 'appeared to
be welded to an orthodoxy' (Derrida 1994: 92). This Marxist ontology, which he
maintains now lives on in the work of Fukuyama, is that which incorporates an
eschatological notion of the end of history (Derrida 1994: 86). Now some might
well interpret Marx's early discussion of alienation as containing just this eschatological notion and deduce from this that there is an effective counter from Derrida
to what I am about to do. To them I should point out that my use of Marx extends
to the separation he makes between philosophical and political questions and in
no way picks up on that eschatology, if, indeed, it is there. There is no other
discussion in this recent work of Derrida's of the argument I am about to take up.)

5 The discussion about Marx, Hegel and Derrida has been mostly about the relation
between Marxist notions of contradiction, practice, etc., Hegel's dialectic and
'différance'. (See, for example, Derrida (1972: 72ff.) and the discussion with
Goldmann in Wood and Bernasconi (1988: 88–92).) These issues are related to
those I am introducing here, although I shall not discuss them directly. For the by-
passing of Marx's argument on the nature of alienation see, for example, Alice
Jardine's confident assumption that Marx's critique of Hegel has been made oti-
ose by Derrida's critique of Hegel. Frustrating, but not remarkable, is the fact that
no argument at all is offered for the assertion that Derrida 'has rendered, at least
for the time being, "Marx" (his texts? "Marxism"?) thoroughly unreadable
through his deconstructions of The Dialectic' (Jardine 1985: 131). Now what
Marx tried to show against Hegel, as I have said above, is that there are two issues
where Hegel identified one. Derrida would show against Hegel that the movement
of 'différance', which is not such as to become resolved in a higher unity, operates
as well as, and coincidentally with, Hegel's Absolute. (This idea might be more
intelligible after reading the exposition below.) It is not at all obvious why the
former criticism should be necessarily rendered 'unreadable' by the latter. There is,
however, one discussion in the literature of Marx's argument about alienation and
its relation to Derrida's deconstruction. Gayatri Spivak (Spivak 1987: 183)
develops, I think, something like the aspect of the argument below devoted to
distinguishing political problems from problems of meaning. This argument is

developed and modified in Spivak (1989). However, I am almost certainly what
Spivak would describe as a 'clarity-fetishist' (Spivak 1989: 206). So I remain tenta-
tive in this opinion, not finding her argument sufficiently clear to be more
confident.

6 Derrida acknowledges the difficulty in distinguishing his ideas from classical theology. The essential difference he wishes to maintain is that the fundamental
movement of 'différance' cannot be conceived as 'an ineffable Being . . . : God, for
example'(Derrida 1991: 76). The reason, as we shall see below, is that the movement of 'différance' is such as to be repressed by conceptions of any original,
given, self-present entities, of which the conception of God is one. My argument,
however, is that whether or not this kind of fundamental movement is conceived
as self-present or not is not as crucial to his argument as Derrida maintains and
the same mistakes arise as in Hegel's blatant absolute idealism.

7 See note 5 above.

8 A significant example of this occurs in the entry for Derrida in *The Concise
Encyclopedia of Western Philosophy and Philosophers* (Urmson and Ree (eds)
1991), the kind of place where one might expect a lucid if brief account of ideas.
The account moves from an outline of Derrida's notion of binary oppositions to
the notion that Western philosophy is dominated by a 'dream of plenitude', as
though the latter has been explicated by the former. Why the presence of binary
oppositions should amount to a 'dream of plenitude' is not spelled out, despite the
fact that it is precisely what the reader would wish to understand.

9 'Such a play, différance, is thus no longer simply a concept, but rather the possibility of conceptuality, of a conceptual process and system in general' (Derrida 1991:
63). And 'What is written as différance then will be the playing movement that
"produces" . . . these differences [which constitute language]' (Derrida 1991: 64).

10 For example, Culler (1983: 61).

11 This argument proceeds in more moves than I have given here. Derrida is mainly
concerned to deconstruct the notion that there are signifieds (concepts, meanings)
independent of the material signifiers by which they are designated (Derrida 1972:
23). The reference theory of meaning underpins the idea of the independence of a
concept from its signifier by supplying an account of the source of meaning,
namely reference, which is compatible with this idea.

12 Derrida (1991: 64).

13 Saussure's famous and now often-quoted statement is this: ' a difference generally
implies positive terms between which the difference is set up: but in language there
are only differences *without positive terms*' (quoted in Derrida 91: 63). Note that
the statement insists only that the positive terms are not part of *the system* of
language, not that they do not exist.

14 Nor does this absurd position appear to be Saussure's, who wanted to deny, not
that relations were between real terms with real properties, but that the specific
properties of any specific term were not relevant to the system of language. The
important point Saussure wished to make is only that it would not matter if 'cat'
were to be used in the way we use 'dog'. But to deny that these specific properties
of terms are relevant to certain concerns is not to uproot the relations they
ground, so leaving them in need of some other explanation. That what I have
described is indeed the reasoning involved is best brought out in the final exchange
between Derrida and Houdebine (Derrida 1972: 91–6). See also Derrida (1991:
63).

15 See Rorty (1967) – the 'young' Rorty – and Olding (1993). What we have here –
and what absolute idealism is almost always about – is the insistence that everything is relational. Relations are therefore constitutive of properties and terms. If
we begin from a 'normal' ontology of things, properties, and relations, what the
absolute idealist does is to insist that the properties and terms are in some sense

illusory or secondary and are determined by the relations. Having done this they are then faced with the problem of explaining the generation of the relations. In this way we arrive at Hegel's Absolute and Derrida's 'différance'. The mistake is the initial rejection of the reality of properties.

16 It would be beside the point here to insist that 'différance' could not be the Absolute because it is not self-present etc. The idealist mistake is in using a concept which has been abstracted from many instances as though it could explain these instances. Compare Marx on the neo-Hegelians in the epigraph to Chapter 5.

17 This is a part of the much more sophisticated account given by Dews (1987: 23–30).

18 '... the subject is not present, nor above all present to itself before 'différance', that the subject is constituted only in being divided from itself, in becoming space, in temporising, in deferral' (Derrida 1972: 28).

19 See Derrida (1972: 9). The latter point refers to Freudian notions that we are constituted by a delay in the satisfaction of the desire for the mother.

20 In the surrational version of deconstruction, the obscurity of the account of the second phase of deconstruction is of little moment. For there, the description functions only in order to identify an alternative theoretical form to the alleged dominant patriarchal theoretical form. I have argued that this identification is necessary as a rallying point and/or as an easy means of denunciation. The fact that it may have no content is then beside the point – indeed it is an advantage, for it prevents crucial claims from being pinned down.

21 See note 10 to this chapter.

22 It is here that the account I gave in note 5 to this chapter of Derrida's difference with Hegel might make some sense. The movement of 'différance' operates both as well as and coincidentally with that of the Absolute, I take it, because it is such as to contain itself in the manner of the Absolute as well as to be more than this containment. It is the latter aspect which Hegel allegedly did not recognise.

23 Roger Scruton (Scruton 1994) argues to the effect that deconstruction has managed to situate itself precisely in that 'God's eye' vantage point on which deconstructionists pour so much scorn. His point is, I think, first of all that what is alleged to be philosophy cannot in principle argue against deconstruction. For if it could, then these arguments, being philosophical (metaphysical), would be able to be deconstructed. But the same applies to any argument – either the argument is itself deconstructive, in which case it is not an argument against deconstruction, or it is not, in which case it can be deconstructed.

24 See Feuerbach, 'Outlines of the philosophy of the future', in Feuerbach (1973) and Marx, 'Economic and philosophic manuscripts' in Marx (1975).

25 Those feminist deconstructionists who uphold the idea that discourse is sexed do tend to revert to something like this position, although, in so far as they have arguments, I would differentiate their approach from that of the kind of deconstruction I have been discussing in Part 2. The 'serious' case for the idea of male and female discourse is discussed in the next chapter.

7 A DIFFERENT DIVIDED SUBJECT

1 I read Ian Hacking's critical discussion of the multiple personality movement (Hacking 1995) only as I was making the final revisions to the manuscript of this book and so I haven't yet been able to adequately work out the consequences of his argument for the position I have advanced in this chapter. It is clear, though, that some reconsideration is required of the assumptions I have made here about the 'splitting' of the personality under the impact of childhood trauma. The problem is not that Hacking has shown that these assumptions are also made by a

fanatical movement in psychology (although this is off-putting) but that he has shown that they do not have a satisfactory basis in evidence (Hacking 1995: 81–112). Nevertheless, I do not think that the substance of my argument will be touched by Hacking's criticisms of these notions. My central point is that political questions are not appropriately addressed as questions of the fundamental nature of 'subjectivity' and that those who turn to psychology for political reasons would do better to focus on contingent personality disturbances. After reading Hacking I now realise that I may have rather too quickly chosen the concepts of 'splitting' and 'dissociation' to describe such disturbances.

2 Kristeva (1986: 28).

3 John Lechte (1990: 34) interprets Lacan's famous statement 'The unconscious is structured like a language' by way of analogy with Saussure's distinction between language as a system, necessary for speech acts, but not referable to by them. My presentation of this point is informed by what I think is Lechte's clear account of the issues.

4 See Freud and Breuer (1974) and Laing (1965).

5 What is said to be at issue are chains of association of ideas which are disconnected from each other. Such chains are thought to distinguish personality fragments or sub-personalities. (This is one of the theses from the literature I accepted at face value until reading Hacking on the multiple personality movement. He establishes that the assumption of a disconnection in the memory chain is far from the only one that can be entertained in order to explain the relevant psychological phenomena. See Hacking (1995: 137).)

6 As, for example, Michael Balint does in *The Basic Fault* (Balint 1968), where he distinguishes pre-oedipal and pre-verbal trauma formation from the post-oedipal, verbal variety, the latter being more accessible to analysis.

7 For some of these see Pinker (1994). In Chapter Two he runs through some of the evidence for the thesis that a disturbance in the language function and psychological disturbance may be independent of each other – a thesis not possible on the 'language constructs the self' approach. In Chapter Three there is an account of some of the major arguments to show that language does not determine our thinking, a thesis which carries the implication that one could well have a concept of the 'I' without the linguistic ability to refer to it.

8 See for example, Braidotti (1989a: 229–38) and Grosz (1989: 91–9) for an argument about Kristeva's lack of feminist credentials, and a reply to the latter in Lechte (1990: 202–4). Also the brief account by Toril Moi (ed.) in Kristeva (1986: 9–12). A defence of Kristeva against this kind of criticism is in Rose (1986: 141–64). Further references to the debate are to be found in Kristeva (1986: 19).

9 My claim here is that central assumptions in Lacan's development of Freud are those reconstructed in the last chapter and to the general effect that there is an unrepresentable and repressed source of meaning which is also the source of the subject/object distinction.

10 See Lechte (1990: 130) on Kristeva's view of the 'place of the father' as the place of society.

11 This is despite the fact that her concerns are not, in the first instance, feminist ones as Lechte (1990: 201) and Toril Moi in Kristeva (1986: 9–12) make clear. Kristeva's own ambivalent attitude to feminism is expressed in her paper 'Women's time' in Kristeva (1986: 187–213).

12 See, for example, 'The system and the speaking subject', 'Semiotics: a critical science and/or a critique of science' and 'Revolution in poetic language' in Kristeva (1986).

13 See 'A new type of intellectual: the dissident' in Kristeva (1986).

14 See, for example, Braidotti (1989a: 233–8); Grosz (1989: 95–6).

15 Irigaray's own book for a more popular audience, *je/tu/nous* (Irigaray 1993) is, on the other hand, written at a level of simplicity which skates over the questions raised here. On the obscurity of Irigaray's writings see Whitford (1989: 106).

16 Kristeva is absolutely explicit on this point:

> In other words, if the feminine exists, it only exists in the order of signifiance or signifying process, and it is only in relation to meaning and signification, positioned as their excessive or transgressive other that it exists, speaks, thinks (itself) and writes (itself) for both sexes.
>
> (quoted in Toril Moi's ' Introduction', Kristeva (1986: 11))

17 See Brennan (1991) for an exploration of the implications of this point.

18 Rosi Braidotti and Alice Jardine are, I think, the most articulate spokeswomen of this position. See Braidotti (1989a, 1989b) and Jardine (1985).

19 See Whitford (1989 and 1991: 75–97) for an interpretation of Irigaray as advocating fundamental changes in the symbolic order.

20 It may be that Rosi Braidotti (Braidotti 1989a), when she insists that the 'crisis' to which poststructuralism sees itself as a response is only a crisis of the male subject, is explicitly following through such a move.

21 The title of one of Irigaray's more famous articles is 'Women's exile' (Irigaray 1990).

22 'Strong difference' feminists tend to be clear that female subjectivity is only a 'becoming' yet to be brought into being and for the most part this is seen as the task of the women's movement. For a clear account see Braidotti (1989a).

23 Irigaray (1981).

24 Irigaray (1982).

25 Braidotti (1989b: 85–105).

26 See Morris (1988: 11–23); Braidotti (1989a: 274–7).

27 It is widely assumed that the Laingian notion of the 'true' and 'false' self implies that the subject is 'given' and that therefore no theoretical account is required. Other versions of psychoanalysis are then contrasted favourably on the grounds that they have an account of the construction of the subject (Mitchell 1974: 243).

28 This characterisation is one which requires reconsideration in view of the reservations about it expressed in Hacking (1995). I am no longer happy with the automatic equation of a splitting of the personality with the breaking up of the memory chain. Nor is this equation necessary for my argument.

29 Freud (1974).

30 The idea that, by and large, psychological repression is of aspects of 'the child' has been developed mainly by Alice Miller in *The Drama of the Gifted Child and the Search for the True Self* (Miller 1983).

31 See Wisdom (1967) on the difference and overlap between psychoanalysis and self-understanding.

Bibliography

Alcoff, Linda and Potter, Elizabeth (eds) (1993) *Feminist Epistemologies.* London and New York: Routledge.

Allen, Reginald E. (ed.) (1985) *Greek Philosophy: Thales to Aristotle.* London and New York: Macmillan.

Althusser, Louis and Balibar, Etienne (1968) *Reading Capital.* London: New Left Books.

Antony, Louise M. and Witt, Charlotte (eds) (1993) *A Mind of One's Own.* Boulder, San Francisco and Oxford: Westview Press.

Bachelard, Gaston (1968) *The Philosophy of No: A Philosophy of the New Scientific Mind.* Trans. G. C. Waterston, New York: Orion Press.

Balint, Michael (1968) *The Basic Fault.* London: Tavistock.

Barrett, Michèle and Phillips, Ann (eds) (1992) *Destabilising Theory.* Cambridge: Polity Press.

Bartky, Sandra Lee (1990) *Femininity and Domination.* New York and London: Routledge.

Beyerchen, Alan D. (1977) *Scientists Under Hitler.* New Haven, CT and London: Yale University Press.

Birke, Linda and Hubbard, Ruth (eds) (1995) *Reinventing Biology: Respect for Life and the Creation of Knowledge.* Bloomington and Indianapolis: Indiana University Press.

Bloom, Allan (1987) *The Closing of the American Mind.* New York: Simon and Schuster.

Bock, Gisela and James, Susan (eds) (1992) *Beyond Equality and Difference: Citizenship, Feminist Politics and Female Subjectivity.* London and New York: Routledge.

Boff, Leonardo and Boff, Clodovis (1987) *Introducing Liberation Theology.* Tunbridge Wells: Burns and Oates.

Bordo, Susan (1988) 'Feminist scepticism and the "maleness" of philosophy', *The Journal of Philosophy* 85: 619–29.

Braidotti, Rosi (1989a) *Patterns of Dissonance.* Cambridge: Polity Press.

—— (1989b) 'The politics of ontological difference', in Teresa Brennan (ed.) *Between Feminism and Psychoanalysis.* London and New York: Routledge.

Brennan, Teresa (ed.) (1989) *Between Feminism and Psychoanalysis.* London and New York: Routledge.

—— (1991) 'An impasse in psychoanalysis and feminism', in Sneja Gunew (ed.) *A Reader in Feminist Knowledge.* London: Routledge.

—— (1992) *The Interpretation of the Flesh: Freud and Femininity.* London and New York: Routledge.

Caine, B., Grosz, E.A. and de Lepervanche, Marie (eds) (1988) *Crossing Boundaries.* Sydney: Allen and Unwin.

Callinicos, Alex (1989) *Against Postmodernism: A Marxist Critique.* Cambridge: Polity Press.
Cameron, Deborah (ed.) (1990) *The Feminist Critique of Language: A Reader.* London: Routledge.
Caute, David (1970) *Fanon.* Suffolk: The Chaucer Press (Fontana Modern Masters).
Chodorow, Nancy (1978) *The Reproduction of Mothering: Psychoanalysis and the Sociology of Gender.* California: University of California Press.
Cixous, Hélène (1981) 'Sorties', in Elaine Marks and Isabelle de Courtivron (eds) *New French Feminisms.* Brighton: Harvester.
Clark, Ronald (1984) *J.B.S.: The Life and Work of J.B.S. Haldane.* Oxford and New York: Oxford University Press.
Code, Lorraine (1991) *What Can She Know? Feminist Theory and the Construction of Knowledge.* Ithaca, NY and London: Cornell University Press.
—— (1993) 'Taking subjectivity into account', in Linda Alcoff and Elizabeth Potter (eds) *Feminist Epistemologies.* London and New York: Routledge.
Cooper, David (ed.) (1968) *The Dialectics of Liberation.* Trans. Constance Farrington, London: Penguin.
Culler, Jonathan (1983) *On Deconstruction.* London, Routledge and Kegan Paul.
De Beauvoir, Simone (1972) *The Second Sex.* Harmondsworth: Penguin.
Depew, David J. and Weber, Bruce H. (1995) *Darwinism Evolving.* London, and Cambridge, MA: The MIT Press.
Derrida, Jacques (1972) *Positions.* Trans. Alan Bass, Chicago: University of Chicago Press.
—— (1991) ed. Peggy Kamuf, *The Derrida Reader.* New York and London: Harvester Wheatsheaf.
—— (1994) *Spectres of Marx.* Trans. Peggy Kamuf, New York and London: Routledge.
Dews, Peter (1987) *Logics of Disintegration.* London and New York: Verso.
Diprose, R. and Ferrell, R. (eds) (1991) *Cartographies: Poststructuralism and the Mapping of Bodies and Spaces.* Sydney: Allen and Unwin.
Docherty, Thomas (ed.) (1993) *Postmodernism: A Reader.* Hemel Hempstead: Harvester Wheatsheaf.
Edwards, Paul (ed.) (1967) *The Encyclopedia of Philosophy.* London and New York: The Macmillan Co. and The Free Press.
Eichenbaum, Luise and Orbach, Susie (1982) *Outside In . . . Inside Out.* Harmondsworth: Penguin.
Eisenstein, Hester and Jardine, Alice (1980) (eds) *The Future of Difference.* Boston: G.K. Hall.
Elam, Diane (1994) *Feminism and Deconstruction.* London and New York: Routledge.
Ellis, John M. (1989) *Against Deconstruction*, New Jersey: Princeton University Press.
Evans, Sara (1979) *Personal Politics.* New York: Alfred A. Knopf.
Fanon, Frantz (1967a) *Black Skins, White Masks.* New York: Grove Press Inc.
—— (1967b) *The Wretched of the Earth.* Harmondsworth, Penguin.
Feuerbach, Ludwig (1973) *The Fiery Brook: Selected Writings.* New York: Anchor Books.
Feyerabend, Paul (1975) *Against Method.* London: New Left Books.
Firestone, Shulamith (1979) *The Dialectic of Sex.* London: The Women's Press.
Flax, Jane (1990) 'Postmodernism and gender relations in feminist theory', in Linda J. Nicholson (ed.) *Feminism/Postmodernism.* New York and London: Routledge.
Fox Keller, Evelyn (1983) *A Feeling for the Organism: The Life and Work of Barbara McClintock.* New York: Freeman.
—— (1985) *Reflections on Gender and Science.* New Haven, CT and London: Yale University Press.

—— (1995) 'Language and science: genetics, embryology and the discourse of gene action', in Evelyn Fox Keller, *Refiguring Life: Metaphors of Twentieth Century Biology*. New York: Columbia University Press.

Fraser, Nancy and Nicholson, Linda (1993) 'Social criticism without philosophy: an encounter between feminism and postmodernism', in Thomas Docherty (ed.) *Postmodernism: A Reader*. Hemel Hempstead: Harvester Wheatsheaf.

Freire, Paulo (1970) *Cultural Action for Freedom*. Harmondsworth: Penguin.

—— (1972) *Pedagogy of the Oppressed*. Trans. Myra Bergman Ramos, New York: Herder and Herder.

Freud, Sigmund (1974) 'Femininity', in *New Introductory Lectures on Psychoanalysis*. Trans. James Strachey, London: Hogarth Press.

Freud, Sigmund and Breuer, Josef (1974) *Studies in Hysteria*. Harmondsworth: Penguin.

Frolov, I. (ed) (1984) *Dictionary of Philosophy*. Moscow: Progress Publishers.

Garner, Helen (1995) *The First Stone*. Sydney: Picador.

Gatens, Moira (1991a) 'A critique of the sex/gender distinction', in Sneja Gunew (ed.) *A Reader in Feminist Knowledge*. London: Routledge.

—— (1991b) *Feminism and Philosophy: Perspectives on Difference and Equality*. Cambridge: Polity Press.

—— (1992) 'Power, bodies and difference', in Michèle Barrett and Ann Phillips (eds) *Destabilizing Theory*. Cambridge: Polity Press.

Gendzier, Irene L. (1973) *Frantz Fanon: A Critical Study*. London: Wildwood House Ltd.

Gerth, H.H. and Mills, C.W. (eds) (1970) *From Max Weber. Essays in Sociology*. London: Routledge and Kegan Paul.

Gilligan, Carol (1982) *In a Different Voice*. Cambridge, MA: Harvard University Press.

Grant, Judith (1993) *Fundamental Feminism*. New York: Routledge.

Grieve, Norma and Burns, Ailsa (eds) (1994) *Australian Women: Contemporary Feminist Thought*. Melbourne: Oxford University Press.

Gross, Elizabeth (1986) 'What is feminist theory?', in Elizabeth Gross and Carole Pateman (eds) *Feminist Challenges*. Sydney: Allen and Unwin.

Gross, Elizabeth and Pateman, Carole (eds) (1986) *Feminist Challenges*, Sydney: Allen and Unwin.

Gross, Paul R. and Levitt, Norman (1994) *Higher Superstition*. Baltimore and London: The Johns Hopkins University Press.

Grosz, E.A. (1988) 'The in(ter)vention of feminist knowledges', in Barbara Caine, E.A. Grosz and Marie de Lepervanche (eds) *Crossing Boundaries*. Sydney: Allen and Unwin.

—— (1989) *Sexual Subversions*, Sydney: Allen and Unwin.

—— (1990) 'Philosophy', in Sneja Gunew (ed.) *Feminist Knowledge: Critique and Construct*. London and New York: Routledge.

—— (1993) 'Bodies and knowledges: feminism and the crisis of reason', in Linda Alcoff and Elizabeth Potter (eds) *Feminist Epistemologies*. London and New York: Routledge.

—— (1994) *Volatile Bodies*. Sydney: Allen and Unwin.

Grosz, E.A. and de Lepervanche, Marie (1988) 'Feminism and science', in Barbara Caine, E.A. Grosz and Marie de Lepervanche (eds) *Crossing Boundaries*. Sydney: Allen and Unwin.

Guess, Raymond (1981) *The Idea of a Critical Theory*. Cambridge: Cambridge University Press.

Gunew, Sneja (ed.) (1990) *Feminist Knowledge: Critique and Construct*. London and New York: Routledge.

—— (ed.) (1991) *A Reader in Feminist Knowledge*. London: Routledge.

Hacking, Ian (1995) *Rewriting the Soul: Multiple Personality and the Sciences of Memory.* Princeton: Princeton University Press.

Haldane, J.B.S. (1932) 'The place of science in western civilisation', in *The Inequality of Man and Other Essays.* London: Chatto and Windus.

—— (1985) *On Being the Right Size and Other Essays.* Ed. John Maynard Smith, Oxford: Oxford University Press.

Haraway, Donna (1991) *Simians, Cyborgs and Women: the Reinvention of Nature.* London: Free Association Books.

Harding, J. (1986) 'Women and science: filtered out or opting in?', Public Lecture given at the University of Sydney, 30th April, 1986.

Harding, Sandra (1986a) 'The curious coincidence of African and feminine moralities', in D. Meyers and E. Kittay (eds) *Women and Moral Theory*, Totowa, NJ: Rowman and Allenheld.

—— (1986b) *The Science Question in Feminism.* Ithaca, NY: Cornell University Press.

—— (1991) *Whose Science? Whose Knowledge?* Buckingham: Open University Press.

—— (1993) 'Rethinking standpoint epistemology: "What is strong objectivity?"', in Linda Alcoff and Elizabeth Potter (eds) *Feminist Epistemologies.* London and New York: Routledge.

Harding, Sandra and Hintikka, Merrill B. (eds) (1983) *Discovering Reality: Feminist Perspectives on Epistemology, Metaphysics, Methodology, and the Philosophy of Science.* Dordrecht: Reidel.

Harris, James F. (1992) *Against Relativism.* Illinois: Open Court.

Harstock, Nancy (1983) 'The feminist standpoint: developing the ground for a specifically feminist historical materialism', in Sandra Harding and Merrill B. Hintikka (eds) *Discovering Reality: Feminist Perspectives on Epistemology, Metaphysics, Methodology, and the Philosophy of Science.* Dordrecht: Reidel.

Haste, Helen (1994) 'The Wife, the Waif, the Warrior and the Warlock', *New Scientist*, No. 1912: 32–5.

Heller, Agnes (1974) *The Theory of Need in Marx.* London: Allison and Busby.

Hewitson, Gillian (1994) 'Neo-classical economics: a feminist perspective', in Norma Grieve and Ailsa Burns (eds) (1994) *Australian Women: Contemporary Feminist Thought.* Melbourne: Oxford University Press.

Himmelwait, Susan and Crowley, Helen (1992) *Knowing Women: Feminism and Knowledge.* Oxford: Polity Press in association with The Open University.

Hobbes, Thomas (1991) *Leviathan.* Ed. R. Tuck, Cambridge: Cambridge University Press.

Hoff Sommers, Christina (1994) *Who Stole Feminism?* New York: Simon and Schuster.

Holland, Nancy J. (1990) *Is Women's Philosophy Possible?* Maryland: Rowman and Littlefield.

Hudson, P.S. and Richens, R.H. (1946) *The New Genetics in the Soviet Union.* Cambridge: School of Agriculture.

Hughes, Robert (1993) *The Culture of Complaint.* New York and Oxford: Oxford University Press.

Huxley, Julian (1949) *Soviet Genetics and World Science.* London: Chatto and Windus.

Irigaray, Luce (1981) 'When the Goods get together', trans. Claudia Reeder, in Elaine Marks and Isabelle de Courtivron (eds) *New French Feminisms*, Brighton: Harvester.

—— (1982) 'One does not move without the other', trans. Rosi Braidotti and Mia Campioni, *Refractory Girl.* No. 23: 12–14.

—— (1990) 'Women's exile', trans. Couze Venn, in Deborah Cameron (ed.) *The Feminist Critique of Language: A Reader.* London: Routledge.

—— (1993) *je/tu/nous: toward a culture of difference.* Trans. Alison Martin, London and New York: Routledge.

Jacobus, M. (1982) 'Is there a woman in this text?', *New Literary History.* 14: 117–41

Jacoby, Russell (1977) *Social Amnesia.* Brighton: Harvester.

—— (1987) *The Last Intellectuals.* New York: Basic Books.

Jardine, Alice A. (1985) *Gynesis.* Ithaca, NY and London: Cornell University Press.

Jay, N. (1981) 'Gender and dichotomy', *Feminist Studies* 7 (1): 38–56. Reprinted in Sneja Gunew (ed.) (1991) *Reader in Feminist Knowledge.* London and New York: Routledge.

Joravsky, David (1970) *The Lysenko Affair.* Cambridge, MA: Harvard University Press.

Kirby, Vicki (1994) 'Viral identities', in Norma Grieve and Ailsa Burns (eds) (1994) *Australian Women: Contemporary Feminist Thought.* Melbourne: Oxford University Press.

Kristeva, Julia (1986) *The Kristeva Reader.* Ed. Toril Moi, Oxford: Basil Blackwell.

Krupnick, Mark (ed.) (1987) *Displacement: Derrida and After.* Bloomington: Indiana University Press.

Kymlicka, Will (1989) *Liberalism, Community and Culture.* Oxford: Clarendon Paperbacks.

Laing, R.D. (1965) *The Divided Self.* Baltimore: Penguin.

Langdon-Davies, John (1949) *Russia Puts the Clock Back.* London: Victor Gollancz Ltd.

Lechte, John (1990) *Julia Kristeva.* London: Routledge.

Lecourt, Dominique (1977) *Proletarian Science? The Case of Lysenko.* London: New Left Books.

Lepervanche, Marie de (1988) 'Introduction', in Barbara Caine, E.A. Grosz and Marie de Lepervanche (eds) *Crossing Boundaries.* Sydney: Allen and Unwin.

Llewellyn, John (1986) *Derrida on the Threshold of Sense.* Basingstoke and London: The Macmillan Press, Ltd.

Lloyd, Genevieve (1993) 'Maleness, metaphor, and the "crisis" of reason', in Louise M. Antony and Charlotte Witt (eds) *A Mind of One's Own.* Boulder, San Francisco and Oxford: Westview Press.

Longino, Helen E. (1990) *Science as Social Knowledge.* Princeton: Princeton University Press.

Lovibond, Sabina (1993) 'Feminism and postmodernism', in Thomas Docherty (ed.) *Postmodernism: A Reader.* Hemel Hempstead: Harvester Wheatsheaf.

MacIntyre, Alasdair (1985) *After Virtue: A Study in Moral Theory.* London: Gerald Duckworth and Co.

—— (1988) *Whose Justice? Which Rationality?* London: Gerald Duckworth and Co.

Mackinnon, Catharine (1991) *Towards a Feminist Theory of the State.* Cambridge, MA: Harvard University Press.

McLellan, David (1989): *Simone Weil: Utopian Pessimist.* Basingstoke and London: The Macmillan Press.

Magarey, Susan (1989) 'Editorial', *Australian Feminist Studies*, No. 10, Summer 1989.

Marks, Elaine and de Courtivron, Isabelle (eds) (1981) *New French Feminisms*, Brighton: Harvester.

Marx, Karl (ed. Lucio Colletti) (1975) *Karl Marx: Early Writings.* Trans. Rodney Livingstone and Gregory Benton, Harmondsworth: Penguin.

Medvedev, Zhores A. (1969) *The Rise and Fall of T.D. Lysenko.* Trans. Michael Lerner *et al.*, New York and London: Columbia University Press.

Meyers, D. and Kittay, E. (eds) (1986) *Women and Moral Theory.* Totowa, NJ: Rowman and Allenheld.

Miller, Alice (1983) *The Drama of the Gifted Child and the Search for the True Self.* London: Faber and Faber.

Mitchell, Juliet (1974) *Psychoanalysis and Feminism.* London: Allen Lane.

Mohanty, Chandra Talpade (1992) 'Feminist encounters: locating the politics of experience', in Michèle Barrett and Ann Phillips (eds) *Destabilizing Theory*, Cambridge: Polity Press.

Moi, Toril (1989) 'Patriarchal thought and the drive for knowledge', in Teresa Brennan (ed.) *Between Feminism and Psychoanalysis*. London and New York: Routledge.

Morgan, Robin (ed.) (1970) *Sisterhood is Powerful*. New York: Random House.

Morris, Meaghan (1988) *The Pirate's Fiancée*. London, New York: Verso.

Morton, Alan G. (1951) *Soviet Genetics*. London: Lawrence and Wishart.

Nicholson, Linda J. (ed.) (1990) *Feminism/Postmodernism*. New York and London: Routledge.

Norris, Christopher (1982) *Deconstruction: Theory and Practice*. Suffolk: The Chaucer Press.

Nussbaum, Martha (1995) 'Letter to the editor', *New York Review of Books*, XLII, 6.

Olding, Alan (1991) 'Women, babies, and bathwaters: some feminist criticisms of biology' (unpublished).

—— (1992) 'Common sense and uncommon nonsense' (unpublished).

—— (1992/3) 'The law of the exclusive muddle', *The Australian Journal of Anthropology*. Special Issue 3: 43–54.

Orwell, George (1950) *The Shooting of the Elephant and Other Essays*. London: Secker and Warburg.

Paglia, Camille (1990) *Sexual Personae*. New Haven, CT and London: Yale University Press.

Patton, Paul (ed.) (1993) *Nietzsche, Feminism and Political Theory*. London and New York: Routledge.

Phillips, Ann (1992) 'Universal pretensions in political thought', in Michèle Barrett and Ann Phillips (eds) *Destabilizing Theory*. Cambridge: Polity Press.

Pinker, Steven (1994) *The Language Instinct*. London and New York: Penguin.

Plumwood, Val (1993) 'The politics of reason: towards a feminist logic', *Australasian Journal of Philosophy* 71 (4): 438–50.

Poole, Ross (1991) *Morality and Modernity*. London and New York: Routledge.

Robinson, Richard (1953) *Plato's Earlier Dialectic*. Oxford: Oxford University Press.

Roiphe, Katie (1993) *The Morning After*. London: Hamish Hamilton.

Rorty, Richard (1967) 'Internal relations', in Paul Edwards (ed.) *The Encyclopedia of Philosophy*. London and New York: The Macmillan Co. and The Free Press.

Rose, Jacqueline (1986) *Sexuality in the Field of Vision*. London: Verso.

Rowbotham, Sheila (1989) *The Past is before Us: Feminism in Action since the 1960s*. London: Penguin.

Sayre, Ann (1975) *Rosalind Franklin and the DNA*. New York: Norton.

Scott, Joan Wallach (1988) *Gender and the Politics of History*. New York: Columbia University Press.

Scruton, Roger (1994) 'Upon nothing', *Philosophical Investigations*, 17 (3): 481–506.

Shiach, Morag (1989) ' "Their 'symbolic' exists, it holds power – we the sowers of disorder know it only too well"', in Teresa Brennan (ed.) *Between Feminism and Psychoanalysis*. London and New York: Routledge.

Shiva, Vandana (1995) 'Democratizing biology: reinventing biology from a feminist, ecological and Third World perspective', in Linda Birke and Ruth Hubbard (eds) *Reinventing Biology: Respect for Life and the Creation of Knowledge*. Bloomington and Indianapolis: Indiana University Press.

Spanier, Bonnie B. (1995) *Im/partial Science*, Bloomington and Indianapolis: Indiana University Press.

Spender, Stephen *et al.* (1950) *The God That Failed*. London: Hamish Hamilton.

Spivak, Gayatri Chakravorty (1987) 'Displacement and the discourse of woman', in Mark Krupnick (ed.) *Displacement: Derrida and After*. Bloomington: Indiana University Press.

—— (1989) 'Feminism and deconstruction, again: negotiating with unacknowledged masculinism', in Teresa Brennan (ed.) *Between Feminism and Psychoanalysis.* London and New York: Routledge.

Stierlin, Helm (1987) 'Existentialism meets psychotherapy', in *Psychoanalysis and Family Therapy: Selected Papers.* Northvale, NJ and London: Jason Aronson Inc.

Strauss, Leo (1953) *Natural Right and History.* Chicago: University of Chicago Press.

Suzuki, David and Knudsen, Peter (1988) *Genethics: the Ethics of Engineering Life.* Toronto: Stoddart.

Tanner, Leslie B. (ed.) (1970) *Voices From Women's Liberation.* London and New York: Mentor.

Tapper, Marion (1990) 'Dichotomous thinking' (unpublished paper).

—— (1993) '*Ressentiment* and power: some reflections on feminist practices', in Paul Patton (ed.) *Nietzsche, Feminism and Political Theory.* London and New York: Routledge.

Threadgold, Terry (1990) 'Introduction' to *Feminine/Masculine and Representation.* Sydney: Allen and Unwin.

Threadgold, Terry and Cranny-Francis, Anne (eds) (1990) *Feminine/Masculine and Representation.* Sydney: Allen and Unwin.

Urmson J.O. and Ree, Jonathan (eds) (1991) *The Concise Encyclopedia of Western Philosophy and Philosophers.* London and New York: Routledge.

Vlastos, Gregory (1981) *Platonic Studies.* Princeton: Princeton University Press.

—— (1991) *Socrates: Ironist and Moral Philosopher.* Cambridge: Cambridge University Press.

Walker, Mark (1995) *Nazi Science: Myth, Truth, and the German Atomic Bomb.* New York and London: Plenum Press.

Wandersee, Winifred D. (1988) *On the Move: American Women in the 1970s.* Boston: Twayne Publishers.

Watson, J. (1968) *The Double Helix.* London: Weidenfeld and Nicolson.

Weber, Max (1949) *The Methodology of the Social Sciences,* trans. E.A. Shils, New York: The Free Press.

—— (1970) 'Science as a vocation', in H.H. Gerth and C.W. Mills (eds) *From Max Weber: Essays in Sociology.* London: Routledge and Kegan Paul.

Weil, Simone (1987) *The Need for Roots.* London and New York: ARK Paperbacks.

Whitford, Margaret (1989) 'Rereading Irigaray', in Teresa Brennan (ed.) *Between Feminism and Psychoanalysis.* London and New York: Routledge.

—— (1991) *Luce Irigaray: Philosophy in the Feminine.* London and New York: Routledge.

Williams, Bernard (1991) 'Saint Just's illusion', *London Review of Books,* 14 (16): 8–11.

Windshuttle, Keith (1994) *The Killing of History.* Sydney: Macleay Press.

Wisdom, John (1967) 'Psychoanalysis', in Paul Edwards (ed.) *The Encyclopedia of Philosophy.* London and New York: The Macmillan Co. and The Free Press.

Wood, David and Bernasconi, Robert (1988) *Derrida and Différance.* Evanston, Il: Northwestern University Press.

Index

A/–A form of dualisms 75, 76, 78, 97
A/B form of dualisms 75, 76, 78, 97
Absolute, the 125, 126, 130, 183n, 185n
absolute idealism 123, 124, 125, 133,
  134, 136, 184–5n
Against Method (Feyerabend) 179n
Algerian National Liberation Front
  (FLN) 15
alienation 118, 122, 129–30, 134, 136
Althusser, Louis 68, 70–1, 174n
'amnesia', feminist: definition of 6;
  explanation of 107
Anderson, John 119
antagonism of the oppressed 27
Apology (Plato) 5, 161n
Aristotelianism 42, 61
Aristotle 76, 170n
'Aryan' physics, compared with 'Jewish'
  64, 174n
'Aufhebung' 130
Austin, J.L. 72
autonomy 30–1; character of 37; denial
  of scientific 89; illusion of 132–3;
  necessary conditions for 38; and need
  for human recognition 30, 51, 53

Bachelard, Gaston 81, 179n
Balint, Michael 186n
Bartky, Sandra Lee 164n
Basic Fault, The (Balint) 186n
binary oppositions *see* dualisms
Birke, Linda 181n
Black Liberation 4, 15–16, 163n
black people, as 'lesser' 35
Black Power 1, 163n
Bogdanov, A.A. 59
'bourgeois' science and thought 59, 63,
  64, 66, 163n
Braidotti, Rosi 138, 144, 145, 182–3n,
  187n

Brecht, Bertolt vi

Christianity, Christian world view 3, 7, 9,
  16, 18, 24, 30, 55, 116, 156, 159, 171n
Cixous, Hélène 174n, 177n
'clarity fetishism' 123
class character of science 59, 63
Cleaver, Eldridge 15
Code, Lorraine 83, 174n, 179–80n
Communism, Communist movement 9,
  11, 162n, 163n, 170n
Communist Party 61, 62, 164n
communitarian theories 47
competitiveness of the oppressed 27–8
*Concise Encyclopedia of Western
  Philosophy and Philosophers* (Urmson
  and Ree) 184n
'consciousness raising' 4, 16–17, 163n,
  164–5n, 166n
conservatism: conservative objections to
  cultural relativism 39; of
  deconstruction 101, 122, 123, 129, 130,
  135; of feminist psychoanalytic theory
  140, 141, 143, 151; of Hegel's account
  of alienation 129–30; of Lacan 142
content versus form 70, 72, 113–15,
  116–18
Crick, Francis 94
'critical theory' 1, 161n, 162n
cultural relativism/relativity:
  conservative objections to 39; 'not
  enough' in conceptions of human
  nature 42; 'too much' in conceptions
  of human nature 42, 44, 47–50
'cyborg manifesto' 74, 175–6n, 178n

Darwin, Charles 94
De Beauvoir, Simone 21
de Lepervanche, Marie 59, 93–9, 180n,
  181n